The Story of Two Campaigns

OFFICIAL WAR HISTORY OF THE
AUCKLAND MOUNTED RIFLES
REGIMENT, 1914-1919.

BY

Sergt. C. G. Nicol.

3rd (Auckland).

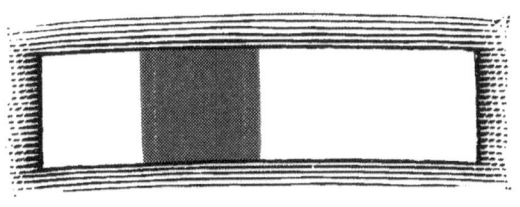

4th (Waikato).   11th (North Auckland).

A.M.R. Squadron Badges and Regimental Colours worn on hat band. The white-red-white strip was taken from the diagonal crosses in the Union Jack.

In Memory

of

The Fallen.

They live in the hearts of their comrades.

Who stands if freedom fall?
Who dies if England live?
— Kipling.

PREFACE

The chief purpose of this book is to record, in as true perspective as possible, the deeds of the Auckland Mounted Rifles Regiment in the Gallipoli and Sinai-Palestine Campaigns. At the same time an effort has been made to reveal something of the spirit of the Regiment, something of the general attitude of mind of its officers and men, which, at times, may have helped it to engage in operations, forlorn hopes and adventures, with the resolution generally associated with regiments with traditions.

The writer begs to acknowledge the assistance at all times given freely by those consulted, and to those who made photographs available for reproduction. Owing to the fact that in the Regiment there was almost community ownership over films and plates, it has been found impossible to state the photographer's name at the bottom of each picture, but among those who obtained many of the finest views are Captain A. Carr, Lieutenant A Briscoe Moore, and Lieutenant H. K. Hatrick. Others who placed their collections at the disposal of the Committee are Major F. Waite, D.S.O., Captain C. V. Bigg-Wither, Lieutenant S. C. Reid, M.C., Lieutenant E. Foley, Captain D'Esterre, and Mr. John Houston.

CONTENTS

CHAPTER		PAGE
I.	Birth of the Regiment...	1
II.	The Voyage to Egypt ...	12
III.	Arrival in Egypt	20
IV.	"An Unknown Destination" ...	27
V.	Gallipoli ...	32
VI.	Defence of Walker's Ridge	42
VII.	The Day After	50
VIII.	Life at Anzac...	54
IX.	Fateful August	60
X.	The Attack Begins	66
XI.	Struggle on the Crest ...	71
XII.	Valley of Torment	77
XIII.	The Last Effort	81
XIV.	Evacuation	89
XV.	Back to Suez ...	93
XVI.	First Action in Sinai ...	102
XVII.	Romani Opens ...	106
XVIII.	Gallop on Katia	111
XIX.	Fight at Bir El Abd ...	116
XX.	Back to the Outpost Line	121
XXI.	Descent on El Arish and Magdhaba	124
XXII.	Rafa—First Fight in Palestine ...	129
XXIII.	The First Gaza	136
XXIV.	The Second Gaza and After	142
XXV.	Tel El Saba ...	155
XXVI.	North to Ayun Kara ...	161
XXVII.	To Jaffa and the Auja ...	167
XXVIII.	The General Offensive ...	174
XXIX.	The Column Goes East ...	177
XXX.	Through the Hills to Jericho	181
XXXI.	Across the Jordan	189
XXXII.	Raid into Gilead	195
XXXIII.	Attack on Amman	202
XXXV.	Jordan Recrossed	211
XXXIV.	Retirement ...	206
XXXVI.	Second Raid into Gilead	214
XXXVII.	Trials of the Valley	218
XXXVIII.	Beginning of the End ...	222
XXXIX.	On to Es Salt ...	227
XL.	The Last Fight...	231
XLI.	The Remaining Enemy—Malaria...	235
XLII	Return Home ...	239
	The Horse-Comrade in Arms	242
	Roll of Honour ...	245
	Honours and Awards	...
	Maps ...	...

Sixty-four pages of illustrations.

COLONEL C. E. R. MACKESY, C.M.G., M.B.E., D.S.O.
First commander of the Auckland Mounted Rifles Regiment.

LIEUTENANT-COLONEL J. N. McCARROLL, C.M.G., D.S.O. with Bar, who succeeded Colonel Mackesy in command of the A.M.R.

NEW ZEALAND MAIN BODY TRANSPORTS AT COLOMBO.

THE BAND. In centre: Major F. C. Wood (Adjutant), Colonel Mackesy, and
Lieutenant Wlralley Stewart (Bandmaster).

The Auckland Mounted Rifles was the only one of the expeditionary mounted regiments which had a band. It differed from the infantry bands in that it was a military combination on similar lines to the Imperial Army bands. It continued as a regimental band, although doing brigade duty, until 1917, when, owing to the depletion caused by casualties and sickness, it became necessary to make it a brigade band, in order to be able to draw players from the other regiments of the brigade, and to increase the total number to 33. The band served with the brigade continuously in the field, and until the armistice spent only a fortnight at the base at Moascar. Whilst quartered in Jerusalem it performed four times each week in the public gardens of the city. Good service was done at both the field hospitals and also at Port Said Hospital by its performances, which were highly appreciated, as they also were by the inhabitants of Richon le Zion, where performances were given on the Synagogue steps each Saturday afternoon, and also concerts in the famous wine cellars of the noted wine distillery of that prosperous Jewish community. Of the original band, six members served through the whole of the war, and returned to New Zealand with the brigade, after doing five years and 19 days' service. They were Lieut. Stewart (bandmaster), Sergt. J. Alec Stewart, Sergt. George W. Stewart, Corpl. G. Smith, Corpl. Leadbeater, and Bandsman C. Bailey.

The Story of Two Campaigns.

CHAPTER I.

Birth of the Regiment.

When the Great War broke out in August, 1914, New Zealand "leapt to arms unbidden." For her "The Day" had come. But it was not "The Day" the Germans had toasted. The people of New Zealand were peacefully inclined. They had not been taught to regard war as a necessity. They had come to a promised land, a land that might be the home of a nation, and all they desired was the opportunity to possess it. True, a system of compulsory military training was in operation, but for home defence only. It was merely a preparation against any possible invader. But at the challenge of militarism to civilisation, the Dominion sprang to arms. The day had come when she was to prove her loyalty to King and Empire, when she was to assume the burden of a free nation within the Empire, when she was to show to the world that Britons of the most distant Dominion were the bone and flesh and blood of the Motherland. Britain's menace was her menace. Her sons were Britain's sons. Her offer to help to the limit of her power, was as inevitable and as certain as the rising of the sun. Within a few days of the declaration of war, the Mother Country had accepted New Zealand's offer of aid, and men of peace clamoured in their thousands to enrol. Never did fiery cross on

Highland hill stir the fighting blood of the clansmen as did the call for men stir the soul of young New Zealand. There was no need to make the call an appeal. The problem of the military authorities during those fateful days of August was not to get men, but to get them slowly enough. It was in this atmosphere of martial ardour and patriotism that the Auckland Mounted Rifles Regiment had its birth. It lacked the advantage of tradition, but its augury was bright.

In speaking of the birth of the Regiment, there is no desire or intention to belittle the value of the three Territorial units of mounted rifles in the Auckland Military District. From these territorial regiments—the 3rd Auckland Mounted Rifles, the 4th Waikato Mounted Rifles, and the 11th North Auckland Mounted Rifles—the Auckland Mounted Rifles of the Main Body of the N.Z.E.F. was officered and supplied with the majority of its non-commissioned officers; its three squadrons were drawn almost entirely from the districts of the three territorial units, whose names they took; but in composition, the three squadrons had practically no resemblance to the territorial units of the same names. They had an entirely distinct individuality, and thus the A.M.R. of the N.Z.E.F. can be said to have come into being at the mobilisation of August, 1914.

No unit under the compulsory territorial training system, with its 18 to 25 years age limitation, could possibly hope to attain to the average standard of the rank and file of the A.M.R. with whom this history deals. The physique of the men was splendid, and from the colonial mode of life they inherited the initiative and resource which make for high military talent. But no regiment of the force contained so many types and represented so many widely-divergent walks in civil life. There were lawyers and schoolmasters and students; there were bushmen and farmers and stockmen; there were tradesmen and labourers and clerks; one single tent in the Epsom camp included a schoolmaster, a barber, a coach driver, an accountant, a carpenter, a farm labourer, a commercial traveller, a farmer, and a lawyer. But a rare spirit of comradeship grew up within a few days in tents, in troops, and in squadrons, and so was born the Spirit of the Regiment which became more and more a living reality as the weeks and months went by, and flourished in glorious maturity on the crags and crests of Gallipoli, along the desert ways of Sinai, and throughout the waterless tracts of Palestine, where was enacted the last and greatest crusade. It was the spirit of the men who, upon the outbreak of hostilities, travelled fast from far back stations by horse and coach and launch and train to be " in time for the war"; it was the spirit which gave the last drop of water; the spirit which does not know when it is exhausted nor when it is beaten. It was the spirit of Kipling's " If "—

" If you can force your heart and nerve and sinew
" To serve your turn long after they are gone
" And to hold on when there is nothing in you
" Except the will which says to them ' Hold on !' "

Within a few days of the call for volunteers, the three squadrons of the Regiment were practically complete, and had commenced training at Epsom Camp, with Lieutenant-Colonel C. E. R. Mackesy in command. Of this officer's distinguished record more will be said later, but something of his character and personality should now be given, because it was largely due to the outstanding qualities of the commander that the Regiment owed its sound and thorough foundations. A tall commanding figure, Lieutenant-Colonel Mackesy was then a man of 54 years, therefore many years over military age so far as it applied to the rank and file. He was a man of wide learning and experience, and there were few men in the Dominion who at that time realised how tremendous the conflict was to be. He was not of those who spoke so hopefully of the "Russian steam-roller," and how speedily it was going to roll up the eastern armies of Germany. It was not surprising, therefore, that the training he prescribed was hard and intensive. The feather-bed soldier had nothing to hope if he found himself under Colonel Mackesy. It need hardly be said, also, that the commanding officer was a strict disciplinarian, but he had no need for a detention barracks, the most dreaded punishment for serious default being to strike the offender's name from the roll. Hundreds of men were waiting to step into every vacancy, so a remarkably high standard of discipline prevailed. It was a unique method of punishment and one of the few occasions it could be practised. It was a modern translation of Shakespeare's lines:—

"He which hath no stomach to this fight,
"Let him depart, his passport shall be made."

Actually, however, a regiment composed of the first volunteers for war has few men of the serious defaulter type, and orderly room appearances were rare, and this continued to be the case with the A.M.R. throughout the whole period of hostilities.

Second in command was Major Chapman, an officer who was to die almost at the beginning of his war service. Hale fellow well met, he won the respect of the men, and they were stern critics. As adjutant the Regiment had Captain Wood, N.Z.S.C., a highly efficient officer. The Regiment was fortunate in its squadron commanders—Major Tattersall of the 4th, Major McCarroll of the 11th, and Major Schofield of the 3rd. All possessed the confidence of their men, many of whom were their personal friends in civil life. So it came about that a very happy family sort of feeling prevailed—so much so that officers and troopers sometimes found themselves on the point of addressing each other by their christian names. Similarly, the happiest relations existed between the troopers and the junior officers.

In dealing with these days when the Regiment was in the making, the work of the sergeant-majors must not be overlooked. All, except one, had come from the Imperial Army. In inculcating a sense of discipline, and in grounding the men in the elementals, these soldiers performed a service of untold value. To illustrate the rawness, in the military sense, of some of the recruits who were so soon moulded into soldiers, an incident of the Epsom parade might be related. One of the frivolities of the moment was for a tent to " count out " another tent in unison. This bright morning one of the sergeant-majors was teaching a few elementary truths to a squad of men who had never been drilled in their lives before. He told them how to " number," and then gave the word of command. All went well until the tenth man was reached, and he, quite unconscious of the enormity of his offence, serenely shouted, "Out." The face of the gallant S.M. was a study, and the homily he delivered is historical.

The matter of the greatest importance in the equipping of a regiment of mounted rifles is the provision of horses, and it was a day of tremendous anxiety for the men when remounts were issued. For days horses had been arriving at the remount depot from many destinations. The pick of the animals had already been ear-marked for the officers, but it was not generally known that all the "old soldiers," who had learned wisdom in South Africa, had paid secret visits to the depot and had noted good animals against the day of issue. Some, in fact, had gone the length of tying small pieces of twine to the tails to aid them in quickly recognising the animals when the descent was made upon them. But on the fateful day, alas, it was not a case of "who finds, keeps." Instead, the remounts were led round in a ring while the troop leaders were given alternate choices; and so it happened that neither the wise ones of South Africa nor the innocents from the pavements and the bush, were allotted the chargers of their choice, and loud were the lamentations. The only cheerful ones were those who had brought their own horses to camp, the instructions being that such horses, provided they were passed by the veterinary officer, were to remain in the possession of the old masters. At that time there were few who were inclined to enthuse over the horses. Even allowing for the usual effects of winter, there was still a look of roughness about the horses, and they were anything but uniform in stamp. Quite a number of the animals seemed to have been badly broken, if broken at all, and generally there was not the appearance of quality one would expect to see in a collection of remounts purchased for war service. One man, a veteran too, rejoiced in a beast which obviously had relations in the kingdom of heavy Clydesdales. She suffered from strangles, and he called her Saucy Kate. Yet events proved that these same horses, excluding Saucy Kate and one or two like her, were the horses which survived the seven weeks' voyage to Egypt, standing all the way, and afterwards carried the bulk of the men through the desert campaign, beating the Arab horses at their own game. Many of these same horses did stretches of 50 and 60 hours without water in that torrid country, and ended their earthly career, after the final surrender of the Turks, at the hands of their own masters, who chose to take this heartbreaking course rather than risk their gallant four-footed comrades falling into the hands of cruel owners and ending their days in slavery.

The only men who evinced alarm about the equestrian qualifications of the troopers were the S.Ms. who had come from the Imperial cavalry. It was quite impossible for them to teach the men a real cavalry " seat "—their only failure—and often they were heard to lament over the " loose seats " of the troopers. " You might be able to stick on," remarked one of the instructors one day, " but I wouldn't say you could ride." However all differences on the question of riding were gradually smoothed out, the troopers admitting that the cavalry style was no doubt pretty, and the instructors at last agreeing that the colonial style was much more effectual than it looked.

The days of August slipped quickly by, and September's days rapidly multiplied, and still there was no definite news of the departure of the Force. Fits of great depression occasionally swept over the A.M.R. owing to fears that colonial troops would not be considered efficient for modern war, that the war would be over before the New Zealand Force could get anywhere, that garrison duty in some inglorious spot would be their portion, and so on and so on. Little did the men dream of the great tasks they would be called on to perform, and the laurels that they or their successors were to bring home. Veterans now smile at these anxieties of former days, but none the less they are a little proud of the spirit from which those anxieties arose.

At last, however, orders came for embarkation, which was carried out at Queen's Wharf, Auckland, on September 22, the bulk of the Regiment going to the Waimana along with the Auckland Infantry, and the balance on the Star of India with the New Zealand Medical Corps. The horses were divided between the two transports. A great crowd assembled to see the vessels draw out into the stream. On the evening of the following day the transports sailed with the small third-class cruiser H.M.S. Philomel as escort. A course for the north was set, the orders being that the ships should join the other eight, with the Wellington, Canterbury, and Otago sections of the Force, in the Tasman Sea. To the astonishment of most of those on board, however, the two transports were re-entering the Auckland Harbour at daylight next morning. It was after-

TRAINING IN EGYPT.
1. Part of Zeitoun Camp. 2. A.M.R. on training trek. Halt on Ismalia Canal, on the way to Delta Barrage. 3. Regiment crossing Barrage Bridge over the Nile.

PART OF THE N.Z.M.R. CAMP AT ZEITOUN, CAIRO.

A.M.R. marching through Cairo on December 23, after Prince Hussein Kamel Pasha was proclaimed Sultan in the stead of Khedive Abbas Hilma Pasha, who had thrown in his lot with Turkey.

TRAINING IN EGYPT.
A.M.R. swimming horses across the Nile below the Delta Barrage.

wards learned that the recall had been issued owing to the presence in Southern Pacific waters of the German cruisers Scharnhorst and Gneisenau, which could have sunk the whole of the then-available escort without running any risk themselves.

In a somewhat depressed frame of mind, the Regiment disembarked three days later. Two squadrons proceeded to Otahuhu and one to Takapuna, where training was resumed until a more powerful escort was obtained. Three long weeks were so spent. On October 10 the Regiment again embarked without any warning, all except one troop being accommodated on the Star of India. On the evening of the following day the two ships, with H.M.S. Philomel escorting, steamed out of the Waitemata to join the rest of the convoy at Wellington. How memorable an event was that final departure! Ashore vast crowds, held by emotions too deep for expression, watched the moving ships get under way. The great dread laid its cold fingers on the hearts of the women, even if some stay-at-home men loudly scoffed at the idea of these soldiers ever getting to the war, which, of course, was then against Germany and Austria alone. It was well for the city and the relatives of the men that the extent of what the sacrifice was to be was not then realised. It was well that no one could know that within a few short months fully one-fifth of those cheering young men of the Auckland Mounted and Infantry units were to give their lives in the cause of humanity, and that almost all the remaining four-fifths were to suffer wounds or the health-wrecking sickness of the Gallipoli campaign. With their splendid band playing the song of the immortal " Contemptibles " of France " It's a Long Way to Tipperary " the men of the A.M.R. took their last farewell of home, and set out on the Great Adventure. The glorious confidence of youth possessed them, an intense patriotism mingled with a keen sense of adventure fired their blood, and a determination to be worthy of the land they represented, shone like a guiding star. These emotions were not openly displayed, however. Then and always the A.M.R. assumed a pose of amused indifference which some of our Allies could never understand.

Wellington was reached on October 14, some hours after the arrival of H.M.S. Minotaur and the Japanese warship Ibuki, which were the adequate additions to the escort. No shore leave was granted to the Auckland men, although it is rumoured that several of them, wearing the uniform of ship's engineers, walked down the gangway to waiting launches and enjoyed good cheer ashore for the last time. Failing the chance of a trip on shore, one of the Regiment's jesters assisted with great alacrity in the loading of stores, hoping that his evil designs might be rewarded. The best " loot " he could get was a case of plug tobacco—but it was not tobacco. Only horse shoe nails were to be seen when the case was opened with great mystery in a dark corner.

At 6 a.m. on October 16, the grey-painted transports, escorted by the warships Minotaur, Psyche, Philomel, and Ibuki, sailed for an unknown destination. It was an event which marks an epoch in the history of New Zealand. It might, indeed, be said that on the day when the Dominion's Main Body Force of 9,000 men sailed to the aid of the Motherland, she achieved nationhood. It was the first great expression of her Imperial obligations, and although her war effort was to reach the then undreamed of total of nearly 100,000 men, it was no mean achievement to despatch within two months of the acceptance of the offer of aid, an equipped force of 9,000 men.

CHAPTER II.

The Voyage to Egypt.

The voyage to Egypt, a destination not then dreamed of, need not be described in any great detail. The first port of call was Hobart, where the troops received an overwhelming welcome, which contrasted with the somewhat restrained farewell the Auckland men had received in their own city. It was realised, however, that the kindly and demonstrative people of Hobart were able to greet the New Zealanders as a compliment to a neighbouring Dominion, and without the personal emotions which must always subdue those who are sending their own kin to war. The Aucklanders were later to realise through their contact with Australian soldiers that the Australians are much more demonstrative people than the people of their own land, and that Australian crowds always give freer reign to their emotions than do gatherings of New Zealanders. This difference in temperament was markedly noticeable between Australian and New Zealand regiments. In action it was observed that the Australians always made more noise than the New Zealanders. Often Australian units, when desperately engaged with the enemy, shouted like a crowd of football barrackers. This was not usually the case with the New Zealanders. When at grips with the enemy they were comparatively quiet, and they fought with a grim determination, never underestimating their foe.

Leaving Hobart the New Zealand convoy sailed to Albany, where were waiting 26 of the 28 transports of the Main Body of the Australian

Imperial Force. It was a wonderful and inspiring sight to see this fleet lying at anchor across the placid waters of King George's Sound, and it afforded very tangible proof of the loyalty of the Dominions, which had been questioned by the German Emperor. Although there was no opportunity for the Australians and their kinsmen from this side of the Tasman Sea to fraternise during the two days spent at Albany, the feelings of mutual esteem which now exist had their beginnings there. Ships greeted ships, and loud and continuous cries of welcome floated across the water. The secret of the atmosphere, which produced common concord among the ships, was that there was mutual understanding, a common impulse having actuated the men, whether from the Never Never or Sydney or Taupo or Timaru.

On Sunday, November 1, the fleet sailed, the Australian cruisers Sydney and Melbourne taking the places of the smaller " P " class ships, which cheered the New Zealand transports on their way as they parted company. The first transport moved towards the open sea at 6 a.m., and the last did not up anchor until 9 o'clock. Next day the remaining two Australian transports from Fremantle joined the convoy, making the total 38, certainly the largest convoy that ever set out on so long a voyage. Although the Australian ships steamed in three lines, with the New Zealand vessels in two lines at their rear, the great fleet stretched almost from horizon to horizon even when sailing orders were being strictly obeyed. Only sailors could understand fully the technical difficulties attending the sailing of so large a convoy, consisting as it did of such a variety of steamers of so varied engine power.

The days, growing warmer and warmer, followed one another with eventless monotony. As is always the case with mounted troops at sea, the men of the Auckland Mounted Rifles spent most of their time among their horses, which required constant attention. The detachment on the Waimana had a particularly hard time, seeing that on that ship they had much more than their complement of horses. Apart from the ordinary duties in feeding and grooming the horses and cleaning the stalls, it was necessary to take a great deal of care of the animal's legs, which were very liable to swell owing to the constant standing. Frequent rubbing and hosing with salt water was carried out with wonderful results. For those not on duty among the horses, ordinary guard duties were found, and on the Star of India occasionally parties were required to transfer coal from a forward hold to the bunkers, bunker space having been reduced by two bunker compartments being used for mess rooms for the men. Incidentally it might be mentioned that in the tropics these mess rooms, being so close to the engine room, became almost unbearably hot, and eating was far from pleasant. Men began to discard one garment after another, until at last some arrived at meals wearing little more than the " uniform " of Gunga Din. Then had to be issued the famous order forbidding men to go about the ship in " a nude state." The man who asked the sergeant-major if he would be regarded as nude if he wore a full bathing suit instead of trunks only, received the fright of his career. The trooper thereupon wrote a letter to a troopship paper that was being produced, suggesting that it was hardly proper for the ship's hose to be left uncovered on the deck in full view of the public gaze.

It was patent to everyone that the destination was somewhere north of the Line, but no one except, perhaps, the commander had any more definite information. This uncertainty appealed to the sporting instincts of one trooper who started a " book " on the hazard. He wrote down some 10 possible destinations, including India and Zanzibar, and he threw in South Africa, seeing that news of De Wet's rebellion had been received. But most of the available cash on the ship was now in the canteen, and no business was done by the sporting individual.

Aided by fine weather, the horses were standing up to their great test of endurance in a remarkable manner. By this time they had learned to recognise the bugle which announced their feeds, and the chorus of glad neighs which greeted this bugle was one of the happiest sounds of the ship.

On November 9, occurred the one sensational incident of the voyage—the destruction of the German cruiser Emden by the Sydney at the Cocos Islands when the convoy was only 60 miles distant. Briefly, the facts of this notable incident are these: About 6.30 a.m. a wireless S.O.S. message, more or less mutilated by a hostile instrument, was picked up from the station on the Cocos Islands advising that a strange warship was at the entrance, and was ignoring the station's messages. The Sydney was immediately despatched to the Cocos Islands by the captain of the Melbourne, who had assumed command of the convoy after the departure the previous day of the Minotaur, which followed the receipt of news of the naval disaster off Valparaiso. The Sydney engaged the Emden by 9.30 a.m., and at 11.20 a.m. she advised that the Emden was beaching herself in a sinking condition. It was afterwards learned that the Emden had crossed the track of the convoy some little distance ahead the previous night, but had seen no sign of it. This may have been due to the great care taken to mask all lights at night. The precautions against detection by the Emden, whose presence in these waters was, of course, known, had been thorough, and it had even been ordered that no empty cases should be thrown overboard lest the hostile warship should be provided with a clue. The excitement on board the transports when the great news was announced was similar to that of Armistice Day.

Veterans of the A.M.R. have vivid memories of many stirring incidents they have witnessed, but one of the great pictures in the gallery of their minds will always be that of the Sydney dashing away to the horizon that morning in November to fight her first fight, and the first fight of the Australian Navy, against the one hostile ship which could have wrought harm to that vast convoy.

On November 13, the New Zealand transports, under the care of H.M.S. Hampshire, pushed ahead of the Australian boats on account of coal and water needs, and reached Colombo two days later. The shore leave granted was greatly enjoyed after the trying days in crowded comfortless ships which did not possess the first essentials of passenger boats in the tropics. The convoy, with the exception of 10 transports which still required coal, sailed on November 17, and reached Aden eight days later. During the run to Aden an A.M.R. mare on the Star of India, in defiance of army regulations, gave birth to a foal, and surviving the ordeal, she was regarded by the experts as something of a miracle. The foal was a fine specimen, but a foal cannot be kept by a mounted rifles regiment even as a mascot, and it had to be destroyed.

The chief memories of that run to Aden are those of a sunrise on a perfectly glassy sea, of the fins of flying fish flashing in the sun, and of hundreds and thousands of porpoises, affected by the martial spirit of the world apparently, manœuvring in troops, squadrons, regiments, and brigades. They moved in troop column, in squadron line, and line of squadrons, the most mobile force that ever assembled.

At Aden the convoy met eight transports on their way to India with British territorial battalions, a cheery crew who insisted upon bestowing large quantities of cigarettes upon the crews of whale boats from New Zealand transports when they learned that cigarettes had been banished from the New Zealand vessels. They also rejoiced in wet canteens, which were painfully absent from the New Zealand troopships.

The colonial convoy, now united again, sailed for Suez on November 26. The days spent in the Red Sea were intensely hot and extremely trying for man and beast. The veterinary officer of the A.M.R., who had lost a remarkably small percentage of horses, and was most anxious to keep up the reputation of his horses, gained a name for professional zeal by commandeering some of the windsails which were supplying a little ventilation to the suffocating quarters of the men in the cavernous place that had once been a hold, and leading them to the horse stalls on the deck above. The troopers, or most of them, were spending the nights on the deck, however, so no one died of suffocation in the dormitories.

Before Suez was reached, instructions were received that the Force had to prepare to disembark in Egypt. Seeing that Turkey was now at war against the Allies, the men of the Regiment were not disheartened at hearing the destination. Those who were still pessimistic over the fear of garrison duty, cheered up visibly when the order came for the sharpening of bayonets and the overhauling of saddlery, and they became quite optimistic when, during the passage of the Suez Canal on the night of December 1, they beheld the very considerable preparations being made for the defence of that vital line of communication. They saw real trenches for the first time, and they exchanged greetings with sentries of many different Indian regiments, who kept watch on the canal banks. This night was the first occasion that guards of the N.Z.E.F. were posted with magazines charged. A previous ship, it was said, had been fired at by scouting Turks or their Bedouin friends, so on each ship a guard was posted to return any compliments of this nature that were offered. No hostile hand disturbed the peace of that extremely peaceful night, however, and the voyagers were able to drink in the wonder of the scene.

The ships, with searchlights at their bows, sending a path of blazing light down the narrow strip of water which is the gateway to half the world, steamed slowly through. The constellations, then strange but to become so familiar to these men from Britain's farthest outpost, blazed with a splendour that intoxicated the senses—the splendour of the orient sky; the eternal desert, so quiet and still and mysterious, so alluring in that strange grey light which hides more than it reveals, whispered its seductive enchantments to these men from the distant green southern islands, and filled their hearts with a strange yearning, and longing to go out into that sandy waste and seek the Thing that called. They were afterwards to know that the soft voice of the moonlit desert was as false and cruel as the mocking mirage when it woos and beckons the thirst-tormented wanderer.

Perhaps the brooding spirit of the old, old land had wakened again at the sound of the gathering armies, and was pondering the stirring days of yore. Maybe it numbered again the legions of its dead, and there was a stirring of the countless bones which lay beneath the all-effacing sand. Perhaps it was the voice of the past telling the tale of history—how the Persian and the Roman had passed that way, how the Crusader in his mail had clanged onward to the battle of the Cross. It may have been that the spirit of the desert whispered of the flight to Egypt of a father and a mother and a Babe. These soldiers, so unlike the warriors who once went that way, gazed in thrilled silence at the scene, but felt more than they saw. It was a wondrous night. Since then they have learned the moods of the mocking pitiless desert; they have suffered its thirst, endured its angry heat, and choked in its storm-lifted dust and sand. They sometimes curse the desert, but the beauty, the charm, the lure, the haunting whispered appeal of that night will always remain with them, for that night they stepped on to the famous stage whereon the greatest drama of all was to be enacted.

CHAPTER III.

Arrival in Egypt.

It was in high spirits that the Regiment landed at Alexandria on December 5, the freedom of movement after being " cribbed, cabined, and confined " for seven weeks, proving the most exhilarating joy. The horses, particularly those of the Star of India which had had more airy quarters than those on the Waimana, came ashore in remarkable condition. They were well-conditioned and glossy coated, and were quite ready to display their colonial conceits to the smaller-framed Arab horses about the wharves. The Waimana contingent had suffered more from the heat, and some of the animals had lost their hair in patches through constant sweating, and the owners, who had travelled on the other ship, had difficulty in recognising their steeds. A few week's care ashore, however, restored them.

At least one official of Egypt had no doubt about the obedience of the New Zealand troops the day of disembarkation. He was a pilot, and he came up the gangway of the Star of India when that vessel was lying hove-to outside the harbour. An A.M.R. trooper had been posted at the top of the gangway with instructions that no one had to be allowed to come aboard. Accordingly the pilot was firmly refused admittance to the ship. " But I'm the pilot," exclaimed that official, as he attempted to push by. " I don't care a d—— if you are Pontius Pilate," calmly returned the trooper, as he held his rifle horizontally across the gangway. " My orders are to let no one aboard." The incident was not noticed from the bridge, and the indignant pilot had to descend to his launch and draw out a little so that he could hail the officer on duty. The trooper in question was not a member of the guard at the Otahuhu camp which "arrested" the hot pie on its way to the officers' mess, and therefore he was not suspected of having been indulging a taste for humour.

The whole Force was transported by train to Zeitoun, an eastern suburb of Cairo, where a camp was speedily established on the very edge of the desert, and it was here that the New Zealanders lived and worked until they were called to participate in the glorious failure on the Gallipoli Peninsula. For the first week or two the A.M.R. concentrated its attention on getting the horses fit for the training ahead. When this was accomplished, the men themselves were ready for the ordeal, the getting of the horses into shape having entailed the tramping of many miles over the desert. It was then that the men began to know the desert as it is—the flats, the high soft sand hills cast up and fantastically moulded by the wind, the rocky slopes, and the flint-like crests—and it was inevitably the crests whereon the troopers were trained in the art of digging trenches. The bulk of the training, however, was in the work mounted rifles are expected to perform in war, with some musketry and bayonet-fighting thrown in. Picture the Regiment in from the desert after a day's training! A dense cloud of dust, rising higher than the cloud that hangs over a column of infantry, is the first sign of the advancing horsemen. The practised eye can readily observe whether the column be mounted or afoot. The dust cloud, hanging thick for half-a-mile behind the tail of the column, comes nearer and nearer, but not at a galloping speed, because the commander does not break from the regulation trot. Finally, the first line of horsemen looms up, but no figure is distinct, and no one identifiable until the line halts. The horses are then led towards the water troughs, but there is not room for all to drink at once. This is not understood by the horses, and those that have to wait, pull and shove and burrow their heads against their masters to reach the water for which their dust-lined throats are aching. While the watering is in progress, one may study the scene. The one colour of both man and beast is a light grey, except where perspiration makes it black. The one colour envelopes the riders' uniforms, the saddlery, and the hair and faces of the men. Looking closer it will be seen that a little ridge of clay encircles the horses' eyes, this being caused by the dust falling on the damp edge. After the horses have been thoroughly groomed, the nose bags with their strict allowance of tibbin and barley, a mixture of the country which the Colonial horses do not yet appreciate, are put on, and then, but not till then, do the troopers get a chance of cleansing their bodies of the coating of grime and grit they gathered on the desert. This was the usual routine during the training days.

Occasionally treks of two or three days' duration were made through the pleasant areas made prolific by irrigation, and these long rides along the paths between the plots of luscious beersim, and through the groves of date palms, were times of placid content, and of rare value in giving the men a chance to study the Fellaheen as he is. One or two trips were made to the Delta barrage, where the horses were swum in the Nile.

In times of freedom, most of the men became tourists, and all the wonders were thoroughly explored, even if time was found to taste the entertainments that Cairo offered. Despite the fixed convictions of many folk who were not there, the nights in Cairo were not wild orgies of dissipation in the realms of vice. Most of the gaiety was of a perfectly innocent character, the soldiers behaving just as well, if not a good deal better than the generality of tourists who go to Cairo.

On December 23, three days after His Highness Prince Hussein Kamel Pasha was proclaimed Sultan in the stead of Abbas Hilma Pasha, the late Khedive, who had shown his colours by going to Turkey after that country had joined our enemies, the Regiment, heading the column, took part in a march of all the colonial troops through Cairo, this demonstration of strength being considered necessary in view of the seething discontent of the Nationalists over the ending of Turkish suzerainty and the establishment of British protection over Egypt. The route led from the main thoroughfares through the narrow bazaars, where the curious eyes of harem women peered through the lattice window screens of the overhanging upper storeys, and sometimes sent eloquent glances when they caught the gaze of the troopers below. A man, whose name shall be Smith, raved about the ravishing eyes of one face at the window, and vowed he would " call," but later altered his mind when he passed an establishment, the entrance of which was guarded by a spectacular gentleman of ferocious aspect—maybe a Montenegrin—who wore in the sash which encircled the top of a pair of very red and very baggy trousers, a couple of revolvers of ancient make and a brace of knives which, Smith observed, were evidences of " a hideously suspicious nature." The mosque area, known to be the centre of seditious sentiment, was embraced in the march.

The display of force may have had good results, for when the Turks made their forlorn attack on the Suez Canal, on the night of February 2—an action in which, to the great disgust of the mounted rifles, New Zealand was represented by the infantry only—Cairo remained placid; the clamour of street hawkers filled the air as it would fill the air if the trump of doom sounded; the gentlemen of importance drank their coffee in the open cafes in all serenity, and smoked the bubbling narghileh; the weird, tuneless music of the kemengeh, the arghool, and the ood, punctuated by the resounding darabukkeh, arose from the malodorous bazaars where the Ghawazee girls danced for the plaudits and piastres of the crowd; and if the students of El Azhar whispered in secret conclave and planned a jehad for the glory of Islam and the crescent, their fantastical hopes faded when the dawn broke on a calmly indifferent city.

In the one riotous incident the Colonial troops were responsible for—the " battle of the Wazza " on Good Friday, which may or may not have had a real cause—A.M.R. men doubtless participated, but the Regiment was able to assume a very virtuous pose, seeing that it was called on to gallop a squadron or two, comprising all the men in camp, into Cairo to line the streets at strategic points. Any other regiment might have been detailed for this duty, but seeing that it was the A.M.R. that the order fell on, the men are still persuading themselves that they must have been the only reliable men of the hour, despite their own doubts

PART OF RUSSELL'S TOP, ANZAC, SHOWING THE SPHINX HEAD.

ANZAC COVE FROM THE SOUTH.

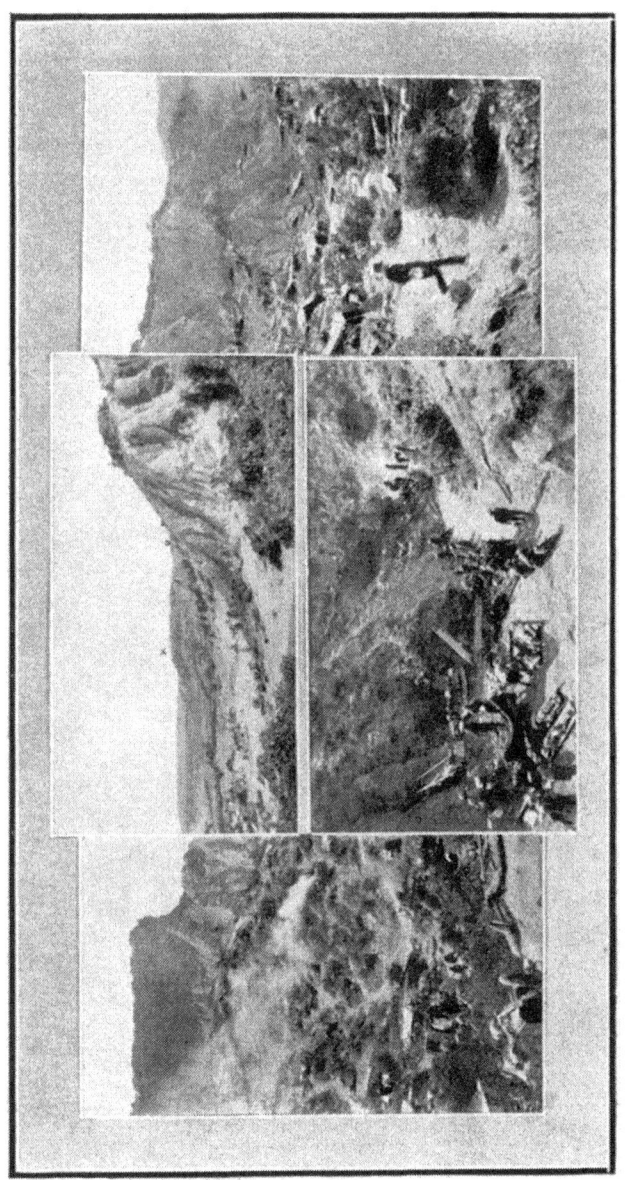

HOW MEN LIVED AND WHERE MEN FOUGHT AT ANZAC.

ANZAC SNAPSHOTS.

1. Periscopic rifle in position. 2. Indian transport mules. 3. Sleeping in support line. 4. The Beach sap. 5. Glimpse of Walker's Ridge. 6. Casualty Clearing Station.

on the question. What they would have done had the riot continued, and they had been required to quell it, no one knows, but there is a legend that " Hassan " Hammond, of the 3rd Squadron, was to be asked to address the rioters after the manner he used to address a team of bullocks which once had the misfortune to labour with him along the bush roads of Te Matakauri. It was considered that no riot could continue in the face of " Hassan's " reasoning.

An important milestone in the history of the Regiment and of the Force, was the day on which General Sir Ian Hamilton, who had come to the East on an important mission, not then divulged, reviewed the whole Colonial Corps, which comprised the 1st Australian Division and the Australian and New Zealand Division. He alone knew what would be required of these troops, practically untried and without regimental tradition behind them, but he has since recorded the high estimate he then placed upon their fighting qualities.

That dusty review will ever remain a bright memory in the minds of the men, for there the Force assembled in full strength on one parade ground for the first and last time. It was a thrilling and inspiring sight, even to those who participated, and it was not surprising to hear that the general described these young regiments as " spoiling for a fight." Whatever warring strategists may say or not say about the Gallipoli Campaign, there is no doubt about the fact that Sir Ian Hamilton has a vigour and personality that appeals to the colonials, and it is certainly a fact that at this review the general rode straight into their hearts. He was as much under inspection by the colonials as they were under inspection by him, and if he were pleased, so were the troops; and whatever happened or did not happen subsequently, the men retain feelings of warm regard towards the Commander-in-Chief. If it was he who was responsible for the failure, the men of the Dominion will be the first to offer excuse. As he rode down the long glistening line of sun-tanned virile manhood, he called cheery welcomes to the officers he remembered meeting when he reviewed the Territorials in New Zealand the previous year, and his smiling but keen eyes seemed to include every man in their searching gaze. After he had gone from one end to the other, the march past took place, the mounted rifles, in squadron column, first going by at the walk and afterwards at a hand gallop, which shrouded a square mile in dust.

CHAPTER IV.

"An Unknown Destination."

A few weeks later an electric current went through the camp when the infantry received orders to prepare for embarkation at Alexandria for a secret destination. It was a sad blow to the mounted rifles again to stay behind while the infantry were sent to war. No one knew what the objective of the Mediterranean Expeditionary Force was to be, but there was not a soul in camp who did not sense the coming of stirring days. In the thrill which the departure of the infantry occasioned, there was an undercurrent of excitement as if the " whispering galleries " of the East had been awakened by prescient voices that spoke of romantic deeds of arms. On the night of the departure, troopers searched for friends along the ranks that loomed through the darkness, grasped hands they never were to touch again, and went back to the tame tiresome tasks of the horse lines. Junior officers of the mounted rifles cursed their luck, and having sat in dismal groups in the mess tent consuming strong waters, they went to bed to dream of anything but the route march ordered for the morrow. But their days went on in the same old way. It has been recorded by a painstaking adjutant that the A.M.R. moved in the direction of El Marg and carried out reconnaisance work, that it took part in operations against the A.L.H. Brigade in the vicinity of Ishkandar Shakir, and that on one sad morning when reveille sounded at 3.30 a.m. it marched against the enemy in the direction of Virgin's Breast.

And while this mimic war went on the infantry were preparing for that audacious landing on Gallipoli.

When, on April 30, the news of the Landing came, the mounted rifles resembled dogs in leash in their anxiety to get away to the aid of the Force which had suffered so severely. A long, restless week went by, and then came the order for the mounted rifles to prepare to go to the front without their horses. The effect of this order on the spirits of the men was instantaneous. The " grousing " discontent that had developed gave place to the wildest exhilaration, which expressed itself in more or less tuneful song. The wave of minstrelsy that swept over the Regiment may not have added much to the art of singing, but it had a meaning which would have given pride to New Zealand, and on that account the fact is recorded. The only regret was that the horses, now trained to a very fine point, were not to share the honours of battle. But while the Regiment would have liked to be used for the purpose it had been trained, there was not a man who would have missed this chance of fighting as a foot slogger.

Unfortunately, no webb equipment was available for the troopers, but from somewhere were produced brown canvas packs which had two arm slings. These crude packs were probably the most " awkward " knapsack equipment ever issued to soldiers, and it was fortunate that they could be dispensed with as soon as the Gallipoli beach was reached. They had to be worn on top of the leather bandolier of the trooper, and they had neither fit, form, nor comeliness. There is some co-ordination and singleness of purpose about the webb equipment of an infantryman, but the disconnected assortment of gear of these troopers—haversack, water bottle, bandolier, overcoat—were all at war with one another, and the result was sad. When ready for the train the men felt like badly-laden camels, and two of them were in such dire straits that they slipped away to the station in a " garry," to the indignation of a sergeant-major of the old school, who demanded to be informed if the men in the cab thought they were " spare colonels or generals or somethin' " and if they intended to drive right into the trenches in their " blasted go-cart." He also wished to be informed if the " spare generals " desired him to send a fatigue party to carry their " luggage " to the train, and get them some wine and a roll and the bosom of a duck to sustain them until their cook got sober. The culprits were glad to escape to the obscurity of an unpleasant fatigue duty.

The strength of the Regiment for embarkation was: 26 officers, 482 other ranks, and 71 horses, the horses being included in the hope that wheeled transport might soon be possible, but they were never landed. The Regiment, with the exception of a small party travelling on the Kingstonian with the horses, embarked on the Grantully Castle, on which was also the 3rd Australian Light Horse, who, like the New Zealand Mounted Rifles, were to fight dismounted. Before the ship sailed, four stowaways were found and sent back to Zeitoun. These four, not quite so fortunate as some others who got to Anzac by stealth, and there were welcomed with joy to the strength of their units, reflected the general feelings of the farriers and reinforcement details left behind, although they had a more irresponsible way of expressing their disappointment. As a matter of fact the farriers of the Regiment had contributed no small amount of gaiety to the camp on the day of departure by their competition for the two vacancies on the war establishment. Someone said that the manner in which the farriers " canvassed " every officer who might be able to support their claim for selection, reminded him of politics in the good old days of patronage.

The transports sailed on the evening of May 9, and after what seemed an endless passage of three days, arrived off Cape Helles, where lay a countless fleet of battleships, cruisers, destroyers, transports, colliers, and small craft of all descriptions. The sight of a " dummy " warship was a rare chance for a humourist, who called on heaven to witness the vanished might of the British Navy, declared his certain conviction that someone was certainly going to be hurt after all, and voiced his intention of going to no more wars until it was agreed that both sides were to fight with bladders on sticks. While the transports lay off Helles (the humorist called it " hell's point," and said he could quite understand why the " old dago " swam it), the men witnessed the Queen Elizabeth shelling, with her 15-inch guns, the Turkish defences on the southern slopes of Achi Baba, the eminence which dominates the southern end of the Peninsula, and they also saw the distant flashes of the field artillery ashore. In the afternoon the transports weighed anchor and sailed north to Fisherman's Hut, which seemed to be the general designation of the colonial position at that time.

While the ships were passing up the coast, those on board were able to study the general outlines of the country. To the north of Achi Baba lay the Khilid Bahr Plateau, but this feature was more distant, some flat agricultural land extending from its base to the sea. North again of this plateau rose the forbidding tangle of ridges, gullies, and crags of Sari Bair, rising by stages to the height of 971 feet at the north end of the range. When the ships hove to off the Fisherman's Hut area, the men saw a sheer clay face rising almost from the beach, and into this ran gorges. In the distance beyond loomed the eminence of what was called Baby 700 and Chunuk Bair, the ground from which the Turk was to dominate the Anzac position—the ground which was to see the troops rise to undreamed of deeds of gallantry and heroism, but which in the end was to put the seal of failure upon an enterprise which will be the nation's pride for aye. At the distance the position seemed so peaceful and still that the mounted riflemen were inclined to believe the rumour that they would have to march some miles before they could smell powder. But they did not then know that birds could whistle in the still of No Man's Land while the trenches on either side bristled with bayonets, and countless eyes kept ceaseless watch, and snipers with fingers on their triggers waited without a movement in their lairs for the reckless or unwary head to show.

CHAPTER V.

Gallipoli.

Soon the destroyer Colne came alongside, and the Regiment, with those ridiculous brown packs up, and all manner of things from shovels to pannikins appended, tumbled down the gangway on to her deck. Most of the men had acquired small bundles of firewood. These had been prepared by some details of the Royal Marine Light Infantry for their comrades ashore, who had taken the place of the New Zealand Infantry, now at Helles, for the Daisy Patch attack. It was a veteran who suggested that the wood ought to be taken, and it was taken, and no one was much disturbed by the wrath of a R.M.L.I. petty officer who had something to say about colonial thieves who would steal the gold out of a tooth. As the destroyer drew shoreward the real nature of the torn, tumbled country became evident, and everyone was prepared to echo the verdict of a tired sailor who said the men who stormed those heights had "done a miracle." Suddenly a few shells burst on the beach, the first evidence of war so far. The next minute Trooper Taylor gained the distinction of being the first man in the Regiment to be wounded. When he was struck no one was aware that spent Turkish bullets, which had missed the trenches on the crest, had been dropping into the sea in the vicinity of the destroyer. Taylor did not know himself that he had been wounded. He thought that some energetic person had brought his rifle barrel into violent contact with his arm, and he turned round smartly to deal with the offender. His surprise at finding that a bullet had penetrated his arm was great.

From the destroyer the men transferred to a barge, which was towed to the beach by a man-o'-war pinnace, commanded by a midshipman who looked as if he should not yet be out of the nursery, but he was a very confident young gentleman. The A.M.R. poured ashore in high spirits. A few worn, bearded men, whose sunken eyes and deeply-lined faces told of the ordeal they had been through, drifted down to the beach, where the troopers were rejoicing as fresh troops usually do. Their cheerful greetings to the men with the sunken eyes brought forth only monosyllabic responses, and one of the weary men was heard to remark to a mate, "You'd think it was our —— birthday." Afterwards the troopers were to know how offensive the bounding, superabundant animal spirits of fresh troops can be to men who are tired beyond all telling.

That night the Regiment bivouacked in the scrub on the steep face of one of the gullies that made a dead end in the cliff face, and all night long the rifle fire on the crest overhead rose and swelled and died away, only to break out afresh more vicious still. At last the Regiment was at war. The brink of the great adventure had been reached, and the peace of mind that comes of sacrifice and of striving in a great cause, the calm that comes in strife to all good soldiers and gives them the power to die cheerfully, began to steal upon them. Next day the Regiment left the gully just before the Turks by means of shrapnel informed them that they had chosen the wrong side if they wanted to bivouack in safety, and relieved the Nelson and Deal Battalions of the Royal Marine Light Infantry in the trenches on Walker's Ridge, the left section of the first crest, the R.M.L.I. leaving Anzac immediately to rejoin the

Royal Naval Division at Cape Helles. The Regiment wound up the steep track leading to Walker's Ridge, looking like a human baggage train.

Walker's Ridge, the right extension of which was afterwards named Russell's Top, after Brigadier-General Russell, the commander of the Mounted Rifles Brigade, was the left section of the precipitous eminence that overlooked the beach. It gained its importance from the fact that it guarded the Nek where the Turkish line came nearest to the beach. It was, moreover, the one point on the left of the whole Anzac position where the Turks had only one line of trenches between them and the sea. Here the enemy, with one successful assault, could immediately breach the Anzac defensive system without being first or afterwards hampered by ravines. To the right of Russell's Top lay Plugge's Plateau, but this was no longer a front line position, the infantry having carried and held Pope's Ridge and Quinn's Post on the opposite side of Monash Gully, which was the extension of Shrapnel Gully, a ravine that ran in a north-east direction from Hell Spit, the southern end of the Landing Beach. The Nek was a narrow piece of ground, sloping slightly towards our line, which lay between the head of Monash Gully and the precipitous ravine which formed the left flank of the position, and which made it almost secure from serious attack from that direction. Beyond this ravine there was no definite trench system, but three outposts had been established on positions that commanded the deres, which ran down to the beach from the mass of tumbled, water-torn country on the north, and, hence, it was not necessary to hold the line running from the left of

Walker's Ridge to the sea. The Nek was a natural bridge between the two lines in this section. While the right section of the position taken over by the A.M.R., in conjunction with the W.M.R., looked across Monash Gully to the "back yards" of Pope's and Quinn's held by the infantry, the centre and left confronted, at a distance that varied from 50 to 100 yards, one of the strongest points of the Turkish line. It was what might be termed a self-contained position, because there was no definite line of communication across Monash Gully to Pope's and Quinn's. Incidentally, Pope's was similarly situated in respect to Quinn's, Dead Man's Gully, which neither side could hold, intervening. These gaps in our line added to our difficulties, but they were not so dangerous as they would appear, seeing that they could easily become death traps for an advancing enemy. The great difficulty of Walker's Ridge was that the area of ground held by us was so small that a second defensive position could not be established. One point on the right of our line was not more than 30 yards from the cliff face, and the left was not much better for rear defences. The only means of reinforcing the Ridge from the beach was via the one steep track that led up the one possible spur. At this time part of our line had "dead ground" in front, which necessitated the driving of saps to give better observation and field of fire. Towering behind the Nek on the Turkish side was the Chessboard and Baby 700. Summed up it was far from being a comfortable position. Its insecurity was typical of the general insecurity of the whole Anzac position.

It was on this eyrie that the A.M.R. learned to war, and a hard school it was. They could have no support from the navy because the trenches were too close, and because it was impossible to get sufficient elevation on the guns. The only artillery available was one Indian Mountain Battery, the guns of which were hidden in pits almost adjoining the trenches. These guns could not be used with any degree of freedom, however, owing to the shortage of ammunition and the superior observation of the Turks. But the mere presence of the guns and the splendid Sikh gunners was a source of strength. No soldiers had better comrades than were these Sikhs, who worshipped their little guns, and lay round them at night with their long curved swords at their hips. How generous they were! How they loved a fight! and how approvingly they smiled at a man who wore a bandage!

When the mounted rifles took over this position, the trench system had not progressed very far, but the men were amazed at what had been accomplished in so short a time by the infantry. Much more had to be done, however, and it was rather fortunate that the Turks were equally engrossed with the development of their defences, " across the way." Within a few days the troopers realised that to be able to dig is one of the first qualifications of a soldier. The first job was to " bring in " the dead ground, and the next was to develop and deepen the maze of communication trenches between the front line and the face. The track leading to the ridge had to be reduced at the steepest points, and it had to be widened at the top to allow for the passage of guns which never came. The task of the ridge was overwhelming, and it became more and more so as death, wounds, and sickness claimed their daily toll.

When the Regiment first came up, the No Man's Land in front presented a ghastly sight. Lying among the bullet-cut scrub were the bodies of friends and foes. One sap passed by two shallow graves where Turks had been buried, and when the trench passed on two pairs of booted feet stuck out through the wall. The weather was intensely hot by day, and the stench of the whole area was frightful. There was no escape from the smell of death, which clung to the men's clothing, and even seemed to permeate the biscuits which, with bully beef and jam, formed the staple ration. Another horror was the flies, which swarmed in myriads in the trenches, preventing men from snatching a little much-needed sleep when the opportunity offered in the daytime, and making eating a misery. It was impossible to leave food exposed, and the only time that the "billies" of bully and biscuit stew were free from flies was when they were on the little smoky fireplaces in recesses of the communication trenches. There was no regimental cooking, of course, rations being issued to sections (four men), who could eat them when and how they liked. Owing to the annoyance of the flies some sections did not eat anything but a dry biscuit during the daytime. To eat biscuit and jam in the daytime a man had to keep moving the hand that held the food. Shrapnel and sniping were often severe, but they did not drive men to distraction as did the flies.

The Regiment remained wonderfully cheerful, however, and even the flies were made the subject of humour. For instance, one man composed the following " verse," which was sung with great gusto to the hymn tune " There is a Happy Land ":—

> This is our hymn of hate, " Gott strafe the flies,"
> Sing it early, sing it late, " Gott strafe the flies."
> Where they come from we can't tell,
> But they surely give us hell.
> We can only sit and yell, " Gott strafe the flies."

Besides flies there were lice, and although most men had the chance of a swim in the sea every few days, no one was quite free of this affliction. But again the humourist found relief in verse, and composed the following to the tune of " The Little Grey Home in the West ":—

> There's a trench on the slope of the hill, called by the Turk, Chunuk Bair,
> That's where we reside in the warm summer-time in a hole that resembles a lair.
> And there's plenty of company, too; how they itch, how they tickle and bite!
> We would happier be with Turk shrapnel for tea than the little grey boys of the night.

With all these discomforts, the exhaustion of labour, the strain of unceasing vigil and shell fire, the lack of nourishing food, and little sleep, there was always a shortage of water and the possibility of no water at all. One pint of water a day was the usual issue. When the Turkish artillery fire from Anafarta, to the north, or from the Olive Grove to the south, sunk a water barge as it approached the beach, there was likely to be no water issue. There on Walker's Ridge the men learned the art of washing and shaving with about three spoonfuls of water, which was all that could ever be spared out of the pint. Later, a well was sunk beneath the ridge, about 30 yards from the sea, but the water was very brackish. Another well was sunk in Sphinx Gully, where the Regiment went to " rest "—the " rest " consisting of sapping in the front positions above instead of watching for the Turk—but the small flow that was obtained was condemned by the medical officer. For men who had to toil so strenuously with pick and shovel in that summer heat of the Ægean, water was the first need, but they had to survive without it.

These were the conditions of life under which the Regiment settled down to the stationary struggle on the ridge, a regiment still untested.

Walker's Ridge was a post of honour, and it stands to the credit of the A.M.R. that they were entrusted with it. But the higher command did not appear to have any doubts about any of the mounted rifles units. It is recalled that when General Birdwood met the colonel, shortly after the arrival of the mounted brigade, he fervently exclaimed, "Thank God you have come, Mackesy," referring, of course, to the whole brigade. Posts of honour, however, are posts of danger and difficulty, and Walker's Ridge was no exception. Apart from the general difficulties common to the whole of Anzac, Walker's Ridge possessed some peculiar to itself—a statement, by the way, that does not mean that other positions of the line did not possess their own particular troubles.

One of the difficulties that beset Walker's when the mounted rifles arrived there was the fire superiority of the Turks.

Their wild fusillades during the night were of little consequence. They did not succeed even in drawing a return fire, and thereby cause a waste of ammunition. But during the long hours of daylight the Turks had us almost blinded. One reason was that they held higher ground, which not only gave them superior observation, but also made it possible for them to have sniping holes beneath their own parapet, often less than 50 yards away. This was an impossibility on our side. Another reason was that the Turks, who, be it remembered, were filled with the confidence of expert marksmen not yet challenged, had prepared sniping " possies " in unexpected places among the scrub outside their line, and on the higher ground behind. The R.M.L.I. had not been able to remove this dangerous sniping menace. Composed mainly of men who had used firearms from boyhood, the Regiment speedily set about killing the sniping.

The supply of a number of periscopes, manufactured by handy men on the beach, partly overcame the disadvantage of holding the low ground, but even then good counter-sniping was difficult, seeing that a man, after spotting a mark through a periscope, had to drop it, pick up his rifle, and expose himself, while he again found the mark, sighted, and fired. Then came another " homemade " invention, in the shape of a periscopic attachment for rifles, which put our men almost on an equal footing with the Turk. It was a slow business to align the sights on a mark when the sighting was done through the reflecting glasses, but it could be done, and it was possible to wait for a movement at a suspected place with the same deadly patience of the enemy snipers in their hidden " possies." The Turks made great rifle practice in shattering the top glass of the periscopes,

THE WATER TANKS IN MULE GULLY, WHICH SUPPLIED RUSSELL'S TOP.

SUPPLY DEPOT IN MULE GULLY, BELOW WALKER'S RIDGE.
The cases contain tins of biscuits and "bully" beef, the main ration of Gallipoli.

BARGE WITH WOUNDED BEING TOWED FROM ANZAC BEACH TO A VESSEL IN THE ROADSTEAD.

AOTEA HOSPITAL, HELIOPOLIS, CAIRO.

but they rapidly lost their confidence. Within a week the men of the A.M.R. had killed a number of Turkish snipers, and had very definitely cooled the ardour of the enemy generally for this form of war. Many of the " cubby holes " beneath the Turk parapet became untenable through the deadly vigilance of our men. One of these holes, a mere stone's throw from our trench, was " spotted " in a somewhat strange way. The back of this hole was usually covered by a piece of sacking when it was not filled by the head and shoulders of a sniper, to prevent the sunlight shining behind it, and so revealing its position. One bright morning the sniper, after withdrawing, neglecting to " drop his curtain," as one cheerful soul described it, and the watchers of the A.M.R. were astonished to see pairs of legs passing at the end of the little tunnel. One man sighted a periscopic rifle on to the hole, and, refraining from firing at the passing legs, settled down to wait for the sniper to " come home." After two hours of waiting a man's head and shoulders shut out the light in the hole. The breathless trooper carefully fired, and he was able to see a body slowly drop downward.

It was evident the Turks were doing a lot of work in front of the A.M.R., and a patrol, under Corporal McDonald, was sent out on May 15th, and returned with valuable information that the enemy were making trenches, etc. On May 16th, a large concentration of the enemy was evident on this front. Lieutenant P. Logan volunteered to reconnoitre the position. Taking Trooper Heays with him, he went out about an hour before dark, and got quite close to the enemy trenches. He came back with the exact positions of the works the enemy were building on the " Nek," information that was very valuable when the attack came.

CHAPTER VI.

Defence of Walker's Ridge.

It was in the early hours of May 19 that the Regiment fought its first fight, and was able to justify the confidence that had been placed in it. It had been known that the Turks had been heavily reinforced at Anzac, and that an attempt was to be made to " push the British into the sea." Accordingly every precaution was taken by the mounted rifles, but it was a most inopportune time to meet an attack owing to the fact that the " dead ground " in the centre of the line was in the process of being " brought in." A sap, about two chains long, had been driven out from the left of the centre at right angles to the fire trench, and another had been started at the right of the centre to junction with the other and form a new line. Between the heads of these two works there was a gap through which the enemy might pour down on the original front line.

On the night of May 18, the 3rd squadron occupied the left, including the new sap which ran out inconclusively at right angles into No Man's Land. Major Schofield was in command of this section. On their right and in the other new sap was the 4th squadron, the 11th squadron being in support behind the two squadrons in the maze of communication trenches that gave no observation and no field of fire. Further to the right was the W.M.R. About midnight a tremendous fusillade broke out from the Turkish line opposite. It was mainly machine-gun and rifle fire, but it was so intense that it killed any observation that might have been made. The night was pitch black, however, and in any case little could have been seen. Everyone was called to arms when the enemy tuned up, and the troops which had been lying in immediate support, filed into the front saps, filling them to their fullest capacity. There was probably a bayonet to every yard. For three long hours they crouched in the narrow saps, which were still without fire steps in many places. The strain of waiting for action is always trying, even to seasoned troops, and it was something of an ordeal for men who were about to fight their first action. But confidence and good humour saw them through.

Finally, at 3.30 a.m., the Turkish fire slackened, and then, after an ominous silence, the enemy sprang to the attack. Cries of " Allah, Allah, Allah," from thousands of throats rent the air—a really fearsome battle-cry, until one gets used to it. Closer and closer came the charge, but still fire was withheld. The squadron officers being scattered among the men made this possible. It was a supreme test of discipline. Not until the first line of Turks was 20 yards away was the order for rapid fire given. The troopers sprang to the parapet like greyhounds, and in a second they were pouring a devastating fire into the approaching ranks. In many cases men were able to remain in position only by bracing one foot against the back wall of the trench. It was not a modern fight. There were no flares to throw out in front and not even any jam tin bombs. It was a battle of bullet and steel.

With the first blaze of fire that pierced the darkness of the mounted rifles line, the first line of Turks seemed to disappear, but other lines came on to meet the same fate. Before long numbers of the enemy were throwing themselves flat to escape from the flying sheet of metal, but at the very place where they should have made the last rush.

Our men began to drop, but even their immediate neighbours were hardly conscious of the fact. The thrill of battle possessed them. Rifle barrels grew too hot to touch and bolts began to get stiff. The imprecations that penetrated the din when bolts jammed, through the heat and grit, were ferocious. The men in trouble were possessed of the healthy belief that if their particular rifles were out of action everything was lost. The end of the left sap became a very warm corner. Here Lieutenant Weir and some of his troop put up a desperate struggle, in which bayonets were used, and drove off three rushes.

On the left, where the old line ran to within a few yards of the gully, matters were in doubt for a time, but Sergeant Thompson, who was killed in August, displayed fine leadership, and the Turks were driven off. It was a small section of the fight, but had it not been for this small body of the 3rd squadron the Turks might have been able to work round the end of the line and penetrate the rear.

The Turks did not appear to have a knowledge of our position and its weaknesses. This became palpably apparent when they failed to concentrate upon the gap between the head of the left sap and the position held by the 4th squadron, to the right. They seemed to lose direction, confused, perhaps, by the angles of the line. The greatest stand of the night was made by a part of the 4th squadron, and it should be described in detail.

Lieutenant J. M. Roberts was in command of the squadron. Captain Bluck, who had been in command of the Waikatos after Major Tattersall had taken the place of Major Chapman as second in command of the Regiment when it left Zeitoun, had been killed by a sniper that morning. Lieutenant Roberts had had only two hours of daylight in which to familiarise himself with the position and make his dispositions. He decided to put Lieutenant C. James, with his troop (the Whakatane Troop), into the new front line, on the right, which, it was obvious, would have to bear the force of the attack. The rest of the 4th squadron occupied the old line, to the right, overlooking Monash Gully, with the exception of Lieutenant Milliken's troop, which was held in reserve. The Whakatane Troop was practically isolated owing to the presence of a small gap between their right and the old line, but this gap was not the menace of the gap on their left, although it made reinforcement and communication difficult. Lieutenant James' orders were to hold the little line for 20 minutes at all costs—and he and his men well knew what the cost would be. They knew that they would have to leave their sap and fight in the open, owing to the fact that in its present state it was merely a deep, narrow ditch, from which they could not fight. It had no fire steps, and it was so narrow that two men could not pass in it. As soon as the attack was launched, Lieutenant James and his men sprang over the parapet, and, lying down in the open, poured their fire into the Turks. Soon they were at point-blank range, and dozens of Turks were shot down at a distance of 10 feet. The miracle was how the little band of heroes was not overwhelmed. The Turks had men enough to sweep through them like a hurricane, but their fire was so well directed, and their demeanour so stubborn, that every rush was crushed, the Turks doing the fatal thing of lying down at the very time their final resolute rush should have been made. It was probably their fear of resolute steel that stopped them. Within a few minutes two-thirds of the troop had become casualties, Lieutenant James being among the killed, but the line held. Then Lieutenant Milliken was ordered to reinforce with the reserve troop, and after him were sent two troops of the 11th squadron, commanded by Lieutenant Finlayson and Lieutenant Logan, Captain Mackesy, of the 11th, accompanying them.

On the whole ridge were only two machine-guns, one of the W.M.R. being at the angle of the left sap and the old line, where it had a wide field of fire, and it did tremendous execution. The other, belonging to the Regiment, was on the right of the Waikatos, but owing to the angles of the new sap and the presence of the steep face of Monash Gully, on its right front, its field of fire was very restricted, and the support it gave was more moral than actual.

As the first streaks of dawn rose above the hills which overlook the field of Troy, the Turks retired at the run. Some, who had been feigning dead, darted back through the scrub, amid showers of bullets. Among the snipers was the colonel, who had been watching the movement from the highest point of the parados. It was the most exposed position of the line, and why he was not shot down is a mystery.

Flushed as they were with success, the mounted rifles did not relax their vigilance. Wearing smiles, and heaven-sent cigarettes in their countenances, they waited for the next attack which was fully expected, knowing that this time the Turk would get it worse than before. But the attack never came. A C.M.R. machine-gun that had been posted on a clay peak in the gorge, on the left, was able to get on to a group of German officers who were conferring in what they had believed to be a safe hollow, and this seemed to end the hopes of the Turks for the time being.

The area of the action was on back yard scale and on our side it was manned accordingly, but the little line had to face a concentration of the enemy that might have been used over a front double the length of the ridge position. Further, the nature of the position had the effect of throwing the whole weight of the attack upon about half our front, in which there was room for less than half the number of bayonets necessary. Yet the attack was utterly crushed, and in about four acres the Turks left nearly 500 dead. The position was held against the principles of war. The whole attack did not extend beyond Quinn's Post, where a very desperate onslaught was beaten off by the 4th Australian Brigade, but nowhere did a Turk enter the colonial line and live two seconds. The total Turkish casualties for the night were estimated at 7,000. The losses of the Regiment were 23 killed, and about the same amount wounded.

A splendid example was set to the men by Colonel Mackesy during the fight. He first appeared, with rifle and bayonet, in the advanced sap on the right. After firing for a time he made his way to the left sap, and finding no room on the parapet, climbed to the parados, which was the highest and most exposed point in the vicinity, and from there emptied several magazines. When the attack was at its height, an " order "—" Cease fire, Australians advancing on your right " was passed down the advanced sap held by the 3rd squadron. In Egypt the men had been thoroughly trained in the passing of orders down a line by word of mouth. On one occasion, General Godley had questioned the Regiment's ability in this direction, and he accepted the colonel's permission to test them. A galloper was started down the line as the verbal order was given to the first man, and the verbal order reached the end before the galloper. Almost automatically, therefore, the order to cease fire was shouted from man to man, and automatically some men took the pressure off their triggers, but the colonel instantly passed back, " Australians be damned! Ask where the order came from?" Back went this order, and no reply was returned.

It was probably the first time in history that a Maori war cry mingled with that of the Mohammedan. The mounted men fought in comparative silence as far as vocal sounds were concerned, but once the Maori haka, " Komate, komate," resounded down the mounted rifle line.

The following morning the regiment received a tribute which made them very proud. It was not from a general but from a squadron sergeant-major who belonged to the old school of the Imperial Cavalry. He was a perfect soldier, but all through the training days he had expressed grave doubts about a regiment that did not worry about its buttons and the brilliancy of its spurs, and which could not see the importance of saluting, and so on. Coming to a group of men with battle stains all over them, he said, " I take it all back. First time in action and steady as rocks. You'll do me." Praise from Sir Ian Hamilton himself could not have pleased the men more.

A staff officer of the brigade related how he had met a party of unofficial reinforcements coming up the track from the beach during the fight. He said he had never seen such a mixture. There were a few A.S.C. men, a couple of Indians, three or four Medical Corps men, and a doctor, all carrying rifles, a sailor, who like many others on the beach proudly sported a pair of riding pants and a wide-awake hat, and finally a midshipman carrying a rifle almost as long as himself. They all wanted to " see the fun," as the middy expressed it. Such was the spirit of Anzac.

CHAPTER VII.

The Day After.

Exhausted though the men were there was no rest for them this day. Parties were set to work to complete the gap in the centre of the line, and everyone else was engaged in making the saps into fire trenches. For a time in the afternoon, rapid fire (the only poor substitute for artillery fire) was opened on the Turkish line with a view to covering an advance by sections of regiments, ordered by the corps commander, the purpose being to destroy the enemy's machine guns. This order was countermanded, however, and fortunately so, for the Turkish line on the Nek was tremendously strong, bristling with a mass of well-concealed machine guns, and, as was afterwards proved by the disastrous attempt of the Light Horse, it was well nigh invulnerable unless battered to pieces by heavy artillery fire. But we had neither the guns nor the ammunition for such preparation, even if this part of the Turkish line had not had the security from barrage fire, which it owed to its nearness to a cliff over 200 feet high, and its proximity to our line. A surprise night attack with bombs might have succeeded, but, lackaday, we had no bombs other than a few of the home-made jam tin variety, and few there were who would not rather have trusted in their bayonets and their rifle butts.

On the 20th, the work on the defences was pushed on, many of the men having had no sleep and practically no rest for 40 hours. During the day the Turk shelled our lines more severely than usual, and among those wounded was Major J. N. McCarroll, the commander of 11th squadron. Fortunately his wounds did not incapacitate him for long. He returned in September, eventually being promoted to the command of the Regiment, and gaining the highest distinctions for his masterly leadership in the Palestine campaign.

Towards evening of this day the men had one of the surprises of their lives. Suddenly hundreds of white flags were waved along the Turkish line, and then large numbers of Turks came out of their trenches, and, still waving the flags, moved towards our lines. Colonel Mackesy immediately mounted the parapet and called on the Turks to stop and state their intentions. He called first in French, then in German, and then in English, but got no reply he could understand. He then told the regimental interpreter to call in Turkish. A Turkish officer replied that they wanted a truce so that they might bury their dead. Such a request by Turks who are notoriously indifferent to sanitary safeguards sounded suspicious. However, the Turks sent forward an officer blindfolded, and he was sent to brigade headquarters while the colonel continued the parley. It was then perceived that behind the unarmed men with flags were many with rifles and bayonets, and above the Turkish parapet immediately opposite, showed the tops of a thick line of bayonets. The enemy were immediately given two minutes to get back to their trenches. It was not promptly obeyed, however, and the whole line opened fire, one of our machine guns accounting for 30 or 40 of the treacherous enemy. Never again was a ruse of this kind attempted.

The following morning the Turks sent in from
Gaba Tepe, on the extreme right, an officer to
arrange for an armistice so that the dead might
be buried. The colonial commander was as
anxious as the Turks to have an armistice for
burials, for many dead heroes of the landing still
lay in the bullet-swept zone, the prone forms all
lying with the head to the foe, speaking eloquently
of the valour of the first fierce charge. It was
most important, however, that the enemy should
not be given a chance of scrutinising our trenches
with all their weaknesses and imperfections, and
some days were spent in drawing up the terms
of the armistice. It was finally agreed that the
armistice should cover the period from 7.30 a.m.
to 4.30 p.m., on May 24; that the Turkish burial
parties were to work on one side and our parties
on the other side of a line pegged down the centre
of No Man's Land; that the bodies of foes found
by either side were to be carried to the dividing
line and handed over; and that rifles were to be
handed to whatever side had owned them.
Parties from each side marked out the dividing
line early in the morning, and then the burial
parties commenced their gruesome task. Here
and there foes fraternised, and sometimes exchanged samples of their rations. But the
majority of our men were too overcome at the
sight of the dead, sometimes lying literally in
heaps, to have much concern with the living. In
front of the Walker's Ridge line lay an Australian
bugler, a mere boy, with his bugle slung across his
shoulders. Nearby lay the body of a New Zealand infantryman, his hands still grasping an
out-stretched rifle, the bayonet of which was in the

body of a Turk. The agreement to carry the Turkish bodies to the centre line could not be carried out owing to their number, and it was mutually agreed that each side should bury all the dead on its side of the line. The work was accomplished by the time appointed and the parties returned to their trenches.

CHAPTER VIII.

Life at Anzac.

At this time the A.M.R. did not occupy the trenches on Walker's Ridge, the Regiment having been relieved by the 9th A.L.H. The A.M.R. was nominally resting in dug-outs on the beach side of Plugge's Plateau, but in actual fact there was no rest on Anzac. There was no rest from shell fire, and no rest from toil. When a regiment was sent to a beach gully for " rest " it meant that it was treated to a more liberal allowance of shrapnel, and more work than usual. When the A.M.R., in these periods of rest, was not carrying water and rations, it was reducing grades on the track to Walker's, or driving new saps or underground galleries in the most advanced positions on the ridge. The men became inured to the experience of digging at new saps a considerable distance from the main line, with parties of the enemy similarly engaged, a matter of 20 or 30 yards away. In the friendly daylight the work in these places was not disturbing, the chief diverting circumstance being when Turkish sentries took flying shots at the shovels when they showed over the top. This amusement became quite popular with both sides, and it was the custom to wave the shovels to signal that the marksman had missed. Those sapping on both sides seemed to think that this little acknowledgement was due to the diligent sentry. During the lonesome night, however, the forward sapping had nothing to relieve the nerves. Frequently men had to work in narrow grave-like places from which a sentry could not be seen, and then the strain was worse than it was under any other circumstance. The Regiment was very emphatic on this point, particularly because they felt that little account was taken in certain quarters of the immense physical and nervous strain imposed by this work. " It's not so bad to go out in a scrap," exclaimed one trooper, " but I object to being speared like a flounder in this ditch. A'course I could chuck a pick, or a spade, or a lump of rock for that matter at a prowling Turk, damn him, but what's he likely to be doin' in the meantime. S'no good me tellin' him that I'm only an amateur sapper, and much too young to die. I don't hold with this dig, dig, digging, and arguin' in point. Why don't we fight the damned thing out." From which, of course, it will be seen that the trooper's nerves were not benefiting much by the " rest." A philosopher, who at the moment was wielding the pick, found some consolation in his firm belief that " the gentlemen engaged in a similar capacity opposite were probably just as funked as he was. He really thought they might heave them over a tin of bully as a sign of sympathy." And then the corporal suggested that if they didn't stop the debate, Abdul would achieve the same result by a sanguinary bomb. Trooper No. 1, having remarked somewhat bitterly that it wouldn't be so bad if the sentry guarding him would sometimes not go to sleep, the operations against terra firma proceeded. The relating of this midnight conversation not only shows the rest-time employments of the troopers, but also indicates the kind of humour that was the law of Anzac—the unwritten law, which ordained everything must be made the subject of mirth, even if it were bitter mirth. Who can say how much of the strength of Anzac had its being in this strange attitude of mind, this determination to jest at hunger and thirst and flies and at death itself? Was it Nature's compensation? Was it the sure and certain consequence of over-taxed bodies and nerves? Was it the outward and visible sign of that strange peace, bred of self-sacrifice, that comes to a good soldier in the struggle and shines brightest when the agony is greatest and death nearest? Was it that of which the great-hearted Grenfell sang in his poem " Into Battle."

> Through joy and blindness he shall know,
>   Not caring much to know, that still
> Nor lead nor steel shall reach him, so
>   That it be not the Destined Will.
>
> The thundering line of battle stands,
>   And in the air Death moans and sings;
> But Day shall clasp him with strong hands,
>   And Night shall fold him in soft wings.

The days wore on—hot days, weary days, and always the daily shelling, always the daily losses through death and wounds and disease, always the same struggle against bodily exhaustion through lack of sleep, lack of nourishing food and incessant toil. Soon most faces took on the " Anzac look," the chief characteristics being the deepening of the lines from the sides of the mouth to the nose. The second period of " rest " was spent in Mule Gully, which ran into the cliff at the point where the Sphinx Head clung to the top of the crest. Here one night the portion of the A.M.R. not on duty held a concert in the darkness, lights at night never being permitted, owing to the danger of detection by the enemy aircraft. The audience sat in groups along the sides of the ravine and had a very jolly time, notwithstanding the fact that transport mules of the

LOOKING NORTH FROM WALKER'S RIDGE, ANZAC.

REMNANT OF THE A.M.R. "COMING OUT" AFTER HILL 60.

1. A.M.R. in Taylor's Gully, Suvla Bay.
2. Bivvies on Gloucester Hill.

ANZAC: THE APEX, WITH CHESHIRE RIDGE IN THE DISTANCE.

Indian Mounted Battery frequently passed through the auditorium. Silent onlookers were the Sikh gunners, who thoroughly approved of such diversions, even if our tastes did not lie in the direction of drum thumping and boisterous mirth.

While in this gully the Turks were regular with their morning and evening " hate " from the guns on Anafarta, to the north, but the dug-outs were all on the " safe " side, and damage was only suffered when men were caught out of their dug-outs. To give more warning than the shriek the shells gave, it was decided to post a man on a pinnacle on the top of the cliff whence he could see the flash of the gun as it fired. His duty was then to blow a whistle. For a time the plan worked well, and it was the best possible plan, seeing that the annoying gun was in a tunnel beyond the reach of the shells of the battleships that had searched for it, only coming to the tunnel mouth to fire. By and bye, the look-out man got tired of looking for the gun to fire, and finally he started to read a newspaper. After that his whistle was rarely before the whistle of the coming shell and he had to be supplanted.

During this period of most laborious inactivity, the Royal Navy, which has been described as " the father and the mother of the Gallipoli forces," kept constant watch and ward. The whole campaign of course depended upon the Navy holding the lines of communication, which were the sea, but in connection with offensive aid, the New Zealanders hold in most affectionate regard the destroyers which night and day patrolled the coast line. What a naval pageant it would have been from the cliff tops had it not been war! Sometimes in the periods of strange stillness that came over the little span of tumbled earth that was Anzac, men would drink in the beauty of the seascape—the blue Ægean glistening in the sun, the Island peak of Samothrace glowing purple through the distant haze, in the middle distance the white sail of some small Greek craft, which gave men visions of the ancient days when the Greeks sailed down that same blue waterway to the classic plains of Troy; and in the foreground the black swift wonderful destroyers of the 20th century, turning in their own length like greyhounds in the chase, and suddenly sending a savage flash of flame from guns that had seen the smoke of an unwary Turkish gun on the distant frowning slopes, for possession of which men toiled and suffered and died.

On May 31, the Wellington Mounted Rifles in No. 3 Outpost, an eminence in the gorge on the left, met serious trouble. In this advanced position, which was really a triangle formed by the junction of Sazli Beit Dere and Chailak Dere, the Wellingtons were suddenly attacked by very large numbers, and although they held on in the shallow trenches against a withering fire and bomb-throwing at close range, they were almost surrounded. During the afternoon they signalled for immediate reinforcements, and the A.M.R., then in the gully below Plugge's, was ordered to prepare for the task. In the early evening the Regiment moved along the beach and got in position at the bottom end of the wide dere. Their aid was not required, however, for after dark the Wellingtons were able to retire out of the untenable position which thereafter was held by the enemy until the great advance of August.

On June 10, a party of scouts, which included a number of A.M.R. men, had an exciting brush with the Turks on the flat which stretched from behind the north outposts to Suvla Bay. This party had gone out on a reconnoitring expedition during the night, and were returning along the sand hills of the beach in the morning when they were observed by the enemy, who despatched a strong party down a water-course that ran right to the beach, with the evident object of intercepting them. From the top of Walker's Ridge the A.M.R. saw the Turkish move, but the scouts did not, and for a few moments the men on the hill felt that the party would be cut off. The scouts, however, saw their danger, and leaving the cover of the sand mounds they took to the hard wet sand at the water's edge and set off at a run. In breathless excitement the troopers on the hill watched the race. Then, just at the critical moment, one of the Indian mountain guns on Walker's Ridge opened fire on the Turks. The shooting was perfect. The shells burst right among the enemy in the narrow water-course, and stopped them just in time to allow the scouts to pass the end and into the outer end of our territory. Then a destroyer, the always faithful destroyer, swept close into the shore opposite the water-course and shelled the Turks in it while the scouts made good their retreat. It was a dramatic incident in which the wonderful luck followed our men.

CHAPTER IX.

Fateful August.

We now approach the month of August which was to witness one of the greatest feats of arms, and one of the most tragic failures in British history; the month that was to see the A.M.R. and all the other regiments of the attacking force from Anzac, cut down to mere handfuls of sick and exhausted men; the month of fate that was to see all the sacrifice of lives, all the imperishable valour, all the striving of naked quivering souls, reap nothing but fame. Before proceeding with the narrative of these events which the written word will never truly describe, some reference should be made to the personnel of the Regiment with which this history deals.

It has already been recorded that Captain Bluck, who had come to Gallipoli in command of the 4th squadron (the original commander, Major Tattersall, having taken the place of Major Chapman as second in command of the Regiment), had been killed, leaving Lieutenant Roberts in command of the Waikatos, and that Major McCarroll, the O.C. of the 11th squadron, had gone away wounded. Many other changes had taken place. Lieutenant-Colonel Mackesy had relinquished command of the Regiment, he having been sent to Egypt to remedy, if possible, a sickness among the horses of the brigade, which was causing heavy mortality. Major Tattersall held the command for a few days and then Major Chapman arrived. Major Tattersall was invalided ill. Captain Mackesy, who had been in command of the 11th squadron since Major McCarroll's departure, had been ordered away for a surgical operation, his place being taken by Lieutenant Herrold. Lieutenant Roberts had been invalided, and Lieutenant J. Henderson took his place as commander of the 4th squadron. Of the junior officers, Lieutenant James had been killed, Lieutenants Logan and Weir had died of wounds, and Lieutenants Abbott and Ruddock had been invalided. Lieutenants Brookfield, Winder and Williams had arrived with reinforcements, and various promotions had been made to commissioned rank. The original adjutant, Captain Wood, N.Z.S.C., who was a source of great strength, still remained, and also R.S.M. Manners and S.S.M. Milne, of the 11th squadron, but S.S.M. Marr, of the Waikatos, had been killed, and S.S.M. Beer, of the 3rd squadron, had been invalided with an attack of fever that was to prove fatal. The manner in which this fine soldier carried on for days when in a high state of fever, not reporting to the medical officer until he was ordered to do so, was typical of the man, and he will always be kept in affectionate remembrance by the Gallipoli veterans of the Regiment.

These changes in the leadership of the Regiment are noted, not only to illustrate the cost of holding the Turks, but also to emphasise the success of the coming advance. Such was the capacity of the rank and file that many changes in leadership did not weaken the Regiment. Many good men had been killed and invalided through wounds and disease, but the spirit of the Regiment, its initiative and resource, its wonderful confidence and its cheerful heart, remained the same.

One would like to speak of the splendid men of the rank and file who died during this three months' struggle. Many names rush to the memory, but it is not possible to mention some without doing an injustice to the memory of others. To record the names of men who had the temperament and the opportunity to do spectacular things, would be unjust to the many who performed the daily and nightly task faithfully and uncomplainingly until death claimed them. They did their duty in the place assigned to them, and if they did not achieve spectacular deeds, their service was none the less true, and their sacrifice none the less good.

Before describing the part taken by the Regiment in the August advance, it will be necessary to give a brief outline of the plan of the Commander-in-Chief, and the object of the attack. The aim was to deliver a decisive blow against the Sari Bair system, from the left of Anzac, by which it was hoped that, with the support of a division landed without warning at Suvla Bay, the dominating crest could be won and held, thus "gripping the waist" of the Peninsula, cutting off the bulk of the Turkish army from land communication with Constantinople, and gaining such a command for the British artillery as to cut off the bulk of the Turkish army from sea traffic. In conjunction, a number of feint diversions were to be carried out in various parts of the theatre of the campaign, and tactical diversions, in the shape of a big containing attack at Helles, and an attack against Lone Pine, on the right wing of the Anzac front. The New Zealand troops were to have the honour of participating in the main thrust, on the left of Anzac. As Sir Ian Hamilton stated in his despatches, "Anzac was to deliver the knock-out blow; Helles and Suvla were complementary operations."

A number of attempts have been made to describe the nature of the four miles of country over which the "knock-out blow" was to be delivered, and many more will be made, but it is doubtful if an absolutely true impression of it will ever be conveyed. Even the camera cannot reveal its real nature. It can give only odd views of gorge and slope and crag, but not a panoramic view, because two-thirds of that desolation cannot be seen from any one point. Had a race of giants transformed a range of hills, 1,000 feet high, into a sluicing claim, they might have left a result something like the features which form the approach to Sari Bair. No grass grows there—only stunted scrub—and there is nothing to bind the clay faces which crumble to the tread in summer, and slide into the deres with the torrential rains of winter. Nor is there any system about the ridges and spurs and gullies. They twist and turn in a most perplexing manner. Deres run abruptly into cliffs; branches from them wander off, and lose themselves. This was the country the Anzac troops, reinforced by some battalions from the new army of Britain, were to advance over in the dark, fighting all the way against a determined foe. The positions to be taken were veritable forts on precipitous heights, requiring of the men the utmost physical and moral effort before the Turks could be assaulted with the bayonet. And it had to be the bayonet and bomb, because the whole scheme depended upon the element of surprise.

The force for the thrust was commanded by General Godley, and it comprised the Australian and New Zealand Division (less the Australian Light Horse who were to hold as many Turks as possible on Russell's Top, Pope's Ridge, and Quinn's Post while the Australian Division did

the same by its operations against Lone Pine), the
13th (New Army) Division, less five battalions,
the 29th Indian Infantry Brigade, and an Indian
Mountain Battery. This force was organised
into four columns—the right and left covering
columns which were to breach the Turkish line
so that the right and left assaulting columns might
pass on to their objectives. The New Zealand
Mounted Rifles Brigade, the Otago Mounted Rifles
Regiment, the Maori Contingent, and the Field
Troop New Zealand Engineers comprised the right
covering column, and it was under the command
of Brigadier-General Russell. Its task was to
gain command of the Sazli Beit Dere, Chailak
Dere, and the Aghyl Dere ravines, so as to enable
the assaulting column to arrive intact within
striking distance of the Chunuk Bair Ridge. To
achieve this object it was necessary to clear the
Turks from Old No. 3 Outpost and Big Table Top
beyond it, and from Destroyer Hill on the right
and Bauchop's Hill on the left.

Each regiment was allotted a particular position to capture, and herein lies the difficulty and
the boldness of the plan. Each and everyone of
these objectives had to be gained, and gained
according to time-table, if the action was to be
successful, and this, be it remembered, by surprise
attacks in the darkness over torn, tumbled country
in which the chances of losing direction were
tremendous. It is the fact that the various posts
were all taken to time-table, that makes this part
of the action the shining example it is of perfection
in execution. The Auckland Mounted Rifles were
allotted the task of taking Old No. 3,
the first operation. This post, or fort, was
connected with Table Top by a razorback,
and it formed the apex of a triangular piece

of ground that sloped down to our No. 2 and
No. 3 Outposts. Since its recapture by the
enemy, on May 30, the Turks, with unstinted
material, had done their best to convert this commanding point into an impregnable redoubt. Two
line of trenches, very heavily entangled, protected
its southern face—the only accessible one—and
with its head cover of solid timber which
could not be seriously damaged by the fire of
destroyer's guns, and its strongly revetted outworks, it dominated the approaches of both the
Chailak Dere and the Sazli Beit Dere. This was
the nature of the position which was timed to fall
at 9.30 p.m. without artillery preparation or
covering bombardment.

Without artillery, and heavy artillery at that,
the position under ordinary circumstances, when
the Turks were prepared, might have defied the
assault of brigades, but the Regiment had to trust
to surprise and the success of a stratagem. For
some weeks the stratagem had been developing,
through what the enemy were led to believe was
the passion of H.M. destroyer Colne for regular
and precise habits. Every night, exactly at 9
p.m., the Colne had thrown the beam of her searchlight on the redoubt, and opened fire for exactly
10 minutes. Then, after a 10 minutes interval,
she had repeated the performance, ending precisely
at 9.30 p.m. The idea was to get the enemy into
the habit of vacating the front line as soon as the
searchlight appeared. The plan was that the
A.M.R. should creep up the ragged thorny slope
when the sound of the destroyer's fire would help
to drown any noise, and the fierce glare of the
searchlight would make the surrounding darkness
doubly dark, and rush the works from a distance
of a few yards the moment the light switched off.

CHAPTER X.

The Attack Begins.

At the appointed hour the Regiment, under the command of Major Chapman, mustering only 381 men, notwithstanding the fact that two drafts of reinforcements had arrived since the Main Body, moved to the attack, taking a winding track through a watercourse until near Fisherman's Hut, thence, in single file, up an extremely narrow and rugged donga to a forward position of assembly, where, with quietness and difficulty, it formed line of squadron column. The men were keyed up to concert pitch and eager for their first offensive action. During the long and arduous period of defensive fighting many had lost vitality and strength, and not a few would have been regarded as sick if they had still been training, but in the excitement weakness was forgotten, and sick men became stalwarts. The hazardous nature of the enterprise was emphasised by the fact that not a cartridge was allowed in breech or magazine. One shot fired accidentally, a light from a slow-burning match which the bombers carried to light the fuses of their primitive bombs, or even a word of command, would have placed the whole scheme in jeopardy. The bombers had to keep their smouldering lights covered, but they also had to keep them in a sufficiently live state to ignite the fuses, and veterans still chuckle over the acrobatic feats of the bombers to achieve both ends. While waiting for the destroyer to commence operations, the silence in that dark ravine was uncanny, and "time was measured by heart beats."

Promptly at 9 p.m. the beam of the destroyer's searchlight cut a bright path through the darkness and her guns began. The Regiment, in formation, slowly crept forward, the 3rd squadron, led by Captain Wyman (Major Schofield having become second in command of the Regiment), being on the right, and the 11th squadron, led by Lieutenant Herrold, on the left, with the 4th squadron in support, finally reaching the outer ray of the searchlight, which was some 25 yards from the trench. Punctually at 9.30 p.m. the second bombardment ceased and the searchlight switched off. Instantly the Aucklanders, spreading fanwise, rushed up the slope. Eight Turks, in a detached post, were bayonetted almost before they were aware of the presence of danger, and the troopers, without the slightest hesitation, dropped down through openings in the overhead cover into the absolute blackness of the trench. The destroyer's bombardment may have had the effect of driving some of the garrison into back saps, but the trench was far from being empty, and some desperate hand-to-hand fighting took place in the dark. The Turks had little stomach for this sort of visitation, however, and those who could, fled. The troopers pressed through the works. One man, in turning the corner of a traverse, found a Turk in a corner, but he had not sufficient room to make a proper thrust, and the unfortunate Turk died slowly. A second later, a Turk fired round a traverse, and two troopers dropped. One Aucklander, in dashing down the trench, bayoneted in fine style a roll of blankets and two or three sacks. Almost before the front line was properly occupied, the troopers were in the second line. So stubborn were some of the

Turks in their defence, that many were concealed feet foremost in holes in the trench walls, from which they fired until the steel did its work.

Very soon the whole position was cleared, and the troopers then set to work to fill the sandbags they had brought, and with them built barriers at various places in the trenches, from which the bombers effectively held off the Turkish counter-attacks during the night. By morning the place was consolidated. The action was a smart, finished piece of work, and the Regiment is very much indebted to the destroyer Colne for its effective co-operation. The Regiment had only 20 casualties this night, while the Turks left 100 dead in the trenches and near vicinity. Unfortunately, among the killed was Lieutenant Harry Mackesy, the Colonel's son, a gallant soldier, who had been commissioned from the ranks and was the brigade's bombing officer.

One of the humorous incidents of the night was supplied by a section of the Maori Contingent, operating in conjunction with the W.M.R. This party lost direction slightly, and they were actually charging a piece of the line taken by the A.M.R., lifting their voices the while in battle cries that had not been heard in war since the pakeha and Maori buried the hatchet. Major Schofield shouted to them in their own tongue, however, and the Maoris grinned, and went to search for Turks somewhere else.

While the A.M.R. were engaged on Old No. 3 Outpost, part of the W.M.R. gallantly attacked Destroyer Hill, on the right, and captured it, and part scaled the precipitous approaches to Big Table Top beyond the A.M.R. objective, and carried it at the point of the bayonet. On the left, the Otago and Canterbury Mounted Rifles were just as successful on Baucop's Hill, the cheers that came through the night gladdening the hearts of the Aucklanders. This series of successes meant that the Sazli Beit and the Chailak Deres and the right branch of the Aghyl Dere were gained. In his despatches General Sir Ian Hamilton said: "Neither Turks nor angles of ascent were destined to stop Russell or his New Zealanders that night. There are moments during battle when life becomes intensified, when men become supermen, when the impossible becomes simple—and this was one of these moments. No words can do justice to the achievement of Brigadier-General Russell and his men. There are exploits which must be seen to be realised."

In a regimental history, space does not permit of the achievements of other units being recorded —that may be safely left in the hands of their own historians—and the advances made by the two assaulting and the left covering columns on the night of August 6 and the following day, cannot, therefore, be described. Suffice it to say that by nightfall on August 7 the left covering force held Damakjelik Bair, where it was hoped to get into touch with the right of the Suvla Bay Division, landed on the night of August 6; the two assaulting columns were on a rough line from Asma Dere to the Farm, to the Apex, which lay beyond Rhododendron Spur, immediately below the southwest shoulder of Chunuk Bair, to the nearest, if the lowest, part of the backbone of the Peninsula. The line formed at the top of the Rhododendron Spur was but a-quarter of a mile from Chunuk Bair, and on it was the New Zealand Infantry.

On the 7th, the A.M.R. was rested in Overton Gully, below the position they had taken. Worn out with their night's fighting, they were able to get some sleep, but they were not immune from shell fire, and 10 men became casualties. On the night of the 7th, the whole attacking force was re-organised in three columns, and the A.M.R. was placed in the right column, under Brigadier-General Johnston. This comprised the New Zealand Infantry Brigade, the Maori Contingent, the 8th Welsh Pioneers, the 7th Gloucesters, the 26th Indian Mountain Battery, and the Auckland Mounted Rifles. This column was ordered to assault Chunuk Bair at dawn on the 8th.

CHAPTER XI.

Struggle on the Crest.

At 2 a.m. the A.M.R. left their crude bivouack, and at 3 a.m. moved off up the ravine, their post being to support the attack. Terrible sights met them. Long lines of stretchers, with their loads of pain, came down the ravine. Stalwarts of the night before, blind with pain and tortured with thirst, were borne seawards, but the beach was to be no haven for them. Owing to the congestion of the wounded, many were to lie on their stretchers until they died; many were to lie until a shell, a kindly shell, put them out of their agony. Who will ever describe the agonies of those days of August? Pushing forward, the Regiment passed the battalions of the dead. At the head of the dere a halt was made about dawn, when the New Zealand Infantry, led by the gallant Colonel Malone, sprang to the attack, followed by the Gloucesters. They quickly gained the crest, the coveted crest, from which men of the New Zealand Infantry were the first to behold the Narrows. It was a tense moment, but how few lived to tell of it! They had penetrated farthest into enemy territory—but to die. As soon as the light was strong enough every Turkish gun concentrated upon the crest, and a battalion advanced from a ridge, 600 yards away, to counter-attack. But between this ridge and Chunuk Bair was a deep ravine, and quickly the advancing Turks were out of sight. Meantime, their artillery and machine-guns swept the crest, and the New Zealanders and Gloucesters were compelled to dig in, a few yards below the crest on their side. Nothing else was

possible, but even below the sky-line there was
little protection, owing to the hail of shrapnel that
came from the guns on Abdel Rahman Bair, to the
north. Soon the attacking Turks had climbed
the ravine, and so narrow was the crest that
they were able to shower bombs into the British
line, which was hardly a trench at all, without
showing themselves. It was a losing fight, but
the infantry, growing less and less every minute,
clung to their position. To make matters worse
the day became intensely hot, and there was practically no water. This was the state of things
when the A.M.R. were summoned to reinforce the
line. But in the tremendous fire that the Turks
had brought to bear on the slope behind the precarious line, the Regiment had been suffering
heavy losses. At 8 a.m. they had crossed, by
small rushes, an intervening ravine swept by rifle,
machine-gun, and artillery fire from the commanding ground on the flanks. Again they had to run
the gauntlet through a deadly barrage, and finally
lie ready to advance in a place that offered no
cover at all. Here discipline was put to a most
severe test. Shells began to fall among them, but
they obeyed the order to lie still, and soon the enemy
guns turned their attention to another quarter.
About noon the A.M.R. were summoned to the
line, and in small parties they dashed down a steep
slope and up a more gradual slope to the line.
They were sent to the left, and started to dig in,
but there was little time to dig. Again and again
came the Turks, and again and again they were
hurled back. Never was there a respite throughout this terrible Sunday. Bombs came over the
crest from unseen hands without cessation. Many
were caught "on the full" before they burst, and
pitched back among the enemy. This was not

ANZAC UNDER SNOW: TROOPER ALLISON STILL SMILING.

WINTER SCENES ON GALLIPOLI: A.M.R. "BIVVIES" IN THE VICINITY OF McCARROLL'S NEST.

MAIN BODY REMNANT AT ZEITOUN CAMP IN NOVEMBER, 1915.

MOUNTED BRIGADE MACHINE GUNNERS, AMONG THE VERY LAST TO LEAVE ANZAC.

done by one man or two, but by every man who got the opportunity. Mason, of the 3rd squadron, was particularly prominent in this respect. Ken Stevens, of the 11th squadron, on one occasion fumbled one of these live bombs, which fell over his shoulder. Quick as lightning he turned round and dropped his hat over it. He himself was wounded by the bomb when it exploded, but the hat undoubtedly smothered the burst and saved others in the near vicinity.

The day grew hotter, thirst tortured this band of Spartans, fatigue dazed them, but doggedly, blindly, automatically almost, they fought on. All sense of time was lost—it seemed that they had been fighting for an eternity. Then came night, but though it brought a cooler atmosphere, it did not bring water, nor did it bring a respite. But the defenders, now few in numbers, hung to the inferno they had gained. Some time after dark there was a call for the A.M.R. to go out and lie ahead of the shallow ditch that had been scraped in the flinty clay. It was then that the men realised for the first time that the Regiment had practically ceased to exist. This advanced post was a living hell, and soon the remnant was called back to the line.

With dawn came another bombardment, but from British guns. Where they were no one can say with any degree of certainty. The navy perhaps! It was probably believed that the position had been lost. It was a tragic anti-climax, just as it was to the Gurkhas, who after gaining Hill Q, to the north, on the same morning, and were pursuing the Turks down the reverse slope, received a salvo of heavy shells. The fire soon lifted from the Chunuk Bair position, but when it was over the enemy continued with bombs. Our guns now began to do some splendid firing, and the bombing slackened. Fewer Turks were seen, no doubt owing to losses and reinforcements being diverted to Hill Q area, where the advantage was taken of the plight of the attackers to launch a sweeping counter-attack, the success of which, combined with the lamentable failure of the Suvla Bay force to push forward, put the seal of failure upon the whole enterprise. A small outflanking effort was made by the Turks, on the left of the New Zealanders, but the party concerned was annihilated.

The greatest vigilance was kept, however, and exhausted though the men were, many did some excellent sniping, being particularly successful against a spot where Turks attempted to run the gauntlet over a few yards of exposed ground. The day was as hot as the one before, and water was as scarce as ever. The wounded lay exposed to the sun at the rear of the trench, and many there died. One man went raving mad, and ran along an exposed place with a tunic over his head, but he fell into the trench before he was hit. Sleepy, hungry, and thirsty, the forlorn hope clung to their 200 yards of line. Some biscuits were available, but the men hardly dare to eat them for fear of accentuating their thirst. Long before this the remnants of the regiments on the ridge had lost all cohesion. The few remaining officers commanded little groups, composed of men of half-a-dozen units. They had long passed the stage when men are strengthened by the presence of their own comrades, and when the spirit of the regiment counts. They had become individualists, but the strangers around them were not men to be watched and weighed in the balance. Everyone knew that everyone had been tested. Death itself had lost its horror. They were too tired to think, too exhausted to care. A fierce fatalism seemed to possess them. A blind indifference to what fate held for them gave a wonderful quality to their courage. Nothing mattered save the holding of the line. No longer did they have any realisation of the fact that their fight was merely a fraction of a battle, that they were merely a link in the chain, a pawn in the game. That little piece of trench was to them a world, a universe, their task the task of a life-time. Every man had reached the point when self was utterly thrown off, when neither life nor death mattered, so long as the task did not fail. They were souls in torment, but it was the torment which comes from fear of failure.

That evening, when they could strive no more, they were relieved. Their place was taken by two battalions, the 6th Loyal North Lancashires and the 5th Wiltshires. Both battalions were wiped out by a terrific attack the following dawn, and Chunuk Bair was lost for good. The attacking force consisted of one whole division, plus three battalions. At 6 a.m. the enemy attempted to carry the advance down the slopes. Line after line came over the crest, to be mown down by the naval and artillery guns, and particularly by the 10 machine-guns of the New Zealanders. Twenty-two lines of Turks came over the crest, but to die.

While this tragedy was being enacted, the A.M.R. was resting in the vicinity of No. 2 Outpost. Its total strength was 66, this including sick men, who had not been in the advance. Of the 288 officers and men who went into the advance only 22 remained: Captain H. Smith, regimental

Q.M., Captain McCormick, medical officer, Lieutenants Herrold, McGregor, and Cobourne, R.S.M. D. Manners, Sergeant Allsop, and 15 rank and file. Worn out as they had been before the fighting, the survivors were now practically shadows of men.

Apart from sheer exhaustion, many of them were suffering from septic sores on their hands, caused by the thorns of the scrub through which they had had to force their way. The sense of tragedy was very near to them—and by a strange irony of fate the place where they bivouacked was known as Eden Gully. The official record in the Regiment diary on August 10 is well worth preserving. All that the acting-adjutant, Lieutenant Herrold, wrote was: "Collected odd men from different parts, and had much-needed rest. Everybody quite knocked up." Major G. A. King, of the brigade staff, took over command of the Regiment, and continued in that position until the return of Major McCarroll, early in September.

CHAPTER XII.

Valley of Torment.

Rarely have men suffered as the wounded of those days suffered, particularly those who were helpless. Away up in the desolate ravines they had to lie until the over-worked stretcher bearers could carry them to the beach. Afflicted with thirst—not the parching thirst that heat and dust and perspiration produces, but the agonising thirst that follows bleeding wounds; the thirst that makes the tongue swell and fill the mouth, that thirst that fills the body with the fire of hell, the thirst that makes men mad. Nor was thirst all. There was the burning pain of open wounds, the torture of the flies around them, the constant fear of again being struck. How awful it is to lie helpless and wonder where the next shell will land! Some of these sufferers lay there until a shell came, and no trace of their bodies was ever found. Others lived to be carried to the beach, lived till they saw across the water the comforting green and red lights of hospital ships, and then died. Some men lay beside the tracks of the pack mules, choking in the dust of the hoofs, but the muleteers could not succour them. The line had to be supplied with ammunition. The wounded must wait. Many of these tortured souls, despairing of the aid they so badly needed, attempted to crawl down the gullies, dragging broken limbs, remaining alive by sheer will and indomitable courage. For thousands of the "fortunate" ones the decks of transports were their hospital. Many arrived at Alexandria and Malta with maggots crawling in the wounds that had never been touched since the field dressing carried by all soldiers had been hurriedly wrapped round them. It was not the result of neglect of anyone—unless the shortage of medical staffs was due to neglect. The officers and crews of these transports did all they could for the men. Firemen, just relieved from the stokehold, became volunteer orderlies, but practically all they could do was to carry food and drink to them, and give quick burial to the dead. But, be it remembered, the big majority of the wounded who got away were under the belief that the crest had been gained and held, and that the campaign was to succeed. Imagine, therefore, their feelings when they learned a week later that the crest had been lost, and that all their suffering had been of no avail. John Masefield, in his epic work "Gallipoli," has given expression to the bitterness that possessed them in the following passage:—"They went, like all their brothers in that Peninsula, on a forlorn hope, and by bloody pain they won the image and the taste of victory; and then, when their reeling bodies had burst the bars, so that our race might pass through, there were none to pass; the door was shut again, the bars were forged again, all was to do again, and our brave men were but the fewer and the bitterer for all their bloody sacrifice for the land they served." But it was never done again. The door was shut and kept shut, until it was opened by the destruction of the whole Turkish Army in Palestine years later. Only the mounted rifles regiments, of the N.Z.E.F., shared in that final victory against the foe that barred the way on the bloody crests of Gallipoli.

Between August 10 and 21, the A.M.R. remained on No. 3 Outpost, the trenches of which they deepened and improved. Two drafts of reinforcements arrived, but not sufficient to bring the

Regiment back to full strength. Indeed, the reinforcements were hardly sufficient to make good the wastage caused by sickness and the daily casualties from shell fire. Diarrhœa became very prevalent, or rather more prevalent than usual. On some days half the men of the Regiment attended sick parade from this cause, and there is not the slightest doubt that most of them would have been sent away to hospital had the need for men not been so acute. But not a man could be spared if he was fit for any kind of duty.

The position was that the Commander-in-Chief had been refused fresh reinforcements from England for another attempt for the all-important crest, and he had to set about the task with the broken brigades he had, plus a yeomanry division from Egypt. These troops, of course, were to fight dismounted. His plan was to assault Scimitar Hill, the fatal stumbling block of the Suvla Bay attack, from Chocolate Hill, while Kaiajik Aghala (Hill 60) was assaulted from Damakjelik Bair by the Anzac troops, the success of which would open the way for a combined converging attack against the W Hills, the last obstacle to the objects of the original scheme. These attacks were made, but neither the A.M.R. nor the W.M.R. participated, owing to their weakness in numbers. New Zealand was represented only by the C.M.R., the O.M.R., and the Maori Contingent. It need not be repeated that the plan failed. The attack against Scimitar Hill cost 5,000 lives, but achieved nothing. That against Hill 60 was only partly successful, and then only from the standpoint of certain units. The New Zealanders gained about 200 yards of the Turkish front line on Hill 60, but neither the Indians and Englishmen, on the left, nor the Australians, on the right, were able to reach their objectives. This action cost the South Island regiments many men, and they were now no better off than the Auckland and Wellington regiments.

On the 22nd, Major C. R. Mackesy, who had just returned from hospital, went out with 50 men to relieve the remnants of the Otago Mounted Rifles in the precarious foothold on Hill 60, being joined the following day by the remainder of the Regiment, which felt that it was again to be considered a fighting unit, seeing that another 50 men and three officers had just arrived from Egypt. The following few days have been described as "very quiet" in the official diary, and, as there is no desire to reflect upon the veracity of the recording officer, the statement must be accepted. It is a fact, however, that during these "quiet" days men were wounded by bombs, and seeing that the Turks were still disregarding the possibilities of the aeroplane for bombing, the inference is that "quiet" is used only in a comparative sense. It is more than likely that everyone had lost all sense of proportion, and after the recent struggle would have classed ordinary shelling as enemy amusements. But the days of alleged quiet were to end suddenly, for another assault was being planned for August 27.

CHAPTER XIII.

The Last Effort.

The objective was again Hill 60, and for the attack only 1,100 men were available. It was the last forlorn hope, probably the most forlorn of all. Such was the condition of the sick and wasted battalions that their strength was gauged solely by numbers, not by units. For instance, the New Zealand Mounted Rifles Brigade could muster only 300 men, and all the survivors of the previous three weeks were sick men. It was a sad, but glorious, spectacle to see the chosen of the various battered brigades moving into position. If ever there is a singer who would compose an epic, let him choose as his subject the last effort of the Anzacs and their brethren at Anzac. If he would "glory in daring that dies or prevails," let him sing of the last dauntless few of the weary veterans who sprang from their trench at 5 p.m. on August 27 into the shrieking field of death, and led the charge. On the right were 350 Australians, in the centre were 300 New Zealand mounted riflemen and 100 Australians, and on the left 250 of the Connaught Rangers. This was Brigadier-General Russell's force. The first line of the attack, in the centre, was led by 100 men of the C.M.R., with 65 of the A.M.R., under Major Mackesy, the second line was composed of the W.M.R. and the O.M.R., and the third of the 100 men of the 18th Australian Battalion.

After a short bombardment, described by the Commander-in-Chief as "the heaviest we could afford," the first line jumped to the attack. In a moment they were under heavy machine-gun fire, and men were dropping on every hand, but there was never a falter nor a stop. The line swept upward and into the first Turkish line, where the defending Turks died or were captured or fled. No force of Turks has ever stood up to British bayonets, and on this occasion the British had bombs as well as steel. Within a few minutes the stalwarts, with all their old-time dash, were pushing on to the next line amid a gale of shrapnel. Many fell, but the remnants of the remnants moved on, and the artillery was able to help them, seeing that guiding flags were carried on the flanks. As darkness fell the machine-guns were rushed forward and got in position. So also was a Turkish machine-gun that the A.M.R. men captured with ammunition, and this gun proved of great assistance during the night. The Australians on the right had not been able to make progress owing to the fire of a battery of machine-guns. The Connaughts, on the left, gained their objective, the northern Turkish communications, in brilliant style, but before midnight they had been out-bombed. Two hundred Light Horse men, the survivors of the great charge across the Nek on the morning of August 7, attempted to recapture the section, but they were driven back to the barricade. Thus, only the 150 yards taken by the New Zealand Mounted Rifles was held.

In this little line, which contained the last of the New Zealanders, a furious bombing duel raged all night, but the men hung on. In his despatches Sir Ian Hamilton said: " Luckily the New Zealand Mounted Rifles refused to recognise that they were worsted. Nothing would shift them. All that night and all the next day, through bombing, bayonet charges, musketry, shrapnel, and heavy shells, they hung on to their 150 yards of trench." The recording officer of the Regiment did not bother about details. He simply said, "A portion of our men still hold part of the trenches at Kaiajik Aghala. They are very tired, and are badly in need of a spell."

At 1 o'clock the next night the 10th Light Horse, who had been brought over from Walker's Ridge—where, by the way, the Nek was still the bone of contention—attacked the lost northern communication trenches on the left, and gained and held them. The hold on this part of the crest was consolidated and held until evacuation. Its possession gave an outlook over the Anafarta-Sagir Valley to the north, and safer lateral communications between Anzac and Suvla Bay. It might have been a tremendous lever had another attempt been made to drive through to the narrows, but that attempt was never made. Instead, Sir Ian Hamilton was recalled, and eventually the evacuation was ordered.

On August 22nd, the Rev. Father Dore, Roman Catholic Chaplain to the Brigade, who was attached to the A.M.R., was wounded. The beloved padre had gone with Captain Jory, the new medical officer of the Regiment, and four stretcher-bearers, to assist with the wounded in Aghyl Dere—wounded of other regiments of course. He was struck in the region of the spine, and would speedily have succumbed if he had been left at any of the dressing stations, but through the devotion of Trooper Foley and others of the stretcher-bearers, he was conveyed to the beach in spite of the system which required the wounded to go from one party to another. The padre returned to New Zealand, but there had to undergo an operation in connection with his wound, under which he died. Few men of the N.Z.E.F. had the wide popularity of Father Dore. Denominational distinctions carried little weight in the Regiment, especially in those days of grim realities, and least of all did they weigh with Father Dore. He was the friend and counsellor of everyone. Wherever he went he took cheer, and raised a laugh when a laugh was badly needed. During the long days of defensive war he made it his business to visit parties in the worst and most dangerous saps, and his magnetic personality always helped to ease the load for over-burdened men. His presence was a better tonic than any the doctor could give, and he will always be kept in affectionate remembrance by Gallipoli veterans.

Another padre who endeared himself to everyone was Chaplain Grant, the Presbyterian Chaplain to the Brigade, who was attached to the Wellington Mounted Rifles. A fine, courageous gentleman, he set a splendid example by his disregard of danger and his devotion to the wounded, and the force lost a true friend when he was shot down in a recently taken trench on Hill 60, while bandaging friends and foes.

On August 29, the remnant of the Mounted Rifles were relieved from the trenches on Hill 60, and moved slightly to the north of The Farm, to Cheshire Ridge, where they lay in reserve until September 4. By this time the only original officers left were Lieutenant Haeata, who had been acting as adjutant since his return in August from duty on Sir Ian Hamilton's bodyguard, and

Lieutenant E. McGregor, who was appointed brigade machine-gun officer. Both officers were invalided sick within a few days. On September 6, Major McCarroll returned to duty, and took over command of the Regiment from Major King, who left for Lemnos to prepare a camp for the Regiment. Lieutenant T. McCarroll, who had won his commission on Gallipoli, became adjutant.

On September 13, after experiencing some cold wet weather, the bulk of what was left of the Regiment left for Mudros, and went into camp at Sarpi. About a dozen men, left behind under Major McCarroll, arrived on September 29. The first parades of the Regiment at Sarpi made pathetic sights. The whole Brigade when it left the Peninsula numbered only 20 officers and 229 other ranks, or about the strength of one squadron and a-half. The A.M.R. Band had arrived, and at one of the first parades of the handful of survivors it played, "Where are the Boys of the Old Brigade." The regiments within a few short weeks had practically vanished, and it can be readily understood that the few who had escaped without wounds had difficulty in controlling their emotions. To honour the veterans it was the custom to parade them in a file by themselves in front of the reinforcements which now were coming in. Words can hardly describe the feelings which the sight of the short lines in front of each squadron produced. In front of one squadron would be four men; before another seven, and so on. The pathetic, nay, tragic sight, made men of our own race silent, but upon a French general it had a contrary effect. This soldier knew little English, but he tried to give expression to the emotions that filled his breast. "It ees—it ees—beautiful," he exclaimed, and his interpretation was really the truest one. In picturing that parade at Sarpi, let us see it as the French general saw it. Let us remember that if the brigade was practically annihilated in a struggle that failed, it was a glorious failure. Let us remember that the men who died on those bullet-swept ridges in a vain effort did not die in vain. They passed in their greatest hour, and they left an example that will never die. For many a hearth-side there was no consolation at the time; sorrow and a bitter sense of loss shrouded the view. But for the nation, and afterwards for the kin of the men who died, there was the goodly gift of a noble example, an inspiration which may be a moving power to generations yet unborn.

At Lemos, the Regiment, with the rest of the brigade, remained until November 10, the days being spent in fairly vigorous training. On the date mentioned the Regiment returned to Anzac. The arrival of reinforcements, and of men who had recovered from wounds and sickness, had improved the strength to 10 officers and 286 other ranks, or slightly over half the establishment. Major McCarroll was in command.

Disembarking at Walker's Ridge pier, the Regiment proceeded to Waterfall Gully. The weather was still fine, although a good deal colder than it was during August, but active preparations were being made against the deluges of winter. For some weeks the chief occupation of the A.M.R. was that of digging shelters, terraces, and what were called "funk holes."

Actually, however, the work of the troops was no longer the point of chief consequence in this campaign. The real front was in London. The prejudices and convictions of London need not be considered here, but the fact is that the forces of evacuation on the home front won the day. Not only could fresh troops not be provided for another attempt against the Turks on Gallipoli, but no less than three divisions of the Gallipoli Army—the 53rd Welsh Division, the 10th Irish Division, and the 2nd French Division —were sent to Salonika to aid the Serbians. So was the seal of final failure placed on the Gallipoli venture.

But the digging went on, and every indication was given to the Turks that they might expect a renewal of aggressive hostilities at any moment. The end was perhaps hastened by the weather breaking on November 27, at which time the A.M.R. was at Gloucester Hill. The intention had been to relieve the 5th Norfolks, but the move of that battalion was cancelled. The result was that when the snow fell on the night of November 27-28, the troops in this sector did not have sufficient dug-outs, and many suffered far more than they otherwise would have done. The snow and cold made life just about as wretched as it could be for men living underground, but these troubles were nothing to those of the following two days, when a fierce blizzard swept over the Peninsula. The heavy seas that arose played havoc at the piers and among the small craft, the trenches became watercourses, many of the deres, once dusty tracks, became impassable for transport, long icicles formed along the parapets, and men became casualties through frozen feet. The sufferings of these days were as intense as those of summer. During the succeeding days the Regiment lived as well as it could in a spot known as "McCarroll's Nest," but they were cold birds, though not in such dire straits as the men further north. There cases of drowning occurred, owing to dammed up water breaking into the trenches. Fine weather set in on December 4, but the losses through frost bite and sickness, incidental to the cold and exposure, had reduced the strength of the Gallipoli army tremendously.

A TYPICAL SECTION OF THE A.M.R.
The leather buckets hanging round horses' necks had to be put on the noses of the animals when on the lines to prevent them sucking the sand for its salt.

SCENES IN SINAI.

1. Dried salt marsh on coast. 2. Sandhill at Romani, where Colonel Mackesy found 45,000 rounds of Turkish ammunition by spearing the sand with his sword. 3. Mount Auckland. Lieutenant Evans in foreground.

THE FIELD OF ROMANI.
1. Looking west from Mount Royston. 2. Boots discarded by the Turks to aid their retreat.

SINAI DAYS.

1. First well dug by Lieutenant Martin and his men. 2. Major C. Schofield "enjoys" a shave. 3. A.M.R. patrol at Duiedar.

CHAPTER XIV.
Evacuation.

On December 8, Sir Charles Munro, now Commander-in-Chief of the Mediterranean Expeditionary Force, ordered General Birdwood, who had assumed command on Gallipoli, to proceed with the evacuation of Anzac and Suvla positions. Of all the hazards of the campaign, the evacuation was probably the greatest. Sir Ian himself had estimated that the operation could not be carried out with less than a 50 per cent. loss, and many officers in high positions were of the same opinion. The only hope of escaping without disaster was to "fool" the Turk. Already he had been "fooled" on several occasions, the habitual shelling of Old No. 3 Outpost, under the destroyer's searchlight, through which the A.M.R. was able to rush the position without heavy loss, being one of the notable examples. But this was a very different matter. Its magnitude would have made the greatest "butcher" in the army shudder. At Anzac and Suvla no less than 83,000 men and their guns and transport had to be taken off, and how could this be accomplished when the position was nowhere deeper than 3,000 yards? At Walker's Ridge the Turkish line was barely 400 yards from the water, and here and at many other places No Man's Land was only 10 and 12 yards wide. This was the task to be accomplished. But once again the seemingly impossible task was accomplished. All sorts of means were used to this end. Days before the actual evacuation was to begin every man who reported sick was sent away, but always at night. In the morning, men who had been taken out the previous night were landed. The greatest activity was kept up by the transport ashore. Men who had gone down the tracks at night were marched back again after daybreak. There is no question that the enemy, despite the mention of evacuation in the House of Commons, believed that another onslaught was in the course of preparation, and their counter-preparations were pushed on with the greatest energy. Daily our aeroplanes reported the construction of concrete emplacements for the guns, which, through the success of the Germans in the Balkans, could now be sent by rail to Constantinople, and right up to the last, new trench works were appearing. The most extraordinary ruse practised by the British Force was that of making the Turks accustomed to long and complete silences. One of these silences lasted for 72 hours.

During these last days the A.M.R. had very few casualties. One of the duties was to send out a patrol each night from the Barricade to Aghyl Dere to patrol the country in the direction of Hackney Wick. This was the last of the Regiment to enter Turkish territory until the Egyptian Expeditionary Force invaded Palestine.

The story of how the entire force was evacuated without the loss of a single life has been fully described in the official history of the New Zealanders at Gallipoli, therefore there is no need again to detail the wonderful feat. On December 14 part of the A.M.R. left Williams' Pier on the Princess Ena, transhipped to the Knight of the Garter, and proceeded to Lemnos. Up till this time the official order had been that the Regiment and other units should go to Imbros for rest, but few who embarked expected to see Gallipoli again. A day or two later, the balance of the

Regiment came away, the last to embark being Captain Smith, Regimental Quarter-master, who had had one of the longest records of continuous service on the Peninsula, and Lieutenant Finlayson. The Regiment went into camp at Mudros East, where the mounted brigade concentrated, and on December 22 embarked on the Hororata for Alexandria.

So ended Anzac. They left it and its graves. They left the trenches, which represented so much physical effort, and the crests, which had been "salted down with the bones" of thousands. They left the little smoking fires beside the "bivvies" that men, with the domestic instincts firmly implanted in their breasts, once called home. They left the place of memories, and can it be doubted that the imaginative thought they saw dead comrades stretch out appealing arms from the slopes? They knew that the campaign had destroyed the flower of the Turkish Army, but that gave no satisfaction at the time. To those who thought, it all seemed wasted effort, wasted lives. Men who had flung themselves time and time again against the enemy with a will that rose above bodily weakness, could not easily reconcile themselves to giving up all they had gained. They could rejoice over the wonderful success of the evacuation when the Turk had been so thoroughly hoodwinked, but deep down they felt the bitterness of failure. Especially was this true of the men who had survived the longest. Now we can view the Gallipoli failure with complacency. We can glory in such a failure, but the remnants of regiments were too close to the thing to see it, and, it must not be forgotten, they did not know how great a thing they had done. Time was necessary to give the true perspective.

How did Gallipoli succeed as far as it did? Because of a quality in the men that would not admit the possibility of defeat; an attitude of mind which seemed to lock their grip; because of an initiative and resource, and a sense of responsibility in the rank and file which made it possible for officers, from generals to lieutenants, to take what otherwise would have been serious risks; and, finally, because of what Major Waite, in the official history of the whole New Zealand Force, has called "a sense of personal superiority over the enemy," because of a cheerful fatalism and an infinite trust in comrades and other units. That, to my mind, sums up the Spirit of Anzac.

Of the causes of failure, history will have much debate. This record is not for the purpose of considering the question, but it is to be hoped that the historians will not overlook the all important fact that on Gallipoli men had to be used instead of shells. Never once did a regiment advance with the help of a real bombardment. Units were practically annihilated in doing the work that in France would have been done by guns. It is a fact that the Turks were not well equipped with artillery and munitions, but they held positions that were fortresses. The greater part of their ground was hidden from the sea, and, therefore, could not be "searched" by the naval guns, owing to their inability to get the required elevation. If the British had had adequate howitzers and munitions, who knows what would have been accomplished?

CHAPTER XV.

Back to the Suez.

When men of the last division to leave Anzac left placards bearing the words, "So long, Johnnie, see you soon at the Suez Canal," they hardly knew how true their frivolous good-bye was to be. The Dardanelles campaign had prevented the Turk from making another attempt against the Canal; but it was only to be expected that, when the evacuation relieved his army, he would turn his attention once again to what the Kaiser had called the "jugular vein of the British Empire." Even if the Turk himself had been willing to leave the British in undisputed possession of the Canal, his German masters would have over-ruled him. To the Germans, the Canal on which the British had to depend for supplying the forces in Mesopotamia and German East Africa, was a prize of the first magnitude. They knew that, even if it could not be held by them, it might be closed for a considerable time by the hulls of sunken steamers, and that even a temporary closure of the waterway might have very serious consequences. They might also have hoped that an attack in force would cause a rising in Egypt, and therefore a further drain on Britain's man power. For political reasons, the Turks themselves had to make an aggressive move. Disaffection was growing in Syria, and the Arabs of the Hedjaz had been giving trouble, which presaged open revolt unless the Turks embarked upon an enterprise that displayed their power.

A constant watch had been kept on the Canal during the Dardanelles campaign, chiefly by Indian troops and British Yeomanry. Danger did not threaten in the shape of attacks in force, but in small parties endeavouring to mine the waterway by night. Mines were actually found in the Canal, and one steamer was holed when passing through one of the Bitter Lakes, but she was skilfully beached, and only a blockage of half a day took place. On another occasion, the presence of mines in the Canal was discovered by a singular form of obtaining intelligence. It was the practice to make a narrow, smooth path on the sand along the east side of the Canal by a camel-drawn brush harrow. This obliterated all foot marks; therefore, if foot prints pointing west were found on the track, it was intelligence of first importance. The presence of these foot prints led to the discovery of mines in the Canal on this occasion.

Up till this time the defences of the Canal were on the Canal itself. The cavalry patrols were based there. The idea seemed to be that the desert was our best ally. When Lord Kitchener visited Egypt, after his call at Gallipoli, he is reported to have said, "Are you defending the Suez, or is it defending you?" An offensive defence was thereupon started. This meant going out to meet the Turk; it meant bases far out in the desert. This involved tremendous engineering undertakings in the shape of a desert railway, a waterpipe line sufficient to supply a large force, and an immense number of camels to convey the water from the bases to the troops ahead.

The route for the railway had to be the coastal route along the line of the oldest road in the world, for here were to be found the main groups of oases. This being decided, it became necessary to render the southern routes impracticable to the Turks by draining off all water supplies. The chief source of supply was that at Er Rigm, at the northern end of the Wadi Muksheib, where the winter rains were dammed up. This source of supply was destroyed by the simple method of digging holes through the thin layer of clay at the bottom to the sandy subsoil beneath. In other places, Roman and Babylonian cisterns which were filled by the winter rains, were pumped dry; and at Jifjaffa an elaborate well-boring plant of the enemy was destroyed by raiders. In this way, all the water of any consequence in the southern desert was cleared, and the Turks were compelled to operate in the north, where our troops and our railway and our pipe line went out to meet them. So began the campaign which was to end in the destruction of the Turkish Army, the liberation of Palestine from the thraldom of the Turk, and the dismemberment of the Turkish Empire. It was the classic battle-ground of history. No less than 26 armies had crossed the Sinai since the beginning of history, and here were men from the Seven Seas about to fight the last crusade. It was war, hard hideous war, but it was romance.

The New Zealand Mounted Rifles was part of the machine which began to move, and it was to be a permanent part. Before the brigade left Zeitoun for the Suez, the New Zealand Infantry were there, but within a month or two all the New Zealand Force, with the exception of the three regiments of the mounted brigade, was sent to France. After training for a month at Zeitoun, the New Zealanders trekked to Serapeum on the Canal, at the northern end of the Great Bitter Lake on the west side. The A.M.R. was now itself again—at least it was back to full strength, but many a horse had a new rider. So many new officers and men were there, that the old family feeling was gone for the time being, but that soon returned as the men got to know one another, and the Spirit of the Regiment lived. Somehow, the Regiment never lost its individuality. Colonel Mackesy was in command again, with Major McCarroll second in command. The trek led along the route of the Ismalia Canal, passing through Nawa, Bilbeas, Abou Hammad, Kasasin (where the battlefield of Tel El Kebir was traversed), Abu Sueir, and Moascar, the journey occupying six days. Heavy rain fell during the latter part of the march, and as one man put it, "the saddles were afloat," with dire results to the saddles. General Murray, who was commander-in-chief in Egypt, inspected the brigade upon its arrival. Through the rain and the rigours of the trek it was not particularly beautiful. "More dubbin" was the brief remark of the general, and of course he was quite right, but, being a general, it was hardly possible to inform him that the brigade had been most resplendent only a few short days before.

A camp was established at Serapeum, and training was resumed; also dubbin. The men revelled in bathing in the Canal, and life was exceedingly pleasant. Occasionally passenger steamers passed through the waterway, the only drawback being that the presence of "bints" made it necessary for bathers to rush to their clothes. It usually happened, however, when steamers surprised the naked bathers that the "bints" scampered first.

It was at Serapeum that the Regiment began "to qualify for dinkum crusaders," as one dissolute character termed it. The band was still off on its travels somewhere about the Mediterranean, and the padre, Chaplain Williams, formed a choir to help things along at church parades. The choir made a joyful noise, and the Regiment thought a good deal of itself. It is a pity that another anecdote of the same period must be recorded, but truth demands. The fact is, the Regiment's language was "frequent and painful and free," and something had to be done about it, no doubt in the interests of the native population. The sergeants, who had established a mess, and were in consequence getting plump and peaceful, were told about the matter, and those worthy gentlemen decided to give an example to the men. It was agreed that every man who swore in the mess should be fined one piastre for each swear. At the end of the first day, it is said, the treasurer was 200 piastres richer. The rule lapsed next day, and of course the only inference is that no A.M.R. sergeant ever swore again. "Hassan" thought that the choir must have done it.

Days of ease are not always good for soldiers, and part of the Regiment became afflicted with pessimism. They knew that the infantry was to go to France, and they began to feel that the mounted rifles were going to be left on the Canal until someone won the war. Fresh batteries of artillery were in the course of construction, and some of the good old veterans of the A.M.R. transferred, and so were lost to the Regiment. Quite a number of the men who had been wounded and had gone to England, were also transferred to the artillery. It should be mentioned that the commander of the artillery stated that he only wished he could get some more men of the type of the troopers who became gunners. Among the officers who transferred to the infantry were Major Wyman, of the 3rd squadron, and Lieutenant E. McGregor, who on Gallipoli had risen to the position of brigade machine-gun officer.

Early in March the brigade marched across the desert to the railhead at Kembla, and took over the trenches and posts held up to then by Australian infantry. This was the first experience of the Regiment in moving over a caravan route with only camel transport, and their first real introduction to the water problem of the desert. Only a few troughs were available at their destination, and it took two hours to water the horses. Few realised that this was to be the ordinary experience of the next two years. The section of trench taken over by the A.M.R. offered new problems. The works were not the usual ditches. Owing to the softness of the sand, the walls had to be built up with sand bags or sacking nailed to wooden uprights. If the wall was torn the sand trickled through and the trench was liable to be blocked. This was not the only trouble, however. When the khamseen blew it nearly obliterated the trenches, and sometimes shifted sand hill crests a number of yards in a single night. When the Regiment arrived, a wind had been doing its best in the interests of the

Turk, and the first task, beyond sending out patrols, was that of digging out the trenches. For the first day or two the horses had to be taken back four miles for water, but after that the supply for all purposes was brought by camel, each camel carrying two 12-gallon fantasses. Needless to say, water for washing purposes was not over-plentiful, but the men of Gallipoli had already acquired the art of washing and shaving in about two spoonfuls of water, and it was speedily learned by the new men. But many felt like the man at Anzac, who, when asked by General Birdwood how he was enjoying his wash, said it was alright, but he wished he was a crimson canary.

While at Kembla a "grain market" was established some miles out in the desert. Its purpose was to get information.

At the end of March the mounted rifles were relieved by Australian infantry, none of the colonial infantry having yet left for France, and they returned to the old camp at Serapeum, but in a week's time moved on to a new camp at Salhia. Here the horses had the benefit of plenty of water and green fed, and they put on condition.

The heat was now trying, and the days grew hotter, but hard work was ahead. On April 23, the brigade suddenly received orders to move to Kantara. It left camp the following evening and set out across the desert on a long night trek. The reason for the sudden move north was that a force of 1,000 Turks had delivered a surprise attack against the unprepared yeomanry at Oghratina and Katia, and against a post held by Scottish infantry at Dueidar. At the two former places the yeomanry were badly cut up, but at Dueidar the Scots checked the enemy and inflicted more losses than were sustained by the British at all three places.

The New Zealand Mounted Rifles established a camp at Hill 70, in the vicinity of Dueidar, and commenced an arduous period of patrol work. Just before the move north a few changes had taken place in the squadron commands. Major Schofield, who had been wounded at Gallipoli, took over the command of the 3rd squadron from Major Whitehorn, who became commander of the 11th squadron, Captain Aldred relinquishing that post and becoming second in command of the 3rd. Major Munro commanded the 4th squadron. While here Lieutenant-Colonel Mackesy had command of the Anzac Mounted Division for a few days in the absence of General Chauvel, the divisional commander, and General Chaytor, the commander of the New Zealand Brigade. Major McCarroll took over the Regiment for the period.

The cordial relations that were established between the Scots and the New Zealanders had their beginning at Hill 70 in a Rugby football match.

A week later the brigade moved to Romani and took over the posts there vacated by the 2nd Light Horse, who went on a reconnoitring expedition a few miles further east. Here water was fairly plentiful in the hods, but usually it was very brackish. It was found that Arab intelligence on the subject of water was not reliable, the natives having no idea of the amount of water required by a brigade. Many extraordinary things were discovered in connection with hod water. One well was not salt, but the water contained a very high content of magnesia. It also contained a neutralising substance which made the water quite safe to drink, but boiling deneutralised it. At another place there were two wells within eight feet of each other; the water of one was very brackish, while that of the other was perfectly fresh, although the intervening sand was quite soft. No explanation could be found for the phenomenon. The most important work for the troopers while at Romani was that of digging wells and making preparations for watering horses quickly. Every squadron was supplied with a pump and a portable trough, which helped matters a good deal.

From Romani the Regiment moved back to Hill 70, and thence to Bir Etmaler, from which place parties were sent out on well-sinking operations. No chances could be taken, and the whole camp stood to arms before dawn every day. Another duty was that of searching the various hods for natives, whose presence was a source of danger. At one hod two Arabs were found by a patrol down a well.

Two intensely hot days were experienced at this time, and man and beast suffered terribly. On May 16, between 11 a.m. and 2 p.m., a temperature of over 120 degrees was registered in a marquee. A patrol of the C.M.R. had 40 cases of sunstroke. The one and only benefit of the heat wave was that it killed myriads of flies, which had become as bad a pest as they had been during the summer days on Gallipoli.

CHAPTER XVI.

First Action in Sinai.

Turks having been reported to be at Bir El Abd and Salmana, some 25 miles beyond Romani, the New Zealand Brigade was detailed to attack them. It was the first definite stunt of the New Zealanders. On the night of May 30, the brigade moved to Dababis. Wells were sunk and a supply of very salty water was obtained, but the horses were so thirsty that they drank it with relish. After resting for the day, the march was continued in the evening. Some distance south of Bir El Abd the 3rd squadron of the A.M.R. was sent by a detour to get behind the post, and, after cutting the telephone wires, to wait to cut off the Turks if they retired when the advance was made by the column. Through some delay, the advance was not made for two hours after the wires were cut by the 3rd squadron—incidentally bayonets had to be used for the job, and some noise was inevitable—and by that time the Turks had got away. The column then moved on against Salmana, which was to be attacked at dawn. The A.M.R. was again detached, and sent to get into position on the south and south-east side. At 4.45 a.m. the Regiment was in position, and the attack was delivered. The three squadrons galloped across the intervening flat ground towards the sand hill, upon which 200 or 300 Turks were in position. The astonished Turks hardly fired a shot, even when the Regiment dismounted near the base of the hill. Fixing bayonets, the troopers rushed the hill, but before they got to the top the Turks were in fast retreat. A brisk fire was opened on the Turkish rearguard, five of whom stood their ground until shot. While this rapid movement was being executed the Regiment came under the fire of the C.M.R., who were advancing from the north-west, but fortunately no harm was done. The 3rd squadron pursued the retreating Turks, some of whom were on foot and some on camels, and succeeded in bringing fire to bear upon them from several eminences, inflicting losses that could not be estimated. At 6 a.m. several hundred reinforcements were seen coming to the aid of the Turks, and, as an action could not be fought so far in the enemy's territory, the squadron was retired. During the action the brigade had the valuable co-operation of an aeroplane, which dropped messages as to the Turkish movements. Only one casualty was suffered by the Regiment, Sergeant Parrish being wounded. This was the first casualty in action of the Regiment of this campaign.

The brigade returned to Dababis and, after resting for a few hours, moved on to Bir Etmaler, arriving at 10.30 p.m. Dog tired, the men were sound asleep the moment the horses had been cared for. At 6 o'clock the following morning they were wakened by the sound of bursting air bombs at the Australian Camp at Romani. It was only a matter of seconds before the Regiment had rushed to their horses and, riding them barebacked, had scattered in the desert, thus removing the target that airmen always look for. It was a strange parade. By the appearance of some men it might have been though to be a swimming parade, although it would have been difficult to account for one bare-legged man carrying his field glasses. The airman did not drop any bombs on the New Zealand lines, but he opened fire with his machine-gun on machine-gun emplacements. The fire was returned by our machine-gunners, but no damage was done on either side. Unfortunately, the Australian Light Horse, whose camp offered a good target owing to its size, lost a number of men killed and wounded, besides many horses.

After a few days spent in patrol and well-digging operations, the brigade once more moved by night against Bir El Abd, but no Turks were encountered. Returning, it was intended to water the weary horses at Oghratina, but the water, such as it was, had practically given out, and it was necessary to push on to Er Rabah, where the same difficulty was encountered. The horses were extremely thirsty when Bir Etmaler was reached at 5.30 p.m. For this expedition the A.M.R. was under Major McCarroll, and the brigade under Lieutenant-Colonel Mackesy. Such night stunts, even though they did not involve fighting, placed heavy responsibilities upon the leadership. All precautions had to be taken against surprise, and only the experienced know the difficulties of moving such a column at night.

The New Zealanders remained at Bir Etmaler until the last week in June, all the time performing arduous patrol duties, which taxed the strength of men and horses. The aeroplane visitation had introduced a fresh burden for those not on patrol duty. Reveille now went at 3.45 a.m., when all horses were saddled to allow of a quick "get away" should air raids take place. Further, the water became very bad, and under all these circumstances the Regiment was very delighted when it was sent back to Hill 70 for a rest. Plenty of fresh water was here available, and the horses had the advantage of shelters from the sun. After the

1. Branding a remount. 2. Hotchkiss rifle pack-horse. 3. "Stew." 4. Hard times.

1. Worn out after night march on El Arish. 2. Machine-gun ready for enemy aircraft. 3. Over the border into Palestine; the first grass.

ON THE DESERT.
1. Hod Amara. 2. Watering horses at Bir et Maler. 3. Laying telephone wire. 4. Another view of Hod.

1. A.M.R. Orderly Room at Mazar. Sergeant (afterwards Lieutenant) E. Foley in foreground. 2. Brigade on the march across the sand. 3. Typical desert hod, or oasis, showing how the sand encroaches.

continuous period of duty at Bir Etmaler, the following message from General Sir Archibald Murray to the brigade was much appreciated:—
" Whatever I ask you people to do is done without the slightest hesitation, and with promptness and efficiency. I have the greatest admiration for all concerned."

Throughout this period, the railway had been forging ahead, and the rails were not far from Romani. With it had come the pipe line, with its pure Nile water, upon which the whole scheme depended. With it had also extended the famous infantry road, which was merely a strip of wire-netting across the sand. The genius who hit upon this simple, but most effectual device, earned the eternal gratitude of the infantrymen and the War Office. On this road the infantry could do infinitely greater marches than on the sand.

CHAPTER XVII.

Romani Opens.

Notwithstanding the fact that it was the height of summer, the Turk was about to challenge. His first concentrations, a few miles east of Katia, were observed on July 19 by General Chaytor and an airman who had taken him out for a "joy ride" after the desert had been reported clear. The force was estimated at 9,000 men with guns. The bringing of heavy guns over the desert for so many miles was a remarkable feat. It was afterwards found that in many places the Turks had made a gun road by digging ditches where the wheels were to run, and filling them with brush, which prevented the wheels sinking in the soft sand.

The Turks started to dig in on a line from Oghratina to Mageibra. All the vital eminences were held in strength, and our patrols were frequently fired on, in some cases by machine-guns. Patrols of the A.M.R., under Lieutenants Reed and Martin, were sent to Bir Nagid, some 15 to 20 miles to the south, to keep a secret watch against the enemy's left. Secrecy demanded that this little post, so far from assistance, must be supplied with rations and water and fodder during the hours of darkness. Camels, of course, had to be used to transport the supplies, and as they took four or five hours to cover the outward journey, this was a matter of some difficulty. The fact that the camel drivers were Mohammedan Indians, under a superb-looking individual who wore a sword, and that the escort was a party of A.M.R. troopers under a corporal, led to an amusing incident the first night, or rather morning. Dawn was just about to break when the loads had been taken off, and there was need for haste if the camels were to be out of sight by sunrise. The Indians did not appreciate the position, and instead of turning back at once, they washed their hands and made ready to pray as the sun came up, the individual with the sword not excepted. The A.M.R. corporal tried persuasion, but that being of no avail, he used the toe of his boot on the head Indian. This form of persuasion was quite effectual.

At the time the enemy's intentions were not known. He was certainly expected to move forward and gain the advantages of the Katia system of oases, but there seemed every possibility that there he would wait for the British to dislodge him. The Commander-in-Chief decided to give him battle on August 13. A considerable force of infantry was in position, but the chief activity for some days was among the mounted troops of both sides. The enemy did not wait to be attacked, however. On July 27 his force, estimated now to number about 20,000 men, made an advance to Abu Darem, in the south, but was checked to some extent in the north by Light Horse and the W.M.R., with whom the latter were then brigaded.

So far the A.M.R. had remained at Hill 70 "standing by." Important patrol duties were daily carried out. On August 1, part of the 11th squadron was sent to establish a strong post to Bir En Nuss, some miles to the east of Dudar, to sink sufficient wells to water a brigade, and part was sent to Bir Nagid to keep a watch on the Turks. These hods were opposite the Turkish left, which was "in the blue," the desert being its only protection, and the troopers looked forward

with the liveliest anticipation to what they hoped
would be a rapid out-flanking movement, the
eternal dream of cavalry. The troops of Finlayson and Alsopp were in touch with enemy patrols,
and were able to send in valuable information as to
the activities of the enemy at Hamisah. On
August 3 the remaining two squadrons relieved
some Light Horse at Dueidar. That night the
enemy force made a general advance, one of the
fiercest fights being a delaying action by a small
body of Light Horse at Hod El Enna. On the
morning of the 4th, the Turks commenced to push
forward their left flank, in a north-west direction,
towards the high ground west of Bir Etmaler, and
soon were on Mount Royston, a high sand dune,
three miles north of Romani. This hill now
became the key to the whole action. Whatever
side held it would have possession of Romani, and
it fell to the New Zealanders to take a prominent
part in the action which regained the hill and put
the seal of failure upon the hopes of the German-
led Turks.

At 7 a.m. the New Zealand Brigade, in which
the 5th Light Horse had taken the place of the
W.M.R. who had been detached for some time,
got orders to move forward. The A.M.R. was at
Dueidar, and got orders to join the brigade as
strong as possible. The 3rd squadron and two
troops of the 4th squadron rejoined the column a
mile and a-half south-east of Canterbury Hill, the
11th squadron and the balance of the 4th squadron
remaining to patrol the Dueidar-Katia road.
About 11.30 a.m. a force of Turks, numbering
2,000, was observed on Mount Royston. About
mid-day, after being heavily shelled by the skilful
German or Austrian gunners on the ridge, a dismounted advance was ordered, the C.M.R. being

on the left, the 3rd squadron of the A.M.R. in the centre, and yeomanry on the right. It was actually an enveloping movement, the New Zealanders moving against the Turkish front and the yeomanry against their southern flank. Enemy advanced posts were driven back, and the 3rd squadron, now supported by Major McCarroll with the two troops and the machine-gun section, again moved forward across the sandy "waves." The warm fire of the Turks was returned vigorously by the A.M.R. machine-guns and the supporting battery, which had brought up its guns with twelve horse teams. Steadily the line moved forward, but surprisingly few casualties were suffered, one of the reasons being the advantage taken by the men of the cover offered by slight depressions, while the dangerous guts, running parallel with the advance, were avoided. It was to be a race against time. If the hill did not fall before nightfall all the effort of the day would be lost, so a general advance was ordered for 4.45 p.m. When the moment arrived, the Turks had begun to feel the pressure of the enfilade fire from the south, and they had already evacuated a position slightly in advance of the base of the hill, and also the left end of their trenches on the ridge itself.

As soon as the final rush began the attackers were met by white flags instead of bullets. About 250 Turks were taken by the A.M.R., including a complete hospital. With the south section of the position taken, it was merely a matter of moments before the whole position was occupied, over 1,000 prisoners being secured besides a battery of mountain guns. The first man to reach the guns was Lieutenant O. Johnson, of the A.M.R., who was killed a few days later. In the latter stages of the action some infantry gave support on the left.

Altogether it was a very satisfactory day's work, and the results were of the highest importance, seeing that the Turkish retirement began almost immediately. The Regiment had carried itself according to its Gallipoli traditions, and they were very tired but very satisfied men who rode back that night to rest after handing over the position to the infantry. But perhaps the proudest man of all was the padre, who had the distinction of getting a piece of metal through his hat without receiving any injury.

CHAPTER XVIII.

Gallop on Katia.

The Regiment nominally bivouacked that night at Pelusium—the Pelusium of ancient history, but now only a spot on the coast with a few ruins. Actually there was little time for sleep for most, and no sleep at all for picquets. It was nearly midnight before the men lay down to rest, and it was only three hours later that they had begun the duties of another day. The watering and feeding of horses began at 3 a.m., the water being brought up by camels, and at 6 o'clock the Regiment and the rest of the brigade moved off to Nuss, where the 11th squadron and the two troops of the 4th squadron who had been detached, were picked up. At 10.30 a.m. the brigade moved eastward in the direction of Katia, the orders being to attack the south-west corner of the hod, where, it was believed, the enemy had some guns concealed. It was decided to sweep down on this part of the hod in a long mounted line, the first men to gallop right through the guns if they were there, and the rear men to bayonet the gunners if there was any resistance. On the left was a Light Horse brigade, then came the 5th Light Horse Regiment, with the A.M.R. next, and the 3rd Australian Light Horse Brigade on the right. The C.M.R. was to be the reserve regiment of the New Zealand Brigade. The troops swung out into open column at 2.30 p.m., and soon were in position to charge. The 3rd brigade did not materialise, however, and therefore the A.M.R. was left with its right flank "in the blue." The gallop was a thrilling spectacle.

The horses simply raced towards the palms, leaving a high cloud of dust behind them. The troopers, expecting the guns to open on them any second, leaned forward in their saddles, and their faces wore the firm hard look which wins battles. The 5th Light Horse fixed bayonets as they rode, and held their rifles as lances. The hod proved to be empty, however, but that fact, not being known, did not detract from the audacious courage of the charge. It was the first time this movement was carried out.

Beyond the hod the regiments dismounted, and in extended order moved forward up the rise in front. As soon as they topped the "wave" of sand, the enemy, from entrenched positions previously prepared, opened a heavy rifle and machine-gun fire, which stopped the advance, and a duel ensued, continuing throughout the whole of that hot thirsty day. Information was received that the enemy were working round on the right and the C.M.R. was put into the gap. The mounted men hung on until dark when a withdrawal had to be started, owing to the Turks bringing up reinforcements, and it being impossible for British infantry to come up in time. The C.M.R. on the right had some difficulty in parting from the reinforced enemy—sometimes a mobile force can get itself into an advanced position much more easily than getting out of it—and the 11th squadron had to be sent to the aid of the Canterburys, and eventually the withdrawal was completed without serious loss. One officer and six men were wounded as a result of the day's adventure. The officer, Lieutenant Taylor, died of his wounds.

Leaving Lieutenant O. Johnston and 12 men of the 3rd squadron as a listening post at Katia, the Regiment rode back to Katib Gannit, arriving at midnight. There were very few men who did not sleep in their saddles as they trekked back, and little wonder too, for they had fought for two days on end with practically no sleep. But rest was still a long distance away, for when an enemy is retreating the cavalry must not rest. For the cavalry there is the constant task of following and harrying the rearguards with a constant eye to unprotected flanks. The unlimited expanse of open desert increased the scope of cavalry work, but the absence of water and the softness of the sand increased the rigours of the work to an unspeakable degree. The bivouac ground was not reached until nearly midnight, and the column was off again at 6 a.m. (August 6) to Katia. The men and horses were thoroughly fagged out by the heavy work and hard conditions, but there could be no rest.

Katia being found clear of the enemy, the brigade was ordered to follow on and gain touch with the Turks. Towards mid-day the advanced scouts encountered the enemy, who were holding an entrenched line to the west of Oghratina. Under artillery fire the mounted men kept in close touch with the foe throughout the day, but the Regiment suffered no casualties. A most interesting incident occurred. The screen discovered that the Turks, in their hurry to get back the previous night, had neglected to cut their telephone wire that led to Katia and to Bayud, in the south. The wires, of course, ran along the ground. A signaller brought up a telephone box and switched on to the line. Conversations in German as well

as Arabic were heard, and Lieutenant-Colonel
Mackesy, who can speak German, went out to
listen, taking with him the interpreter who knew
the Turkish language. In this way everything was
heard and understood. It was ascertained that
the retreat was to continue. Von Kressenstein
was heard to say: "I will give you the orders for
to-morrow later," but unfortunately he did not
give them on the telephone. While lying beside
the wire the colonel was able to study the bursting
of shells from an uncomfortably close position.
He observed that shells do not have as good an
effect when they strike yielding sand as they do
when they hit solid earth. At dusk the brigade
withdrew to the Er Rabah, but kept touch with
the enemy by patrols. Patrol duty is never easy,
but in their present state of fatigue the men who
had to go out to peer and watch and listen this
night were not to be envied. During the day
Lieutenants Reed and Martin with patrols were
lent to the 52nd Infantry Division, and they succeeded in capturing eight camel men and four
ammunition camels.

At 3 a.m. the brigade was again astir, and
was off at 4.30 to bid good morning to the Turks,
whose main position was now Oghratina. The
brigade remained in reserve throughout the day,
the 5th Australian Light Horse Brigade making a
demonstration. It was shelled again, but no
casualties were suffered.

The next night was spent at Rabah. At 4
a.m. (August 8), the force was again on the move
eastward, and found Oghratina to be evacuated,
the enemy holding a position in strength two miles
west of Bir El Abd. That night was spent at
Debabis with patrols keeping touch with the
Turks. On a board at Oghratina was found a

message which confirmed the belief that Lieutenant Alsopp and his patrol had been taken prisoner on the night of August 3. The message read: "Here was a German artillerie observation post. and had seen all the movements of the English cavaliere. Lieutenant Alsopp, A.M. Rifles, now prisoner of war—a gentleman—had eaten in our batterie." The facts of this misfortune were that Lieutenant Alsopp, with eight men, had been posted at Nagid for the express purpose of giving information to the troops behind. Someone without authority ordered them to Abu Raml, further south, where they were out of touch with the troops they were intended to serve. That night the Turks made their advance, and the little party was enveloped by two columns and captured. The only man who escaped was Sergeant Cheetham, who had been sent out to ascertain if there was a way of escape. When he returned with the information that there was a way he found the post gone, the Turks having already arrived. In the darkness the sergeant made his way back to safety, galloping between the Turkish columns.

The ground the British troops now occupied was in a filthy state, the smell of the dead bodies of men and animals being atrocious. But there was more to contend against than the unpleasant evidences of a hurried retreat. Cholera infection was abroad. When a notice was found above a grave stating that the patient had died of cholera, it was believed to be a piece of Turkish bluff, but soon the fact was established that cholera had occurred. Prompt measures were taken, and the troops were forbidden to drink from any of the wells. As a result the danger was averted, the only case occurring in the regiment being that of a man who disobeyed the order.

CHAPTER XIX.

Fight at Bir El Abd.

There was little rest for the brigade on the night of August 8. Bir El Abd was to be attacked at 6 the following morning, and the lines were awake and busy at 2 a.m., when horses were fed. The brigade moved out at 4.30, and at 5.15 the advance screen supplied by the A.M.R. was in touch with the enemy. (How simple it is to say that a screen was in touch with the enemy! How easy to say it, but what of the bullets that whip the morning air and the anxious peering eyes that must miss nothing, and the furrowed brow of the lieutenant who must be certain that the messages he sends back by flag are perfectly true. Yes! it is much easier to say that the screen gained touch). Leaving the horses under the cover of sand dunes the troopers, in open formation, moved forward to the attack, from a point about one and a-half miles west of and overlooking Bir El Abd. Splendid covering fire was provided by the Somerset Battery. The front line of the A.M.R. comprised the 3rd squadron on the left, and two troops of the 11th squadron and one section of machine-guns on the right. On the Regiment's left were the C.M.R., with Australians beyond them, and on the right was expected to come the 3rd Light Horse Brigade. The 3rd brigade again failed to get up, and again the Regiment had its right flank "in the air."

On the left of the hummocky country to be traversed was a ridge running forward from Bir El Abd, and on it were the Turks who, if unmolested, would have made it particularly hot for the attackers, but the moment the advance was started Lieutenant Hinman's machine-guns sent a deadly sheet of metal along the crest and cleared it. The absence of the brigade on the right soon began to have serious consequences. At 6.45 it was reported that enemy reinforcements were coming over the long ridge south-east of Bir El Abd, and the Regiment had to extent its front to a considerable extent. Major McCarroll went across to command this section, taking with him two troops of the 4th squadron. Advancing by troops the regiments made steady progress. At 9 a.m. the right flank was reinforced by one squadron of the 5th Light Horse. About 11.20 the C.M.R. and the left flank of the A.M.R. had to retire a distance owing to enfilade fire and, with the continued pressure against the unprotected right, the situation began to look ugly. Half-an-hour later the Turks counter-attacked with two battalions, each numbering 500 or 600 men. Aided by the Somerset Battery, the Regiment was able to hold its ground until the arrival of small reinforcements and a W.M.R. machine-gun section. The enemy then opened up a heavy artillery fire, which continued until 3.30, when he launched a second counter-attack, before which the C.M.R. had to retire.

During the afternoon the Turks sent in three fresh battalions against the left, and although the fighting did not develop into a hand-to-hand affair, it was warm enough for anyone. By 3.15 the A.M.R. reported that it was holding the enemy well, but at 4.15 a retirement was ordered. This presented a problem of difficulty, especially in view of the signs of another counter-attack. It had been observed, however, that the machine-guns used by the enemy were of German make. It was thus known that their field of fire was limited. Accordingly, it was decided to move back slowly to a point where the horses could be brought up, and then rush off the two flanks at a wide angle, which would prevent the machine-guns getting round on them. This was done, leaving only a small body in the centre. When the time came for this section to move, the enemy machine-guns were apparently fixed on the flank routes taken by the others. Instead of going by the flanks the men mounted their horses and galloped straight over the ridge immediately in rear. So successful was the movement that only one casualty occurred among the last section as it got away. Mention should be made of the splendid work of the machine-guns under Lieutenants Hinman and McCarroll in covering the respective withdrawals of the right and left sections. Some delay occurred in starting the final withdrawal on account of the shortage of sand carts for the wounded, but all the wounded were successfully evacuated before it began. The Regiment's casualties for the day numbered 11 killed and 19 wounded. The A.M.R. lost two particularly fine officers in Captain O. Johnson, who was killed, and Lieutenant A. M. Martin, who died of wounds. Lieutenant Martin had done splendid work in finding and developing water.

This was the last fighting the Regiment engaged in at this period. The Turk, menaced on the southern flank by the Camel Corps, and on the rear by the mounted troops, who had so thoroughly proved themselves, hurried his departure, and within a couple of days patrols had penetrated beyond Salmana without meeting the enemy. For some days the Regiment was bivouacked at Bir El Abd doing patrol duty and helping to bury the dead and the bodies of animals. Plenty of evidence was found of the havoc the guns had caused among the enemy transport camels. Romani was a most decisive victory. Nearly 4,000 prisoners were captured and the Turkish casualties were estimated at no less than 7,000. Thus, over half the force that had come across the desert was accounted for. The Regiment had its full share of fighting. During the week the men had little sleep, little water, and only "hard tack" and bully beef for food. The heat had added to their trials, which did not end with the battle, however, for patrol duty beyond Salmana was the usual routine. "It's a hell of a life," wrote one man during these days. "We need a spell, and so do the mokes. At Bir we found lots of beer bottles. Empty, of course. If ever I get out of this don't talk desert to me. The only shelter from the sun is what we can rig up with our blanket. All manner of insects attack us at night, and at dawn they are relieved by an army corps of vicious flies. Anyhow we got an onion issue to-day, and they say the railway is coming on fast. I suppose we are dinkum crusaders, but we don't look it or feel it. In the next war I'm going to be a rum buyer in Jamaica."

A few days after the last of the fighting, Brigadier-General Chaytor had to go to hospital owing to his Gallipoli wound giving him trouble, and in his absence Lieutenant-Colonel Mackesy took command of the brigade and Major McCarroll of the Regiment.

A week later the brigade moved to Hod Amara, beyond Abd, where it took over the outpost line, and made a reconnaisance over the rough ground north of Salmana and the island of El Galss, which is separated by a very shallow strip of water which dries up in summer. No traces of recent occupation by the enemy were found. It was a long, rough ride, but most interesting. En route a number of dry salt "lakes" were crossed, the horses' hoofs not making a mark on the hard crystal bottom. There was good fresh water in the vicinity of El Galss, sometimes in proximity to very salt wells. Patches of water melons and fig trees were found, and the fruit tasted like food of the gods after the fare of the recent hard days, but many suffered terrible pains afterwards. Lieutenants Finlayson and Coates acted as guides to the brigade on this expedition.

A couple of days later an enemy airman dropped three bombs on the Amara Camp, but did no harm. It was at this time that the 3rd squadron commander, Major Schofield, who had been seriously wounded on Gallipoli, broke down in health, and went away for good. He was succeeded by Major Bennett.

The brigade remained at Amara until September 11, the only diversions being provided by enemy 'planes, which usually appeared overhead at breakfast time, but usually passed on. A shift was then made back to the old camping ground at Bir Etmaler, where a well-earned rest was enjoyed. Reinforcements were received, and the old hands were sent away on leave to a splendid camp, established for the convenience of leave men, at Sidi Bishr, on the coast at Alexandria. A pleasant month was so spent.

Meantime, the railway was pushed on with remarkable speed, and all that troubled the workers and their protectors was air raids, which, however, rarely did any damage.

On October 22 the New Zealand Mounted Brigade was shifted up to Bir El Abd with camel transport, which was suggestive of further adventures.

IMPORTANT BRANCHES OF THE SERVICE.

1. Signaller Clark cutting enemy telephone wire at Magdhaba and "teeing in." 2. Cacholet camel for conveyance of wounded. 3. Ambulance sand cart. 4. Signallers' pack horse. 5. Camel transport. 6. Evacuation of wounded.

CAPTURES.

1. Turkish field kitchen. 2. A desert well. 3. The buggy obtained at Magdhaba.

THE FIELD OF RAFA, WHICH WITNESSED A PERFECT ENVELOPING ATTACK.

1. Date palms and tomatoes near Gaza. 2. Tamarisk tree near Kalassa. 3. Esani, on the Wadi Ghuzze. 4. A bivvie in the desert.

CHAPTER XX.

Back to the Outpost Line.

From Abd it moved on the next day to Bir El Ganadil, where it took over the forward outpost line from the 3rd Light Horse Brigade. Here the men were back again to the old duties of scouring the desert night and day. Within a few days the Regiment was moved forward to Bir El Kasseiba, and so the work went on. An important part of the duties in this forward position was that of locating and developing water. Our air force was constantly active, and various means of replying to questions dropped by the airmen were devised. For instance, a party would be marched round in a ring on the south side of the column to indicate "no." The life was hard, but now that the winter season was well on, it was healthy. Fresh goat meat was now included in the daily ration. Daily, Bedouins and their families were brought in and sent back to live at the expense of the nation, and in this connection some of the patrols had quite new experiences. On one occasion a woman rebelled against leaving the little hod, and the junior lieutenant in charge of the party felt nonplussed. He strongly objected to meeting with the modern woman movement away out in the desert. He got the rebels in, of course, but felt aggrieved. Later, the reason for the conduct of the woman became plain, and it proved that she was not a modern woman after all. Another batch was brought in, some of them with babies, belonging to the first lot. Apparently the babies had been left some distance away, but the mothers could not explain. One woman told an Egyptian cameldriver that she had left her baby in a bush, and when she was told to go and get it she kissed the feet of her guard and wept for joy. The cooks that evening prepared condensed milk for the babies, to the delight of the troopers, who had remarks to make about the start of the regimental nursery, and the appointment of a sergeant nurse.

Towards the middle of November, the Regiment moved on to Bir El Mazar, a spot some 20 miles east of Bir El Abd, which the railway was now approaching. The other regiments of the brigade were scattered about the neighbourhood, and keeping guard over several miles of front. There were no palms at Mazar, but good water was found. The ruins of an ancient Norman Church were found on the coast not far away from the camp. So rapid had the progress of the railway become, that on November 26 the brigade had to move on once more, their base now being El Mustagidda, a few miles from Mazar.

On the following day, Captain Finlayson and Lieutenant M. E. Johnson, with a party of eight men, left on a reconnaisance of the road to El Arish and of enemy works at Masmi, three miles south-west of the town. This entailed a long detour into the desert to the south from Bir El Gererat. This part of the journey had to be covered by night, and solely on compass bearings. The last five miles had to be covered after daybreak. The patrol was able to ascertain that there was no serious opposition around Masmi, but saw one or two small patrols. Our patrol was not observed, and got back according to time-table with all the necessary information. The total distance travelled was 46 miles. About this time camel patrols made similar expeditions to other points of the desert, and thus its topography and the dispositions of the enemy were thoroughly investigated. During the succeeding days considerable activity took place among the air forces of both sides, and the mounted regiments became inured to the experience of scattering when the Taubes appeared. Early in December, all four brigades of the Anzac Mounted Division were on the front, and the two infantry divisions were up with the railway. El Arish was to be the next objective, but before the blow could be struck the railway had to be brought as far as Kilometre 128, and a great supply of water accumulated. This was absolutely essential, because the desert to the south in this region was the most waterless tract of the Sinai. Fortunately what water there was, was fresh, the brackish wells having been left behind. By December 20, the preparations were complete for the advance, which, owing to water troubles, had to be swift and sure. Any lengthy delay would have meant disaster to the mounted brigades which had to deliver the blow.

CHAPTER XXI.

Descent on El Arish and Magdhaba.

On the afternoon of December 20, the A.M.R., again under the command of Lieutenant-Colonel Mackesy, General Chaytor having resumed command of the New Zealand Brigade, left Mustagidda, and after watering at New Zealand Valley, four miles to the north-east, moved on to Gimai, where it joined up with the rest of the brigade. The Regiment, which had been detailed to form the advance guard, had barely time to draw rations, drinking water, and fodder, the latter being the mobile ration of pure barley, before it had to move off into the night. The distance to be covered was over 20 miles, and it had to be done solely by compass bearing. The first 15 miles had to be due east (90 degrees) and the remainder at 40 degrees. The route led across trackless desert covered with sand hills, which all looked alike.

The task of guiding the Anzac Division fell to the lot of Captain Finlayson, of the A.M.R. The difficulties of his job that night cannot be over-estimated. In the first place he had to estimate the distance covered. Further, he had to be guided by the stars, but, unfortunately, stars have a habit of moving across the heavens, therefore a new star had to be chosen every now and again. The system adopted was that they should ride at an even walking pace for 50 minutes and then halt for 10 minutes, when bearings were to be checked. From this the distance covered could be estimated with some accuracy. Every 25 minutes the officer and his assistant had to select a fresh star as the guiding mark. They also had to make allowances for detours, which sand hills sometimes made necessary. This was before the days of the oil bath compass, which may be read with accuracy while riding, therefore the bearings could only be checked when they dismounted every hour. Notwithstanding the tremendous difficulties the march continued throughout the night with absolute precision, and at dawn the brigade was at Masmi, a truly remarkable achievement. From Masmi the brigades moved to their places, and by dawn El Arish was completely invested, Yeomanry being on its west side, the New Zealand Mounted Rifles and the 3rd Light Horse Brigade on the south-west, the Camel Corps on the south, and the 1st Light Horse Brigade on the east. It was found clear of the enemy, and immediately occupied. The town, which consisted of the usual mud brick buildings, covers a considerable area, and is only about one mile from the sea. Besides a mosque and a number of well-built public buildings it had once had a fort, but this had already been reduced to ruins by shells from monitors out at sea.

With El Arish in our hands it was possible to take immediate action against Magdhaba, some 24 miles up the Wadi El Arish (the Biblical River of Egypt), which had a garrison of 2,000. The mounted troops turned south to this new "job" the following day. At 10.30 a.m., on December 22, the 3rd squadron was ordered to proceed up the wadi to Bir Lahfan, and there await the arrival of the brigade if water was plentiful. The squadron's report being favourable the brigade moved out from El Arish at midnight. Every effort was made to preserve silence, and smoking was not allowed. The guns, however, made a tremendous row on the hard surface of the wadi. But the noise was not sufficient to keep the troopers from sleeping in their saddles, seeing that they had had no sleep the previous night.

Early that morning Magdhaba was surrounded, and it fell to a bayonet attack at 4 p.m. Some 1,200 Turks were made prisoners, and all the guns and material in the post captured. Great difficulty was experienced in getting water that night, but at 10 p.m. the Regiment had secured wells. The A.M.R. was left to clear up the field of action and destroy the serviceable buildings. Apart from the six field guns captured, which were sent into El Arish, there was a four-wheeled buggy, and there was wild mirth among the men when two troop horses were yoked into it. "Make the old nags think of market day at Pukekohe," remarked one man as two spare horses gaily trotted off with the vehicle. The Regiment left for Masmi at 2 p.m., and, after a halt at 5 o'clock, continued the march which was to bring them " home " for Christmas Day. A mistake was made in leaving the wadi too soon, and the Regiment got lost and had to wait through the intensely cold hours until dawn before it could find itself. It was rather an unfortunate Christmas morning, and it has been recorded that the cheerful trooper who suggested that they might employ the time by singing carols got a frigid reception. Even the horses seemed to realise that they were missing something, for one officer who went to sleep at his horse's head was wakened by the beast banging him with the empty nose bag.

The A.M.R. did not have a cheerful Christmas. Utterly worn out by the work of the previous days and nights, they spent the day in slumber. The cooks did their best to put on something out of the ordinary, but the plum pudding was hardly sufficient to keep the thoughts of everyone from wandering to the desert route from Mustagidda, along which they had had to discard the parcels that had arrived from home just before the ride began.

Periodically the Sinai Army was, in the language of the service, de-loused. This very necessary operation was simple, each man's clothing and blankets being placed in a steam disinfector for 20 minutes, at the end of which time the " Bedouins of the seams " were done with this life—or theoretically so. But a de-lousing parade of the A.M.R. at El Arish had perils for the men as well as for the creatures for which it was called. A party of men, more or less naked, were waiting for their clothes to come out of the disinfector when a Turkish aeroplane came over and dropped a bomb not far away. The Regiment, as usual, scattered with their horses, and the rather bare party had to gallop off as they were.

At El Arish the mounted men rested in great discomfort, for the weather turned wet and cold. The nights were most uncomfortable, because all the shelter that was possible was what could be obtained by rigging up ground sheets or blankets over the holes the men scraped in the sand. After a few days the A.M.R. moved to a new bivouac close to the beach, passing on the way a long convoy of the prisoners taken at Magdhaba, and the wounded, who were conveyed on sledges or in covered-in sand carts. It had been intended to take the prisoners and the wounded to Egypt by sea, but the heavy weather made that impossible. It was a memorable sight, which contrasted sharply with the scenes of the previous months. Twenty yards away from the long column of defeated Turks the breakers rushed up the sandy shore. In the mist out at sea lay a number of vessels of the Royal Navy, recalling Gallipoli memories.

At the new bivouac site, wells were speedily sunk only 100 yards from the breakers, but the generous supply of water obtained was almost free of salt. The reason appeared to be that there was a hard strata below the sand which held the rain water.

On December 29, General Chetwode, who had been in command of the Desert Column during the recent operations, inspected the New Zealand Mounted Rifles, and in addressing the men said that in the history of mounted war the recent action of the division created a record. He said he had expected big things of the division, but not so much as it had accomplished. For the first time in history, British cavalry had reconnoitred, attacked, assaulted, and stormed a position. Afterwards he expressed his personal thanks to Brigadier-General Chaytor for the good work of the New Zealand Brigade.

The weather continued bad. On the last day of this eventful year there was a howling gale, which turned the beach into a boiling, seething, roaring line of white foam. One of the small steamers which had been landing stores on the beach was driven ashore. During the gale a supply of fresh meat for the A.M.R. was buried by the wind-shifted sand, and it had to be dug out. The stew on that occasion was more gritty than usual.

CHAPTER XXII.

Rafa—First Fight in Palestine.

The rest at El Arish was to be of short duration. The mounted division, having proved its capacity for sudden night dashes across the desert, was on the move again at dusk on January 8, the objective being Rafa, a police post, consisting of a few tumbled-down buildings on the frontier, 30 miles away. This day the Wadi El Arish was in flood, but it was forded without difficulty, the spate being more remarkable for its width than for its depth. The column assembled at a point four miles east of the wadi on the road. The intention was to surround the strong Turkish entrenchments, the New Zealanders again being part of the force to be thrown round the redoubt. Sheik Zowaiid was reached by 10 p.m., when a halt was made for three hours. This enabled the horses to be fed, but owing to the intense cold the men were unable to get any sleep. As a matter of fact they could not lie down, but had to tramp up and down to keep up their circulation.

As dawn approached the "Camels" and yeomanry moved off to the north-east, to get into position for their attack from the west and south-west. The Light Horse and the New Zealanders continued east, the first task being that of rounding up the Bedouins, believed to be hostile, living in and around the village of Shokh El Sufi, four miles south of Rafa. The A.M.R. threw a cordon round the village, and soon had collected a large crowd of yelling natives. Two unfortunate incidents proved the wisdom of the precaution taken to remove the Bedouins. One A.M.R. man was shot dead by an Arab, who then escaped on the trooper's horse. At another tent the Arab owner suddenly drew from his clothing a sabre, with which he struck one trooper over the head, knocking him unconscious, and then galloped off on the soldier's horse, taking his rifle with him.

The troops were now in Palestine, the A.M.R. crossing the border at 6 a.m. Colonel Mackesy was the first to cross the line. They were also out of the desert. Much of the land was in barley or grass, and the flocks and herds of the natives dotted the landscape. There were no fences to hamper the movements of the cavalry—there is not a fence between the Suez and Constantinople—and the men rejoiced at the firmer " feel " beneath the hoofs. The field artillery, which accompanied the brigade, was able for the first time in the campaign to move at the gallop.

At 6.45 the brigade formed up behind a ridge which gave good cover, and from which the best view of the enemy works could be obtained. They consisted of a series of strong redoubts, connected by a maze of saps on the top of a huge mound or hump, the approaches to which, on all sides, were smooth grassy slopes of a mile or more. It was anything but an easy position to attack, and everyone expected that it would cost many lives. At nine o'clock the brigade was ordered to move north to get into position to attack the right flank works, and to cover the northern flank to the sea. Half-an-hour later it crossed the ridge and moved forward in column of troops extended. The Turkish artillery opened fire, and the pace was increased to a fast trot. For about a mile the horsemen were in full view of the redoubt, but the enemy gunners never got the range. Notwithstanding the shelling, many Arabs, with their flocks, were along the line of the advance. Grazing donkeys seemed to realise that big events were afoot, and galloped as fast as their legs would carry them alongside the excited horses. On reaching a point about two miles from the Turkish position, the men were dismounted, and immediately sent forward in extended order.

The C.M.R. was on the right of the line, with its right flank on the white sand hills that border the sea, and then came the 3rd and 4th squadrons of the A.M.R., the 11th squadron being held in reserve. The W.M.R. was the reserve regiment, part of which moved in support of the C.M.R. and part remained behind the A.M.R. to watch for enemy reinforcements towards Shellal and Khan Yunus. The C.M.R. occupied the village of Raffa as it moved to its position, and intercepted some retreating Turks and Germans, and also a camel train. At mid-day a combined attack by the brigade was commenced against part of the enemy position known as Green Knoll Redoubt. On the left of the brigade, the 1st Light Horse Brigade was operating, but some of the W.M.R. reserve had to be put in to fill a small gap between the brigades. Steadily the line moved forward by sections under the splendid covering fire of the Inverness Battery and our machine-guns and rifles, which made the redoubt look like a smoking furnace and kept down the enemy fire to a considerable extent. The covering fire saved many lives, for there was not an inch of natural cover over the whole mile of grassy slope that had to be traversed. Soon after the advance began the 3rd squadron of the A.M.R. was withdrawn, and the 11th was sent in on the right of the 4th, the reason being that in their position the 3rd could not make headway, except at heavy cost, which was not necessary, seeing that two sections were compelling the Turks to evacuate this part of the redoubt. Between 2 and 3 p.m., the 3rd squadron was sent in to reinforce the line, which, by 3.30, was far enough advanced to make the final assault. At 3.45 orders were issued for a general attack, but they did not reach the New Zealand Brigade until after 4 o'clock. At the same time came the information that the Turkish reinforcements were only two miles away. This menace against the rear of the troops on the eastern side of the redoubt, combined with the fact that darkness was fast approaching, made it essential that a decision must be immediately forced or a withdrawal made. For the New Zealanders, at least, a withdrawal would have been as costly as a charge, owing to the absence of cover. A little later an order was issued instructing all brigades to withdraw. It reached the Australians, the Camels, and the yeomanry, who immediately commenced to retire. It did not reach the New Zealand Brigade at the same time, and at 4.30 p.m. the New Zealanders, notwithstanding the fact that they saw the Australians on their left moving back, rose to the final charge with the bayonet. It was magnificent. The last 200 or 300 yards were covered in two grand rushes, and cheering madly, the men were into the first trenches. The surviving Turks surrendered. After a short pause the line swept forward against the next position—Sandy Redoubt—but before the gleaming bayonets were within striking distance, the garrison stood up and surrendered. When the Australians saw the New Zealanders charge, they turned at once and rushed the trenches above them.

A little later the Camels and yeomanry also returned to the attack, but they met little opposition. The Turks had had enough, and everywhere they threw down their arms. Within a few minutes the whole of the position was in British hands. Victory had been snatched on the call of time with the sun going down. But for the good fortune which prevented the New Zealand commander getting the order to withdraw in time for him to stop, the day would have been lost. There are many veterans who argue that even if the order to retire had reached the line it could not have have been obeyed because the men had reached the point when the last charge is inevitable and when soldiers become individualists. Whether that be so or not, the fact remains that the resolute action of the New Zealanders turned incipient failure into outstanding success. Not only was the night descent upon Rafa, over 30 miles of sand, a brilliant lesson in mobility, as one war correspondent described it, but the attack after the investment was a model piece of work up to the point when the action was almost broken off. As for the final charge of the one remaining brigade, words can hardly do it justice. It was everything that a charge should be, and more. It was the personification of that indomitable courage which achieves the impossible. An authority has stated that in such a well-sited and highly developed position two British battalions could have beaten the onslaught of a division. Early in the day it was ascertained that the German commanders believed it impregnable to attack of the mounted men. A captured German officer, to whom the colonel of the A.M.R. spoke, said that the attack could not succeed, and he was a very surprised man when he learned that the position had fallen.

The British casualties were surprisingly light for such an action. The New Zealand Brigade lost 17 killed and 92 wounded, the list for the A.M.R. being four killed, three died of wounds, and 41 wounded. The wounded included Major Whitehorn, Captain Aldred, and Captain Finlayson.

The total enemy losses were about 300 killed and about 1,600 prisoners, only 160 of whom were wounded.

Never did prisoners find themselves on the march quicker than did the Turks and Germans taken at Rafa. Owing to the proximity of the reinforcements, with whom the W.M.R. was still engaged, they were hurried back to Sheik Zowaiid, and the bulk of the mounted men with their horses, which had been without water since the previous night, went back too. The ambulance had to remain to evacuate the wounded, however, and a regiment of Light Horse remained to protect them.

Thereafter, Rafa, which had witnessed one of the most perfect operations in the history of mounted warfare, remained an outpost position until the railway came forward. So did the desert army, having fought and toiled and endured through fiery heat and raging thirst, through choking winds and bitter cold, come to the borders of the Promised Land, its pastures gay with glorious flowers. It was for many a wonderful moment of their lives. Here they stood, victors so far and confident of the future, at the gateway of Palestine, whence came the very principles of truth and justice and right, for which the war had been waged. They were to tread holy ground. For them their fighting was to be the battle of the Cross, and whether religious convictions were strong or weak, the thought appealed to the slowest imagination. They were stirred in a way that neither the physical fatigue nor the drudgery of army life nor the system which kills individuality, could lessen.

CHAPTER XXIII.

The First Gaza.

The historic town of Gaza was to be the next objective, but once more the army had to wait until the railway " caught up " before the blow could be delivered. Gaza was strongly held. It was the right flank of the new Turkish line, which extended over the 30 miles to Beersheba and into the high ground beyond, and preparations had to be made for an attack by infantry, in addition to flanking movements by the mounted troops. After Rafa, the A.M.R., with the rest of the brigade, returned to Sheik Zowaiid, and thence to Masaid, near El Arish, where a bivouac was established. Here Major Mackesy rejoined the Regiment, and took over the 3rd squadron.

On February 22, the whole mounted division was ordered forward on an expedition against the enemy positions in the vicinity of Khan Yunus, the main purpose being to capture a certain hostile sheik and his following. The early part of the night was spent at Sheik Zowaiid, the march being resumed at 1 a.m. At dawn, the advance guard came into action against the enemy trenches two miles and a-half south-west of Khan Yunus. The A.M.R. was held in reserve, and so did not participate in the action early, in which the Turks evacuated their lines and retired to high ground on the outskirts of Khan Yunus, where there were strong earth defences and cactus hedges. A continuance of the action was not feasible, and a withdrawal was ordered about 7.30 a.m. The hostile sheik was not secured, but valuable information as to the nature of the country and the best routes

RIDERS OF THE SAND.

1. Lieutenant A. Carr, Corporal Gillespie, and Troopers Hartley and Glass. 2. A section bring in an old Bedouin and two children found in a state of starvation.

1. Hotchkiss Section.   2. Fresh milk at Khan Yunus.

THE ATHLETIC SIDE.

1. Boxing on the desert. 2. A.M.R. football team, which never nad its line crossed; winners of the Anzac Cup.

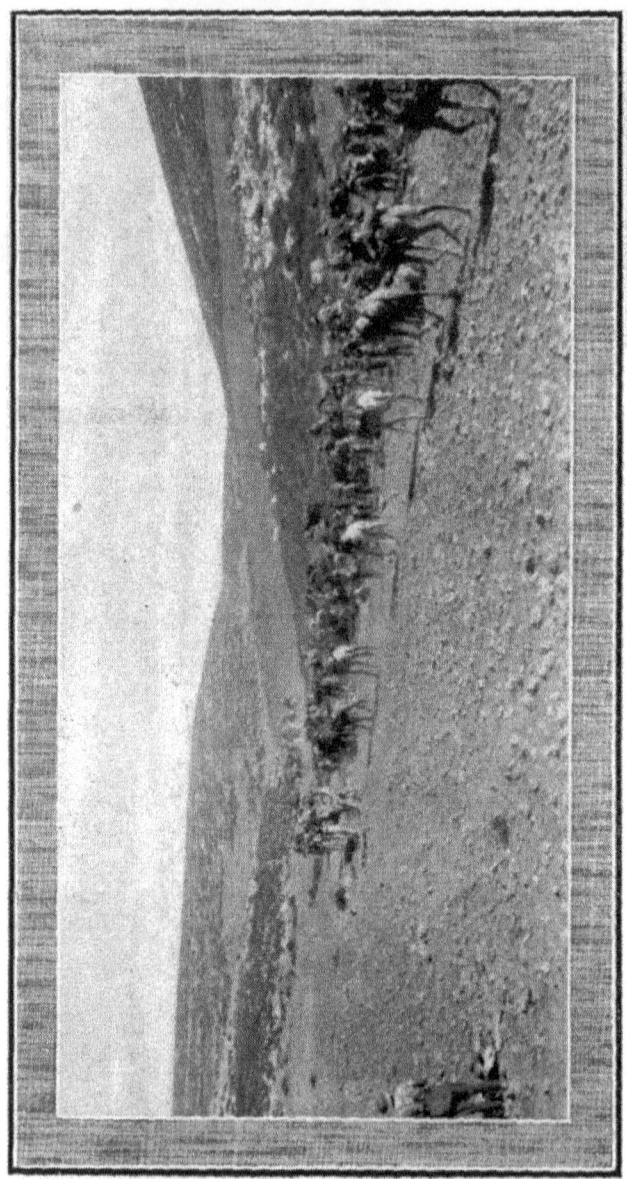

NORTH OF BEERSHEBA: REINFORCEMENTS ARRIVING TO HELP THE NEW ZEALANDERS.

for the various arms was obtained. Thereafter, Sheik Zowaiid was the base of the brigade. A few days later the brigade, with the A.M.R. supplying the advance and right flank guards, reconnoitred the country beyond Sufi, where enemy patrols were pushed back by the advance guard, no casualties occurring. This kind of work continued for some time without interruption or event, beyond the more or less sporting minor affairs with enemy patrols, the collective result being that the advancing railhead was effectually guarded, the country thoroughly explored, and water developed.

On March 10 the brigade was moved to Bir El Malalha, on the coast, but, as was remarked by one man who had not forgotten the slur cast upon the mounted rifles by some fool who had placed in a gift parcel a note stating, " I hope this does not fall into the hands of the cold-footed mounteds," they did not spend the time wading in the sea and holding picnics. The " picnics " took them on reconnoitring expeditions towards Gaza, and to lonely outposts to keep watch on the enemy patrols. The foolish people who imagined that the mounted men were enjoying a high time of lotus-eating, would have received a rude shock had they been taken on one of these night patrols, to spend a sleepless night on top of a sand hill far from their Regiment, and to be shot at by a hostile patrol in the morning. This work the men accepted as a matter of course. They did it uncomplainingly, but they objected seriously to home-fire burners belittling them.

The feature of the topography which called for special duty was the Wadi El Ghuzze, a watercourse dry except during winter rains, which runs north and south a few miles west of Gaza. The crossing through this wadi had to be carefully studied in view of the coming operations. It was not a particularly deep watercourse, but usually its banks were too steep for the rapid passage of troops.

The brigade came up to Dier El Belah before the attack on Gaza on March 26, and from there moved off at 2.30 a.m. to get behind the town to keep back Turkish reinforcements and attack the position from the flank while the infantry made the frontal attack. Crossing the Wadi El Ghuzze at El Jemmi the brigade moved to Tellul El Humra, the 2nd Light Horse Brigade going further north to cover the ground to the sea. The 4th squadron was detached to oppose reinforcements advancing from the direction of Huj, while the 11th squadron and one troop of the 3rd went on a similar mission towards Tor Dimre, further north. At 4 p.m. the 22nd mounted brigade and the N.Z.M.R. attacked Gaza from El Meshahera, the remaining portion of the A.M.R. being held in reserve. Meeting with little resistance, and impeded only by cactus hedges, this part of the attacking force entered the outskirts of Gaza, and the town was theirs for the asking. But orders for withdrawal were issued, and when questioned they were made insistent. Accordingly, the mounted men were withdrawn—the most tragic and inexplicable episode of the whole campaign. There was no serious danger of the enemy reinforcements coming into the fight from the rear, nor was there any other reason why the Turks should have been handed back the town, but it had to be done. The A.M.R., less the 4th squadron, got back to Dier El Belah early the following morning. They were very tired, but even fatigue was forgotten in their disgust at being pulled out of a great victory. Their spirits went down to zero, and a period of dark depression was ushered in.

During this night the 4th squadron, which had been left at Huj to delay reinforcements, had to retire in face of the reinforcements which pushed forward as soon as the retirement took place. Leaving Huj at 3 a.m. they had to ride all night, going at a smart pace for some miles, to avoid being captured. But, as usual, they found something to laugh about, which after all is the saving of many a soldier. They had captured one Turkish infantryman, who was wearing all his equipment. This unfortunate Turk had to be brought along, but as he could not be mounted he had to run, clinging to stirrups on either side. When a halt was called the prisoner, with set purpose on his features, took off his equipment, each part of which he flung to the ground with an angry grunt. Then he smiled cheerfully, and indicated that he would be much happier to go on without it. "I don't blame the poor devil," said one of the Waikatos. "I wouldn't care to train for a marathon with a pack up, but why didn't the lunatic tell us he wanted to drop it."

During the succeeding weeks the New Zealanders had the doubly distasteful job of holding an outpost line over country which they felt they had completely secured when they made the dash for Gaza, and of digging strong posts on important features. The Regiment, in its dashing desert work, had almost forgotten the tremendous digging of the Gallipoli campaign, and the men were hardly stimulated by the obvious purpose of these operations. Were they to assume the defensive, or settle down to a stalemate?

At this time four Hotchkiss automatic rifles were added to the equipment of each squadron. These guns further increased the offensive and defensive strength of the mounted rifles, which, having already machine-guns and Lewis rifles, possessed stronger striking power than any mounted regiments in history. All this complementary armament was carried by pack horse, and therefore it possessed the same degree of mobility as the regiments.

The outpost lines held by the mounted regiments often covered a number of miles, squadrons being detached, but always there was the closest touch between them and between the headquarters of regiments and brigades. At night time the outposts could always communicate with their base by means of signal lamps, and by flag or helio by day. It was a stimulating, if common, sight on a sunny day to see the helios flashing their messages across the sky. The soldier takes the signal service as a matter of course, just as he does the medical service, the supply and transport service, and all other services upon which the whole fabric of an army rests. But it is only doing bare justice to the men concerned to place on record the splendid work they invariably performed. The A.M.R. was always fortunate in its specialists, as it was in its supply officers and transport men, who toiled out of the limelight, but often in great danger. They were always good game for hostile airmen, and they did not have much of "the fun."

During April, the transport services performed a tremendous task in building up a great water reserve at Tel El Jemmi, on the Wadi Ghuzze. The water was brought by camel (for the most part) from the wells at Belah, and it was stored in tanks and canvas cisterns. Squadrons were told off to unload this water, and the magnitude of the supply may be gauged from the fact that on one day the 11th squadron of the A.M.R. unloaded 60,000 gallons. It was on this water-carrying duty that old Bob Hammond tried the experiment of threatening an enemy airman with a lousy shirt. The shirt was all he had, and he thought it was better than nothing. The facts of the affair were that Bob's shirt had been riding on the load, the day being hot, and the soldier in question having no great liking for unnecessary clothing. The shirt either fell or jumped off the load, and Hammond wandered back to get it. An airman swooped down very low, and opened his machine-gun on him. With the bullets kicking up a lively dust around him, Hammond seized the shirt and flourished it vigorously at the Taube, which thereupon departed. It is not known whether the airman was scared of the living shirt or was overcome with mirth.

CHAPTER XXIV.

The Second Gaza and After.

The second attack on Gaza was commenced on April 17, the main attack being delivered by the infantry divisions which could be supplied from Belah, where the railhead now was. The mounted division was used to protect the right flank of the infantry.

The operations of the New Zealand Mounted Rifles commenced on the evening of the 16th. The object was to demonstrate against Abu Hareira, and so prevent the enemy from detaching troops to reinforce Gaza. During the night the Regiment moved with the brigade to Shellal, arriving there at 3 a.m. At dawn, horses were watered in the wadi, and a move was then made to a point half a mile east, where men and horses were fed. Enemy aircraft being very active, the 11th squadron was detached to bring rifle fire to bear on them, the result being that the hostile airmen kept at a higher altitude. At 9 a.m. the Regiment moved with the brigade to an eminence overlooking Hareira, Sheria, and the Turkish railway line running laterally between Gaza and Beersheba. The 4th squadron was detached to watch these places, observing much activity among the enemy forces, and the striking of tents. Throughout the day the regiment was frequently under machine-gun fire from the air, but no casualties were sustained. That evening the brigade, in accordance with previous instructions, moved back to Shellal, arriving at 10 p.m. During the day the infantry had advanced against Gaza, and had seized the Sheik Abbas-Mansura ridge.

The following morning the brigade again moved out to continue its duties in containing the enemy forces in this area, and protecting the right flank of the infantry. On the march the A.M.R. acted as advance guard to the brigade. By midday the 3rd and 11th squadrons, who formed the screen, were on the ridge running south-east towards El Buggar, driving the enemy advanced posts before them. On being relieved by a squadron of the C.M.R., the 3rd squadron withdrew, and with headquarters moved to El Girheir, whilst the 11th squadron established observation posts on the ridge from the road at Imsiri to a point one mile south-east of El Girheir. Again aircraft were active, flying low to deliver bursts of machine-gun fire. Our men replied with volleys. After dusk the brigade returned to Shellal to feed and water, but not to rest. Shellal was reached at 9.30 p.m., and at 11 p.m. the regiments were on the move again, the destination being El Mendur, which was not reached until 6 o'clock on the following morning (April 19).

This day the mounted division was required to be more aggressive than it had been during the operations, the infantry having been unable to make progress. At 9 a.m. the 3rd squadron of the A.M.R. was detailed as a guard to a battery of artillery, and proceeded with it in the direction of Atawineh, where the guns got into action, the 3rd squadron going into the firing line on the right of the W.M.R. Throughout this long hot day the squadron lay in a patch of high barley under very heavy rifle and artillery fire, and lost one killed and 17 wounded. It withdrew at 8 p.m. with the uncomfortable feeling that very little had been achieved. The other two squadrons had an easier

day, being held in reserve behind a hill west of
Atawineh. They were often menaced by aircraft,
however, and two men were wounded through
this cause. This day saw what was practically
the end of the second battle of Gaza, the plain
hard facts of which were that the Turks with
strong forces, plenty of artillery and munitions,
good defensive positions, and an invaluable railway running behind their front, were more than
a match for the desert column. With the conviction that Gaza could have been taken three
weeks earlier, when the mounted troops were withdrawn from their position of mastery, the men,
after these operations, came as near as ever they
did to "getting their tails down."

The Regiment, with the rest of the brigade,
remained in the forward positions of this area
until the end of the month. Some trench digging
at various strong posts was necessary, but the
most arduous duty was that of night patrolling
along an extensive outpost line. Whole regiments
had to be used on these forward positions, and so
dangerous was the situation regarded that the
outposts had to report hourly during the night.
The base of the A.M.R. was at Karim Abu El
Hiseia, on the Wadi Ghuzze.

At this time a number of changes took place
in commands. Brigadier-General E. W. C.
Chaytor, C.B., C.M.G., was promoted to the
command of the Anzac Mounted Division; Lieutenant-Colonel C. E. R. Mackesy, D.S.O., after
acting as brigadier for a few days, was appointed
Administrator of the Khan Yunus-Deir El Belah
area; Lieutenant-Colonel W. Meldrum, C.M.G.,
D.S.O., who had been in command of the W.M.R.,

became Commander of the New Zealand Brigade; Major J. N. McCarroll took over command of the A.M.R., and was promoted to Lieutenant-Colonel; Major C. R. E. Mackesy, who had been in command of the 3rd squadron, became second in command of the Regiment, and Captain T. L. Ranstead, who had been signalling officer to the Regiment on Gallipoli, and who had seen almost continuous service, took over the command of the 3rd squadron; Lieutenant W. Haeata, who had been acting as adjutant for some time, took over the duties permanently, Lieutenant J. Evans, who had rendered brilliant service as adjutant throughout the campaign, being transferred to the New Zealand infantry in France.

In connection with the operations in the second battle of Gaza, the names of Captain A. C. M. Finlayson, Sergeant Dunbar, Lance-Corporal K. M. Stevens, and Trooper K. Bishop, were brought under the notice of higher authorities.

The Regiment had richly earned a rest when it was relieved by infantry on April 29, and moved back to bivouac, at a spot one and a-half miles south-west of Fara. For some weeks the weather had been hot, and during the last week the dreaded wind had come with its suffocating heat and blinding dust. Fara was not a rest camp, of course. The term "rest" is used only in a comparative sense, as it always must be in respect to mounted troops who have to keep the enemy and his movements under close surveillance over miles of country. At Fara, the Mounted Rifles and kindred bodies were what might be called the antennae of the army, but they were also the sting. Sometimes moving in force, sometimes in

small bodies, the desert horsemen kept guard over
the territory east of the wadi. Occasionally
enemy patrols fired on the screen, but history does
not take much notice of such incidents. It is the
kind of work that is covered by the communique
which says that patrols were in touch with the
enemy, but quiet prevailed along the front. In
addition to this highly-important duty, road-
making was carried out and water developed in
the wadi. Time was found, however, for football
and sports.

A force of 2,500 Turks was reported to be
advancing towards Fara from Beersheba on May
10, and the New Zealand Brigade was ordered to
move out that night, push the enemy screen back,
and test the strength of the force at El Buggar.
The A.M.R. acted as advanced guard to the brigade, with the 3rd squadron in the van. Turkish
patrols retired before the advancing screen, and
no action eventuated. Valuable information as to
the nature of the country was obtained, however.
The road was found to be fit for the passage of all
arms and wheeled traffic, the country being easy
rolling downs, carrying stunted crops and some
grass. Water cisterns were found at Kh Khasif
and El Buggar. On this stunt the men had their
first glimpse of the minaret of the mosque in
Beersheba.

It was at this time that the men were issued
with gas helmets and trained in their use. Parties
were marched through dense clouds of gas, and
they felt very sorry for themselves. To add to the
discomforts, which, with the approach of summer,
were not light, inoculation against typhoid and
cholera was carried out. During the month a
considerable amount of barbed wire defence was

put into position along the British line—ominous preparations which were hardly calculated to give encouragement to the desert cavalry.

The most important aggressive operation of the period was the destruction of the southern sector of the Beersheba-El Auja railway. In this successful raid the New Zealanders were used to hold a defensive line between the Imperial Mounted Division, which demonstrated before Beersheba, and the Australian Light Horse. The Australians performed their demolition work about Bir Aslui, while part of the Camel Corps, which had moved south from Rafa, operated on the line near the terminus at El Auja, close to the Turco-Egyptian frontier. No opposition was encountered, and the railway was rendered useless, many viaducts and a large bridge being destroyed.

At the end of May, the Regiment, with the rest of the brigade, moved back to a bivouac ground at El Fukhari, where a new " home " was speedily established. The weather was growing hotter and the flies came in myriads. Training in manœuvres, bomb throwing, and musketry was carried on, the range shooting being most important in view of the fact that Mark 7 rifles had been issued in place of the old Mark 6 type. Then the band came up from Rafa, and apart from the trials of summer, and the occasional visits of enemy aircraft, life was considered quite satisfactory. There was no want of applicants for leave to Cairo, however. Early in June a new bivouac was established at Tel El Marakeb, near Khan Yunus, where the training, which is rest, was continued, and later, another shift was made to Kazar. At this time the following names were brought under the notice of higher authorities:—

Captain A. C. M. Finlayson, Lieutenant C. V. Bigg-Wither (regimental quartermaster), S.S.M. H. Eisenhut, Q.M.S. J. Patten, and Trooper A. T. Buckland. Advice was received that Colonel Mackesy had been awarded the C.M.G. and R.S.M. W. Palmer the Military Cross.

On the night of July 3-4, the New Zealanders moved east in support of the Australian Mounted Division, which had to reconnoitre the country in the Shellal-Beersheba-Asluj area. By morning the Regiment was in its appointed position, west of Taweil El Habari, where the squadrons, particularly the 11th, were vigorously shelled, but the shelter of the wadis prevented any casualties. Here a remarkable incident was witnessed. A British aeroplane landed on open ground between the advanced division and the reserves. In a twinkling the Turkish artillery had the range, and the pilot was forced to bolt on foot. Fully 100 shells burst round the 'plane, which everyone thought must have been damaged. Later the pilot, unseen by the Turks, crept back to his machine, and starting the engine careered along the road to safety. He could not rise owing to one wing being broken, but the machine rushed along the road like a motor-car, to the great joy of the horsemen. The New Zealanders withdrew during the afternoon, and watered the thirsty horses at Fara, the first watering for 31 hours.

The following day the "bivvies" which covered the "arm chair" holes in the ground were folded up and a shift was made to Fara, where a standing camp of tents was taken over. Patrolling work was resumed. Five patrols of one troop each were sent out to the outpost line, and soon renewed their acquaintance with the

Turks. At Kh Khasif a squadron of cavalry was seen watering their horses, and Hotchkiss and rifle fire was brought to bear upon it. The Turks did not wait for any more water.

On July 8, during a reconnaisance by the Anzac Division, the New Zealanders saw for the first time the new Commander-in-Chief, Major-General Sir Edmund Allenby. The presence of the great soldier in the forward zone was more than a tonic to the regiments which were still suffering from the Gaza fiasco, and his personality began to have a wonderful effect throughout the entire force. "He'll do us," was the colloquial verdict. In this expedition the advance reached within four miles of Beersheba. The Turkish guns were busy during the day, and much activity was seen among the Turkish forces, which, no doubt, feared an attack.

A couple of nights later the brigade left on a silent stunt with the idea of rounding up any Turks believed to be in the habit of frequenting the Khasif-El Buggar area. Leaving the horses at a safe distance, the positions were surrounded on foot, but the Turks were not there. At this time the squadron commanders were Captain Ashton (3rd), Major Munro (4th), and Captain Finlayson (11th).

On July 12 there was another foray. At Khasif a troop, under Lieutenant Tait, encountered three troops of enemy cavalry, and forced them to retire, after a short encounter. The Somerset Battery came up in the afternoon to shell an eminence known as Hill 630, but the Turks did not wait for the attentions of that excellent battery. The Turkish gunners did their best to spoil the work of Lieutenant Hatrick and his signallers, who were using helios, but fortune again attended the signallers, and no harm was done. A day or two later the Regiment took over part of the advance defences, the 3rd squadron going to Z Redoubt at El Ghabi, the 4th squadron to Y Redoubt at El Jezariye, and the 11th squadron to X Redoubt at Um Ajua. These redoubts were already entrenched, and were protected with barbed wire. The most serious disadvantage of this duty was that horses had to be taken to Gamli, four miles away, for water, the 30 transport camels of the Regiment being unable to bring up the necessary supplies. Owing to the large proportion of the men who had to be on patrol duty and on guard in the redoubts at night, this stretch of duty was arduous. On July 19 there was a mild scare, patrols from Fara encountering a strong force of Turks in the fog early in the morning. The A.M.R. remained in the redoubts, but the rest of the brigade moved out with the division, and infantry came up to support the Regiment. No action eventuated, but casualties occurred through shell fire.

The Regiment returned to Fara on July 22, but excursions and alarms continued to be the order of life. The weather was very hot, the men became worn out, and there was a great deal of sickness. Patrols ventured right into what the Turks regarded as their territory, and often were under fire. One day the report came in that the Turks were evacuating Beersheba, and this had to be investigated. Of course the information was incorrect. The following day there was a reconnaisance to the Wadi Imleih. After the fog lifted at 8 a.m., a patrol, under Lieutenant M. E. Johnson, located a Turkish post, and two troops under Captain Finlayson were ordered to capture it. They moved into the Wadi Sheria, and then under cover of artillery fire they rushed the post, but the Turks fled. The A.M.R. men gave pursuit, one troop galloping along the north bank of the wadi, and the other along the south bank of the Wadi Imleih, and came within an ace of cutting off the Turks. Heavy fire from the Sana redoubt forced the troops to retire. Four Turks were killed and a number were wounded. Later, the Somerset Battery directed its fire against Sana, 7,000 yards away, and so well was it directed that the Turks were made to clear out in disorder. Corporal E. J. Coleman, who turned back and rescued under fire a man who had his arm broken when his horse was shot, was recommended for reward. He was given the Military Medal. It was a very gallant rescue.

By the beginning of August, new infantry divisions were appearing on the front, the railway had reached Shellal, which was as far as it could go, and there were signs of another forward move. Acutally the army was being organised for the next blow, but the hour was not yet ripe, and the endless game of night and day riding had to go on. The squadron commanders remained the same, except that Major Ranstead, upon his return from hospital, took over the 3rd squadron, Captain Ashton becoming second in command of the 4th squadron.

A very fine piece of work was carried out by Lieutenant M. E. Johnson and a patrol of four men, on the night of August 7. It had been reported that the Sana Redoubt was being filled in, and definite information was wanted on the point. The party went to Khirbit Erk during the afternoon, and after dark rode due north for a mile and then east for an hour. Owing to the brightness of the moonlight the party had to wait until midnight before venturing further. They succeeded in getting close to the redoubt without being detected, and at a distance of from 250 to 150 yards they reconnoitred the post, gaining definite information that the trenches were not being filled in. Small parties of Turks were seen in all quarters of the works.

The prevalence of fog at this time added to the troubles of patrols, and was responsible for some incidents which afterwards were considered amusing. Often patrols moved out in the darkness with the object of "beating" the Turks for valued observation posts at dawn. One foggy morning several patrols got into a bad state of nerves owing to the screen losing direction, and after riding around for a time coming up in rear of the party which they had been expected to protect. Later one officer rode across to the officer of the next patrol, and said he was certain that some men were in front of him, and he was very anxious to know if the screen of his friend was in its right position. Of course it was, how could his screen lose itself, was the reply. Later the first officer informed his brother that he would not dream of casting reflections about his men, but that he could swear that a horse that had loomed up and disappeared again was very much like Baldie of the second troop. "Of course there was no need to worry about the fellows getting lost," remarks the ex-officer long after.

N.Z. MONUMENT AT AYUN KARA.

1. Primitive plough at work in the Valley of Ajalon.
2. Bedouins described as allies.

ORANGES AT LUDD

THE AUJA NORTH OF JAFFA, WHERE A SHARP ENGAGEMENT OCCURRED.

"An officer doesn't need to worry with men of such capacity. Even if they do lose themselves in the fog you can bet your boots that you'll hear where they are mighty quick if they run into an enemy patrol. And if nothing happens you can rely upon them pulling into some dump before long. It's easy to be an officer with such men." On the other hand we find ex-troopers yarning over the days that have been, and some one is bound to remark that the great thing on these night adventures was to have officers they could trust, and then they will start to extol Bobbie This or Magnus That or Mervyn So and So, or Sinclair Whathisname, who did honour to the King's commission, and never, never lost themselves. And when long after the days of stress, officers and rankers indulge in expressions of mutual admiration, you realise what a happy family it was, and you get the key to the secret of many things.

The men and horses were badly in need of the rest which commenced on August 18, the Regiment and the rest of the brigade going to Goz Abu Um El Dakeir, on the coast, in the vicinity of Khan Yunus. Never did men more enjoy sea bathing than did the grimy sun-baked men from inland. The sea itself was hot—as warm as No. 6 at Te Aroha, remarked one man— and horses and riders disported themselves in the surf like porpoises. Then there was fruit to be had from Khan Yunus—prickly pear and watermelons, and for some there was leave to the rest camp at Port Said. Of course the usual athletic epidemic broke out during the life of ease by the vitalising sea, taking the form of boxing on this occasion. Each evening burly brown giants pounded each other in the "stadium," and one man with an eye for muscular strength, formally called upon Richard the Lion Heart to "trot out his ironclad pugs." The shades of Richard remained mute, but doubtless they were there.

On September 18, the New Zealanders, much improved in health, moved to Fukhari, taking the place of the 4th Light Horse in the support line. They arrived at the new bivouac ground in a severe dust storm, which continued for a number of days with maddening persistency. The most of the month was spent in strenuous training and practise of all kinds, but time was found for football matches. But there was not to be much more time for play.

CHAPTER XXV.
Tel El Saba.

About October 20, General Allenby began to make his concentrations for his attack against the Gaza-Beersheba line. The New Zealanders formed part of the Desert Mounted Corps concentrating about Khalasa and Asluj, from 15 to 20 miles south of Beersheba.

At 5 p.m. on the evening of October 25, the brigade started for Esani, 15 miles to the southeast, and after a cold ride reached their destination at 1 a.m. In this locality was seen a new ration dump, which was being built up by night by steam tractors. A few nights later the brigade moved to Khalasa, 10 miles further south, and the next night continued on another 15 miles to Asluj, due south of Beersheba. No fires were allowed this night, and water and bully beef formed the supper. At 6 p.m. the following evening, the brigade started on the trek north to the attack on Beersheba from the east. The route for the first 10 miles followed a splendid metalled road, over which the guns and wheeled transport held exclusive rights, the column being a triple one. The road was left when the Wadi Imshash was reached, the column then moving almost due east along the bank of the wadi for another 10 miles, when it turned due north along a winding track. At 2 a.m. a halt was made while the W.M.R. went forward to surround a post at Goz El Shegeib, where a body of enemy cavalry was suspected to be. The post was found clear of the enemy, and the march was resumed at 3 a.m. At dawn the brigade was three or four miles south of the Beersheba-Bir Arara Road, to the southeast of Tel El Saba, a strongly-held peak over 1,000 feet high, which dominated the eastern approach to Beersheba. At 8.30 the road line was reached, the A.M.R. then being in reserve. At 9 o'clock the A.M.R., with the Somerset Battery attached, received orders to advance on Saba, the C.M.R. being on their right and the 3rd Light Horse on their left. The advance was started immediately, the 11th squadron, under Major Whitehorn, forming the advanced guard. The advance followed the line of a wadi, which offered good cover, and in which pools of water were found for the thirsty horses. The discovery of this water was of great importance. Leaving the wadi the 11th squadron came under long-range machine-gun fire from Saba. The ground traversed was flat and open, but it was intersected with many watercourses, which gave good cover.

At 1,800 yards from the enemy position the 11th squadron dismounted, and continued to advance on foot; the other two squadrons (the 3rd being under Captain Ashton and the 4th under Major Munro) rode on under cover of the north bank of the wadi to a point 800 yards from the objective. From this point the 3rd and 4th squadrons moved on foot into position on the left front of the 11th. The advances were made a troop at a time, the machine-guns being pushed on to give covering fire. The 3rd Light Horse regiment came into action on the south side of the wadi, and brought covering fire to bear on the position. The Somerset Battery gave considerable assistance with a well-directed fire against machine-gun positions, the exact locations of which were communicated from the attacking line. It was the first time the experiment of putting a battery under the commander of an attacking line was tried, and it proved highly successful. The battery commander received his orders direct from the regimental commander, who was never far from the firing line, and always in a position to see the effect of the covering shells. Thus no time was lost in correcting the range of the guns, a signaller with flags passing on the messages given to him orally by the Auckland colonel. It was only a matter of minutes before several changes in the range were flagged back, and the shells were bursting right over the machine-gun emplacements of the enemy. "That's the stuff to give 'em," ejaculated Lieutenant-Colonel McCarroll as he saw the goodly sight., Immediately this remark was sent back as a message by Lieutenant Hatrick, who doubtless had his tongue in his cheek as he did so. After the fight the battery commander, an Imperial officer, inquired who sent this message. "I could not find it in my book of signals," he said, "but I would like to say that we understood it perfectly, don't you know. It was—eh—rather novel for the service. What! It is to be preserved in the record of the battery as a memory of you fellows." At 2 p.m., when the Regiment was in line, orders were issued for a general attack ten minutes later. Promptly to the second the line moved forward in short rushes, the covering fire of our artillery and machine-guns being excellent. At 2.40 a hill 400 yards east of Saba was rushed, and 60 prisoners were taken, and also three machine-guns, which were immediately turned against Saba with splendid effect. After a short "breather" the Regiment moved on against Saba. Steadily the line moved on, the old indomitable spirit sending joy to the heart of the colonel, who knew that nothing could stop that line of bayonets. At the exact moment the Regiment rose for the charge, but already the hill was won, the garrison retiring precipitately. A total of 122 unwounded and 10 wounded prisoners were taken by the Regiment, besides four machine-guns and a large amount of war material. The A.M.R. suffered practically the whole of the brigade's casualties, having held the post of honour. It lost six killed, including Captain S. C. Ashton, and 22 wounded, including Lieutenant W. H. John, a Main Body man, who had been promoted from the ranks. His injuries proved fatal. Captain G. S. Cheeseman assumed command of the 3rd squadron upon the death of Captain Ashton.

How the tide of battle rolled on, crumpling the Turkish left, and within a few days carrying the whole of the line from Gaza to Beersheba, has been related in other histories. During these wonderfully successful operations the New Zealanders were used in pressing the left flank of the enemy. After spending a night and day in consolidating the Saba position, which was shelled and bombed from the air, the A.M.R. sent forward the 3rd and 11th squadrons to take a turn of duty on the outpost line. The water trouble now began to reach the severe stage. So far the horses had been watered in surface pools in the Wadi Saba, but this supply soon gave out. The men had by now consumed their iron rations, but their greatest concern was for their horses, which had carried them so far and endured so nobly. On November 2, the W.M.R. and the C.M.R., which had been engaged with a force of 400 cavalry to the north-west of Kh El Ras, and the 4th squadron of the A.M.R., moved to Bir Imshash and took up an outpost line facing east and covering the wells in that locality, the other two squadrons of the A.M.R. arriving that evening. In this area some dozen wells were located, but they contained only a few inches of muddy water, and this had to be drawn up in buckets, which were filled by men who descended. It can be readily imagined how slow a process this method of watering was, but when everything possible had been done the thirst of the poor animals was only stimulated. During the next few days the Regiment, when not out on the outpost line, was ranging the countryside in search for a little water. On the 4th, the brigade was rushed to the Wadi El Sultan to support yeomanry who had come into action. This day neither the men nor the horses had any water. The following day the C.M.R. and the Waikatos pushed forward their line some 800 yards, and were heavily shelled. A counter-attack was attempted against the left of the C.M.R., and the 3rd squadron of the A.M.R. was ordered to support, but the attack was repulsed. During the day, water for the men was brought up on pack horses, but there was none for the horses, which by midnight had been without a drink for 48 hours. The " Camels " were due to relieve the mounted rifles, but as they did not materialise, it was decided to lead the horses to Beersheba, 14 miles distant, to get a drink. This day the Regiment lost one man killed and four wounded, but the C.M.R. suffered heavily.

On the morning of November 6, the Camel Brigade arrived, and the sorely tried New Zealanders moved back on foot to Mikreh, a distance of five miles. The Camel Brigade did not have too much water for themselves, but the New Zealanders were in such dire straits that they gave them 150 gallons. This worked out at half-a-pint per man. Everyone was tempted to gulp the water, but most took only a sip, and boiled the rest for tea. The state of fatigue of most of the men after this rigorous week of trekking and fighting, revived memories of the Gallipoli August. That night the led horses arrived back from Beersheba, and the Hotchkiss gun pack horses, which by this time had not had a drink for 72 hours, had to start on the 10 miles journey to Beersheba to be watered. Truly the horses of the mounted rifles " did their bit " towards the defeat of the Turks. On the 7th, 8th, and 9th the Regiment had to send the horses to water at Beersheba, and it says a good deal for their stamina that only 50 had to go to hospital.

On the 10th, the W.M.R. and the C.M.R. moved back to Beersheba, but the A.M.R. had to remain for another day on the outpost line, watering horses with the greatest difficulty at Makruneh. On the morning of the 11th, the Westminster Dragoons arrived at the inevitable trot, to relieve the A.M.R., and never were the Dragoons more popular.

CHAPTER XXVI.

North to Ayun Kara.

When the Regiment started for Beersheba to rejoin the brigade, it actually began one of the most notable treks of the campaign. It left at 12.30 p.m., and just had time to draw fodder and rations and water for the horses before moving on with the brigade on a 60 mile ride across Philistia, to the left flank, which was still moving north behind the retreating Turks. Sheria was reached by midnight, after which the pace became much slower than it had been owing to some wadis having to be crossed in single file. Some men and horses fell down the steep banks. At 3.30 a.m. a halt was called, and the tired men tumbled off their horses almost asleep. Rain fell before the march was resumed at dawn, but few there were who felt it. At 7.30 Jemmaleh was reached, and there a halt of two hours was made. Some water existed at the place, but it was guarded by engineers, who refused to allow it to be used.

Pushing on through the rich rolling country, over which there was much wreckage of war, the New Zealanders arrived at Tel El Hesy at 1.30, finding some fine pools of water in the wadi, the result of the rain of the previous night. The north side of the wadi had been heavily entrenched, no doubt as a second line of defence. The march was continued at 2.30, the brigade passing through the lovely emerald village of Bureir, and on to Hammame, where it was bivouacked. Over the last few miles the pace was very poor, owing to wadis having to be crossed in the darkness. They " boiled up " that night with muddy water secured at Hesy. When dawn broke they found that they were in the orange-growing country. The horses were taken two and a-half miles to the sea coast for water, and the men drew drinking water at a German mill. Fodder and rations did not come until late, and when the Regiment moved on again the horses had had only eight handfuls of barley each. That night the Regiment bivouacked two miles north of Kh Sukereir, and the following morning, each man carrying fodder and rations for two days, it moved on to join the other regiments of the brigade, which that day was to fight the battle of Ayun Kara, its most severe engagement of the campaign.

The C.M.R., who were the advanced guard, got into touch with Turkish outposts at 11 a.m. They pushed on, but by mid-day were definitely checked. Orders were immediately issued to attack the enemy, whose main positions were on a series of hills, with long slopes between them and the sand hills of the coast. The C.M.R. was on the right of the line, the W.M.R. in the centre, and the A.M.R. on the left. The regiments advanced in line of troop column, and soon were under long range machine-gun fire. There being some high ground on the right front of the A.M.R., the 3rd squadron, under Major Twistleton, was sent forward to secure it, the other two squadrons taking cover from direct fire in depressions. As the W.M.R. pressed on towards the main position, some cavalry appeared on the left front of the A.M.R., and Colonel McCarroll, who had been viewing the position from the 3rd squadron's hill, ordered the 11th squadron to advance as rapidly as possible to ascertain the strength and position of the threatening force. Heavy rifle and machine-gun fire prevented the squadron getting to the required position, so two troops of the 4th squadron (Lieutenants M. E. Johnson and Ryan) were detailed to gallop straight at it. This sudden and vigorous move evidently upset the enemy, for they reached the spot with very few casualties, the enemy retiring quickly. Under cover of the fire from the 3rd squadron the other two troops of the 4th squadron pushed on to secure some high ground to the left of the W.M.R., who continued to advance steadily. As soon as the 4th squadron had gained their objective, the 3rd squadron was drawn into support, and the 11th was sent forward on the left of the 4th. Covered by the 4th, the 11th advanced steadily, but for some time they did not reach any point where they could get a view of the enemy, although heavy rifle fire was coming down all the valleys from the higher positions of the Turks. At 2.15 the patrols of the 11th located some of the enemy concentrating in the orange groves nearby, and Lieutenant Jackson's troop pushed well forward and found that the enemy was advancing rapidly. Colonel McCarroll galloped forward, and, seeing that the troop was being attacked, sent in every available man, including signallers, gallopers, and batmen to reinforce, and signalled to the 3rd squadron to come up. Major Twistleton brought his men up at the gallop in fine style, losing only two horses, although two or three bullet-swept zones were traversed, and dismounted his men within a few yards of the line. Lieutenant S. Reid's troop was sent in on the right, but heavy enfilade fire gave them a severe time, and the few men who were not killed or wounded had to be called back.

At 2.45 the enemy, under cover of heavy artillery fire, started a strong attack. Several of the Turkish machine-guns now began to make their presence felt, and the commander brought up his machine-gun section, which opened a counter fire. The action in this part of the battle now became a machine-gun duel, it being impossible for Colonel McCarroll to move his men until the opposite machine-guns were silenced. After a furious fusillade the Auckland machine-gun sergeant, in worried tones, reported his gun out of action. "That's all right," replied the Colonel, " so is the Turk's," for at the moment the enemy guns were abandoned. Meanwhile, the W.M.R. had pushed up the hill on the right, and there came under a very heavy fire. Two troops of the 3rd squadron were sent further to the right, to a spot where they could bring enfilade fire against the Turks assembled in a valley. The Hotchkiss guns and machine-guns, under Lieutenant Kelly, were also sent in, and did great execution. Afterwards they described this chance as "the machine-gunner's dream."

While this drama was being enacted, the counter-attack was rapidly developing. It was estimated that fully 600 fresh infantry were flung against the Regiment, which by now had suffered very severe casualties. In many places the attackers got within bombing distance of the thin line. The A.M.R. men on one small hill having been all killed or wounded, the Turks established themselves on it and brought an oblique fire against the main position. The situation was now very serious, and two orderlies were sent with orders for the fourth squadron to come up, but both were wounded. Eventually a message was got through, and the Waikato stalwarts, led by Major Munro and Lieutenant Johnson, raced across the fire-swept area—a sight worth living to see. They regained the hill, and in spite of heavy opposition worked round the enemy's left, and were able to enfilade the main line. This move nonplussed the Turks, who then fled in disorder towards the orange grove, under the heaviest fire that could be put across. Colonel McCarroll had just collected his squadron leaders to organise pursuit when he was wounded in the neck and then in the shoulder. Major Whitehorn then took command, but the colonel before receiving medical aid, rode to brigade headquarters and arranged for support in the event of a night attack. The Turks kept up a heavy artillery fire until dark, after which the victorious troopers consolidated their position and removed the wounded.

The A.M.R. lost heavily, 15 being killed, including the gallant Lieutenant J. D. Stewart, of the 3rd squadron; 74 wounded, including Lieutenant-Colonel McCarroll, Captain Twistleton, M.C., and Lieutenants K. J. Tait, M.C., S. C. Reid, G. L. King, C. G. R. Jackson, and E. A. H. Bisley. Captain Twistleton and Lieutenant King died of wounds. The W.M.R. lost 8 killed and 44 wounded; the C.M.R., one killed and six wounded; and the machine-gun squadron, eight killed and 18 wounded. The Turks, who retired during the night, lost 160 killed and 250 (estimated) wounded. The Turks who made the counter-attack were part of a fresh force that had just arrived from its victories in Roumania, and they apparently were unprepared to meet troops of the quality of the desert horsemen. One wounded prisoner remarked to an Aucklander, "Inglizee no run," and he seemed to be rather perplexed over the fact that a thin and outnumbered line had refused to budge in the face of what seemed inevitable disaster. The secret of the victory was the simple fact that the mounted riflemen were actuated by a spirit which did not permit of retreat being considered when committed to a definite action. It was the same attitude of mind which defied set principles of war on Gallipoli. It had its foundations in an extraordinary confidence, resolute and highly capable leadership, and the sense of personal responsibility which possessed the men of the Regiment.

The following morning the village of Ayun Kara was reported clear of the enemy, and, with a company of "Camels" on the left and the 1st Light Horse on the right, the brigade moved forward towards Jaffa, meeting with no resistance. On the way they passed through the village of Richon le Zion, where for the first time they met Jews. One member of the community was a brother of Rabbi Goldstein, of Auckland. The joy of these people at being freed from the tyranny of the Turks was unbounded. They treated the New Zealanders most hospitably—an exceedingly pleasant experience after the tremendous effort they had just made, and the harsh hungry times spent in the south with its hostile Bedouins.

CHAPTER XXVII.

To Jaffa and the Auja.

Jaffa was occupied without opposition, the Turks falling back to the line of the river Auja, a few miles further north. While this fighting had been taking place, great success had been achieved to the south. Ramleh, on the Jaffa-Jerusalem railway, was taken; and the enemy, whose receding line extended in a south-east direction from Jaffa, had reason to feel anxiety for Jerusalem itself.

With its bivouac in the suburb of Sarona, the original home of the German Colony, on the north-east outskirts of the town, the Regiment did duty on the outpost line and in the town itself. After living by desert ways for so long it was no small novelty to garrison such a fine town as Jaffa, with its wide streets, gardens, and trees. In normal times Jaffa had a population of 60,000 people, including 30,000 Moslems, 10,000 Jews, and 10,000 Christians, but during the war its population had gone down considerably, and it had lost its prosperity, partly through there being no fuel for the engines which had been used to pump the water from the wells to irrigate the orchards. Within a few days of the British occupation, Jews and Christians, who had been expelled by the Turks, started to return, bringing their goods and chattels in all sorts of conveyances.

The names of the following officers and men were brought under notice in connection with the month's fighting:—

On November 1.—Lieutenant K. J. Tait, Signal-Corporal G. S. Watt, Temporary-Corporal O. F. T. Young, and Troopers W. R. D. Laurie, J. Wilkinson, and J. Smillie.

On November 8.—Lieutenant S. C. Reid, Sergeant C. N. White, Corporal H. D. Aitken, and Trooper D. Pilcher.

On November 14. — Acting-Captain W. Haeata, Sergeant-Trumpeter J. L. Morgan, Corporal A. G. De Lautour, Lance-Corporal F. H. Hardie, Temporary-Sergeant M. Gilbert, and Troopers H. Underwood and W. H. Jefcoate.

On November 24 and 25, the New Zealanders took part in a very stiff engagement against strongly reinforced Turks on and beyond the Wadi Auja. The purpose of the action was to secure control of the bridge and fords, and to contain as large a number of the enemy as possible by creating the impression that a further move northwards was contemplated.

On the 27th, the brigade was relieved on the outpost line facing the Auja, which now carried a considerable volume of water, by the 161st infantry brigade. At 1 p.m. the C.M.R. opened the ball by galloping across the ford near the mouth of the river, and securing the ground which dominated it. Then with the W.M.R. they turned east and cleared the enemy from their positions on the ridge overlooking the bridge, taking Sheik Muannis and Khurbet Hadrah at the gallop, and securing some two miles of country on the north bank of the stream. It was a very smart and spectacular piece of work. While this operation was being carried out the 4th squadron

JUDEAN HILLS IN SPRING.

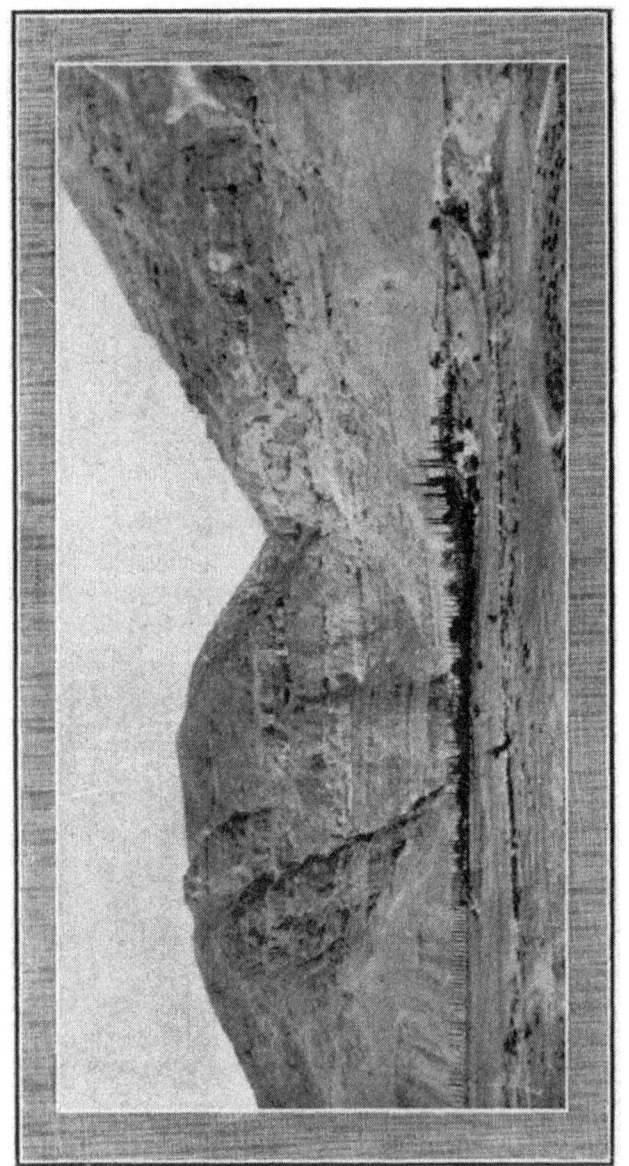

JEBEL KURUNTUL, NEAR JERICHO.

1. The spot where Christ is said to have been baptised. 2. Olive tree in the Garden of Gethsemane.

THE JORDAN VALLEY.
1 and 2. Post watching a ford. 3 4 and 5. Glimpses of the river.

of the A.M.R., under Major Munro, demonstrated in front of a ford some two miles above the bridge.

As soon as the north bank had been cleared by the W.M.R. and the C.M.R. the infantry crossed the bridge, and the 3rd squadron (Captain Cheeseman), and the 11th squadron (Captain Herrold) of the A.M.R. moved to the outpost line beyond the infantry, the two squadrons being under Major Whitehorn. Two squadron posts, with two machine-guns, were established in front of Hadrah, the other regiments holding similar posts between them and the sea. All was quiet until 2.45 a.m., when a small mounted patrol of the enemy appeared in front of the forward post of the 3rd A.M.R. The patrol retired under the fire of the troopers, but half an hour later heavy fire broke out on the left flank of the thirds, and they were compelled to retire to a pre-arranged line of resistance. Our machine-guns opened a rapid fire for 15 minutes, and for another brief space there was quiet. At 3.45 the enemy made another advance, supported by heavy rifle and machine-gun fire, and the advanced troop of the 3rd squadron found itself outflanked on both sides. It fell back on the rest of the squadron, but the Turks, in strong force, swarmed forward, and the squadron, as soon as it got its led horses sent back, retired to the position held by the machine-guns. Communication with headquarters was now impossible owing to the wires having been cut by enemy fire. Eventually two messengers were sent out, advising the infantry of the situation. By 4.30 the enemy were between the two squadron posts of the A.M.R. The machine-guns on both sides opened up, and the enemy continued to press forward, getting close enough to use bombs. The position of the 3rd squadron became untenable, and with the machine-guns the troopers were compelled to fall back upon the infantry at 5.45. The 11th squadron was able to remain in its position, and opened fire on the force now pressing the 3rd squadron and the infantry. About 8.30 the infantry, under the covering fire of the two A.M.R. squadrons, fell back on the bridge. By this time 12 enemy guns were firing on Hadrah and the bridge. The A.M.R. horses were still on the north side of the river, and as the bridge was impassable the "Number Threes" were ordered to race for the ford near the mouth. It was one of the liveliest gallops horse-holders ever had. Speed was the one chance of getting the horses out of the closing vice, and speed was secured, notwithstanding the fact that some of the men were leading six horses. Although under fire for most of the way, the horsemen, with their arms almost out of the sockets, reached the ford without serious loss and plunged through to safety. A few of the men decided to risk swimming the river rather than running the gauntlet to the ford, and somehow got across. The casualties among the horses and the men who led them would have been heavy had not the Turks, who tried to intercept them, fired as they ran. Meanwhile the dismounted squadrons held on to the north bridgehead, and after all the infantry were over the 3rd squadron rushed across, some by the bridge and some through the water. It was not until then that any artillery support was given. The Somerset Battery and the guns of the infantry brigade opened on Hadrah, and this enabled Captain Herrold and his squadron, who had been within an ace of being cut off, to move down the bank and cross at the bridge. The W.M.R. and the C.M.R. had a very similar experience further down the river, having to hold on to cover the retirement of the infantry. Afterwards some crossed dismounted at the ford near the mouth, and others by boat.

At the bridge the A.M.R. and some 30 Tommies, who had not departed as fast as some of their comrades, formed a line covering the south bridgehead, and, as the belated artillery concentrated on Hadrah, a party of the A.M.R. forded the river and brought back their own and infantry wounded through the waist-high stream. This gallant work was done under fire.

The Regiment's casualties were: 1 killed, 1 missing, and 19 wounded, including Major Whitehorn, who had been in command of the Regiment since Lieutenant-Colonel McCarroll was wounded. Major Munro now assumed command of the A.M.R.

After the struggle on the Auja, the New Zealanders went into bivouac about half-a-mile southeast of Sarona, a step rendered necessary through the wonderful accuracy of the Turkish guns which ranged right on to the Somerset Battery, the guns of which had to be removed at the gallop. There was every reason for supposing that German residents of Sarona were signalling information to the Turks. The infantry brigade, it is understood, investigated the spying, and executed the culprits. For some days the guns of both sides were constantly in action, and fighting occurred further inland. Two destroyers arrived off Jaffa, and assisted the British guns by bombarding the Turkish lines. To relieve the transport which had had an extremely hard month, small vessels landed stores at what answered for a wharf at Jaffa. The Regiment's chief concern was to build up its strength again, and a considerable number of men and horses came up to fill the many gaps.

Some men will remember Jaffa chiefly for its oranges, its wines, and its howling jackals. In connection with oranges there was quite an entertaining incident. For some time the men had been suffering from septic sores, a very painful and uncomfortable trouble, in enduring which they had displayed their usual uncomplaining fortitude and that fine comradely spirit in relieving those most afflicted. General Chaytor, on being informed by the medical authorities that oranges would probably cure the men, requisitioned oranges, and had them issued. The army supply authorities said there was no authority to issue fruit, but the issue went on with splendid results. Finally the general found authority to issue vegetables, and he proved that oranges were vegetables. As to wine, the soldiers were forbidden to purchase it, but the orders were not proof against the genius of " old soldiers " and wine was secured, although on one occasion the thirsty souls had to go the length of parading a bogus guard to relieve the infantry doing duty at the wine store. Lieutenant Briscoe Moore states in his excellent book, " The Mounted Rifleman in Sinai and Palestine," that one trooper on being questioned why he had been to the wine store, replied brazenly that he had gone to get his horse a feed. Considering the potency of much of the grape juice, it is highly probable that he did. And then the jackals! These animals made mournful music throughout the nights. One man declared that there were at least 100,000 jackals in one orchard, and he had not been to the wine press either. At sunset the first of the animals began to pipe up, and the combined choir was soon going full blast.

CHAPTER XXVIII.

The General Offensive.

On December 4, the New Zealand Brigade moved east to Sakia, and there relieved a battalion of the Camel Corps in the trenches, the horses being left a mile away. Here they remained, while was enacted the greatest event of the war—the advance which forced the Turks to evacuate Jerusalem. In the actual move against the Turks which drove the infidel from the Holy City, the New Zealanders had no part, but already they had contributed to that end by their resolute fight at Ayun Kara, which forced the Turkish right further north, and the action on the Auja, which drew against them some thousands of the enemy who otherwise would have been used further south.

Advancing through the rain and mist the infantry had reached the outskirts of Bethlehem by the evening of December 8, with cavalry already across the Jericho road, where it turns east from the Valley of Jehosaphat. Panic broke out among the defenders, and during the night the Jews listened with joy to the sounds of the retreat. After four centuries the Turk was flying headlong from the scene of his worst tyranny. By a happy coincidence the day was that of the festival of Hanukah, which celebrates the recapture of the Temple by Judas Maccabæus from the heathen Seleucids in 165 B.C. The day of deliverance had come. The Arab prophecy, that when the Nile flowed into Palestine, the prophet (Al Nebi) from the west should drive the Turk from Jerusalem, had been fulfilled.

On December 11, the Commander-in-Chief made his formal entry into the city. All units of the army were represented at this historic ceremony. The 20 men from the New Zealand Brigade rode 40 miles over the hills to be present, arriving with the grime of war upon them and their accoutrements, just one hour before General Allenby walked through the Jaffa Gate with the representatives of the army behind him to the citadel below the Tower of David, from the terrace of which was read in seven languages a proclamation announcing that order would be maintained in all the hallowed sites of the three great religions, which were to be guarded and preserved for the free use of worshippers. The simplicity of the ceremony was in sharp contrast to the pompous entry, through a new gap in the wall, of the German Kaiser in 1898.

After spending several cheerless days in the wet trenches, the A.M.R. proceeded to Jaffa, where it came under the orders of the 52nd Infantry Division, the W.M.R. and the C.M.R. going back to bivouac at Ayun Kara. While at Jaffa the Regiment again came under the command of Major Whitehorn, who returned from hospital. A few days later the A.M.R. relieved a brigade of infantry on the left of the Auja line, the horses being sent back to Jaffa.

On the night of December 20, the 52nd Division crossed the Auja, and carried the enemy positions on the north. The A.M.R. returned to Jaffa for their horses, and on December 22, moved to the scenes of their fighting on the north side of the Auja, and put in a strenuous day on patrol in advance of the infantry. The A.M.R. then moved back to Jaffa and thence to Esdud, 30 miles south, near the coast, to rejoin the brigade. They marched via the Yebna Bridge (Yebna is the Jamnia of the New Testament period and the Ibelin of the Crusades), and thence along the sand dunes to the brigade bivouac south of Wadi Sukereir. It was one of the most severe marches the Regiment had ever done. Heavy rain fell continuously, and a cold wind raged. The night of December 24 was spent beyond Ayun Kara, the men being drenched to the skin. Pushing on the following morning the bedraggled column struck seas of mud on the Yebna plain, horses going down and being got up with great difficulty. The limbers at some places were right under water. Then the Wadi Sukereir had to be swum. The fact that it was Christmas Day may have had something to do with it, but the fact is that the men's cheerfulness seemed to increase with every new misery. There was no bully beef that evening, but a little of the salt flat substance that the army calls bacon was available, and some sort of a meal was therefore made at the sorry-looking fires. The doctor was in fine mood for a meal, and he had an extra ration for himself.

On January 12, the brigade moved north to Richon le Zion, the Jewish village near to Ayun Kara, and there tents were provided, and training and football again became the normal life. Soon after the shift, Lieutenant-Colonel McCarroll returned from hospital and resumed command of the Regiment. Major Whitehorn became second in command. During this period no fighting of any importance took place. The Turks had established a line running round the north of Jaffa to the north of Jerusalem, Philistia and the greater part of Judea had been occupied, but before a further advance could be made the army had to be reorganised.

CHAPTER XXIX.

The Column Goes East.

The next offensive operation was a movement against the enemy's left, the object being to drive the Turks from their positions covering Jericho from the west, to occupy the town temporarily to allow of it being examined by political and intelligence officers, and to clear the valley west of the Jordan as far north as the Wadi El Aujah. The role of the Australia and New Zealand Mounted Division was to assist the infantry by threatening the retreat of the enemy through Jericho, and afterwards to throw out protection round Jericho for at least 48 hours.

On February 15, the Regiment left Ayun Kara for Bethlehem. The route was not the usual one through Latron and Amwas, but by devious tracks across the hills. "This will be great," exclaimed the padre. "We will see the most interesting part of Central Palestine." "You can have it all for me," replied a trooper, with an eye to his steed, and, no doubt, more than a thought for the long climbs leading his mount. However it is yet too soon to speak of the hills. The first stage of the journey was south-east across the plain to the Junction Station, the point where the line to Beersheba met that to Jerusalem. They passed through pleasant country, the vineyards about to burst into leaf, and the almond trees in glorious bloom. The little Bedouin village of Akir was on the route, looking anything like the great Philistine city it once was. On all sides barley crops were sprouting, and the primitive farming operations of the country were going forward. The night was spent at the Junction Station. The following morning the march was continued, the route turning south-east from the railway a few miles beyond the station, and leading immediately into the hills. The ancient road was in quite fair order, and the day's march to Zakariyeh was pleasant. The wild flowers which were blooming in profusion among the rocks of this wild region were a perfect delight. The colours of the anemones were beyond description. Here and there among the hills were passed small cultivated patches, and the growth of grass was amazing. Near Zakariyeh, a high point not unlike Gibraltar, where they bivouacked that night, was the place where "David did the shanghai trick," as one youthful veteran described the duel between the shepherd boy and the Philistian giant. One man surveyed the scene of the exploit in silence. He noted the pebbly bed of the old brook, and finally drawled, "Well, the shepherd bloke had stacks of small arm ammunition anyway." Some of the boys visited the village nearby, and had a rummage through what had been a sheikh's harem. In a bag on the wall was found the sign of the eternal female in the shape of black powder for darkening the eye-brows. The most junior lieutenant was advised to try it on his upper lip. The watering of the horses was a tedious job that night, all the water having to be drawn up 30 feet from a cistern.

Soon after leaving the bivouac the next morning, the horsemen found themselves on a sharp ascent. Bleak, barren, rocky ridges stretched as far as the eye could reach. A halt for lunch was made on the watershed, and then the route led down by steep grades. Finally, the

Hebron road was reached, and it was followed to within a mile of Bethlehem, where they bivouacked for the night among the rocks and boulders. The horses that evening drank water from Solomon's Pools.

The Regiment remained in bivouac the following day (February 18), and many men took the opportunity of visiting Bethlehem. All around were fine olive groves and vineyards and crops of barley on the little terraces which represented the labour of thousands of years. The great centre of interest was the Church of Nativity, which is built on the site of the Manger. Who could have dreamed when the Regiment left Auckland that men of it, before they returned, would stand in the accoutrements of war on Christendom's holy place. Who could have imagined that the paved streets of Bethlehem would resound with the march of New Zealand horsemen as they moved forward to the conquest of Jericho?

The next day (February 19) the column moved east to its difficult task across the hills. Already the W.M.R. had gone out to assist the 60th Infantry Division in its attack on El Muntar, some 10 miles east-north-east of Bethlehem. The A.M.R. was on the way at 9.30 a.m., the "road" being little more than a goat track. At 11 a.m. they started to descend to a wadi by a track that was so steep that the men had to lead their horses. Camels, of course, were the only means of transport on this march, and the drivers had a very arduous time in getting the clumsy brutes through. Muntar having been taken that morning, the mounted men pushed on over the unspeakable track along the bed of the wadi. The scene was an impressive one. On either side towered high cliffs, and among the heights could be seen flocks of goats tended by Arabs, who played on the old-fashioned pipe as they led their flocks. At nightfall patrols were sent out, and the brigade, now joined by the W.M.R., bivouacked.

CHAPTER XXX.

Through the Hills to Jericho.

At 3 a.m. the next morning, the advance was continued. The W.M.R., dismounted, was sent forward on the right, while the C.M.R. was ordered to occupy the high ground to the left. At 4.30 the column, led by the A.M.R., started to move forward in single file. It was nearly nine miles long, and looked like a giant brown snake drawing itself across the hills and ravines. The descent was steep and stoney, and one cheerful soul named it the "Gaby Glide." Unfortunately, the "glide" was over rocks and loose shingle, which even the led horses negotiated with difficulty. For the camels it was as uncertain as a greasy boom, and the ungainly animals sprawled, and "split" and stuck, and sometimes came to grief. The camel is not built for acrobatics of the kind. As regimental headquarters, at the head of the column, was making the last glissade from the pass into the wide valley after daybreak, enemy guns opened fire from two high hills, Tubk el Kaneitera and Jebel el Kalimun, which commanded the approach and completely dominated the valley. The ranging was bad, however, and only one horse was hit before headquarters was behind the cover of little hillocks which were scattered over the valley. The enemy gunners still had an excellent field of fire, but, fortunately, they frequently changed their targets, and thereby aided the attackers. When the A.M.R. swung out across the valley in fairly open order it became apparent that the C.M.R. had missed their objective and taken the wrong ridge. The positions of the enemy in front of the A.M.R. were very strong, the W.M.R., on the right, had encountered opposition, and generally the situation looked anything but encouraging. With the artillery and machine-guns sweeping the valley, the A.M.R. commenced to press forward. Of course, there were no guns to support them. Before long the 11th squadron, which had entered the valley as the vanguard, was ordered to cross the track and get under the cover of a low ridge, but the track was swept by machine-gun fire, and the move had to be abandoned. It was then decided to " plug in " from the front, and troop by troop, the squadrons galloped forward from one piece of cover to another. The machine-guns with the Regiment attempted to give some covering fire, but little impression could be made on the nests of machine-guns firing from well-prepared positions on the heights.

While the A.M.R. had been working up the valley in this manner, the attack to the north by the infantry, who had advanced along the main road, had been developing well. The C.M.R. had got into its correct position, and had started to co-operate with the A.M.R. by excellent fire on the Turkish positions. Towards mid-day, a lull in the enemy's fire gave the 11th squadron a chance to rush the first position, on the right side of the valley, which in addition to its operations against the A.M.R. had been a factor in holding up the W.M.R. The garrison retired in haste before the dismounted rush of the North Aucklanders. Meantime, the 3rd and 4th squadrons were pushing on against the left and centre. A brigade of Light Horse from the rear had been sent to work round the enemy's left, but the movement was necessarily slow, owing to the tracks having to be negotiated in single file. To the north the infantry had succeeded in ousting the Turks from their first positions, and this gave them gun positions, the fire from which compelled the enemy to remove the higher tier of machine-guns on Kalimun. The A.M.R. horses were now ordered up, and in one furious charge the hill was taken. The garrison did not wait, but bolted down the other side. Very soon the Turks were shelling the crest by guns in the open, only a mile away. It was the first time Turkish guns went into action in full view.

The taking of these positions did not clear the way to the Jordan Valley, however. Four or five miles further, stood the frowning peak of Nebi Musa, said to be the burial place of Moses. This formidable position was reconnoitred, but as the daylight was fast waning it could not be attacked that day. The Regiment spent the night on the line gained. Strong posts were established in front, and then rose the eternal question of water for the horses. The horses of one squadron were sent four miles up the wadi to a well. Owing to the time occupied in drawing up the water in buckets these horses were away for four hours. It was therefore decided to do no more watering that night, otherwise the men would get no sleep at all.

When dawn broke there was no sign of the enemy on Nebi Musa, and it was soon ascertained that the position had been evacuated. The column continued its march down the desolate valley. The track became narrow and steep, and in places it was bordered by a precipice. Then rain began to fall, and the track became dangerous. A descent into the rocky bed of the wadi was therefore made, and down it the men and animals stumbled in single file. The brigade column stretched out to a distance of five miles, and offered

a splendid chance to the enemy. A couple of
well placed machine-guns could have done terrible
havoc, but the Turks had gone. No doubt they
had been hurried by the fact that the infantry
were pressing along the main road further north.
About 9 a.m. a gap appeared in the hills ahead,
and soon after the mounted men were issuing into
the historic battleground of the Jordan Valley. A
few miles to the south lay the Dead Sea, to the
north lay Jericho, and seven or eight miles to the
east, across the winding Jordan, rose the Hills of
Moab and the country of Gilead.

The enemy was in fast retreat across the
plain, and hopes were entertained of cutting some
of them off, but while the New Zealand Brigade
" dribbled " out of the hills, valuable time was
lost, and the main force of the Turks was across
the Jordan by the Goraniyeh Bridge before the
rear parties could be threatened.

Jericho, which looked well from a distance,
proved to be horribly dirty. Australians had the
honour of being the first into it. Away beyond the
Jordan could be seen a Turkish camp. The
A.M.R. bivouacked on the west side of the valley,
with the Mount of Temptation towering above
them. The other regiments were ordered to watch
the line of the river from its mouth to El
Ghoraniyeh Bridge. Major Munro, of the
A.M.R., was appointed military commandant of
Jericho.

When a party of A.M.R. men visited the
town the next day they were disgusted at the dirt
and squalor. In a hospital, or a place that
passed for such, were a number of typhus cases,
and among them was a man who had been dead

RAID TO AMMAN.
1. Camel transport in the Hills of Moab. 2. A.M.R. after crossing the Jordan.

VIEW OF THE JORDAN.

INTO GILEAD: THE WADI KELT.

TROOPS WINDING DOWN THE SLOPE TO THE JORDAN AT JISR ED DAMIEH.

for some time. An Austrian nurse, who had remained to look after these patients, bowed pleasantly to the men, and said, " How do you do," in English. An English-speaking family told them amusing yarns about the Turkish Corps commander, who had had his headquarters in the town. It appears that his habit was to drink much wine at dinner. Then he would lean back and exclaim, " This is the war for me, but to complete the picture bring me a nice girl." He had a very poor opinion of German officers, and made no secret of his belief in the ultimate defeat of the Turkish Army.

In the Greek church they found a picture of St. George that had been mutilated by the Turks. This was interesting, in view of the fact that the Turks named the British mounted forces " St. George's cavalry "—the idea, no doubt, coming from the design on the handle of the cavalry sword.

On February 22, the whole of the mounted troops, excepting the A.M.R., moved back to Bethlehem, the W.M.R. and the C.M.R. returning thence to Ayun Kara. The A.M.R. was attached to the 60th Division to act as corps cavalry, its job being to patrol the Jordan, or as near to the Jordan as the enemy would permit. The patrols came in for a good deal of shelling, and among the first men to be wounded was that fine troop leader Lieutenant McCathy.

During the first few days the road leading to Jerusalem was crowded by the ever-pitiful refugees. Among the crowd were to be seen barefooted women and children carrying huge loads. Although these folk of many races were leaving their homes for their own good, and were under the care of Britain, which always feeds the people of a country she conquers, their present tribulations were saddening.

For those who were interested in Biblical history, this wonderful, but rather desolate valley, was crowded with interesting places. A mile north of Jericho, beside the ruins of the first Jericho, was Elijah's well, the source of the water supply of the town. This was the well which the prophet is said to have turned from brackish to sweet water.

A reconnoitring stunt was carried out on March 2. The infantry brought forward their guns, including four 60-pounders which were attached to the A.M.R., and the old, old valley echoed to martial music of a very different kind from the trumpet-blowing which the Israelites once indulged in with good effect around the walls of Jericho. The A.M.R. pushed ahead towards the bridge, but the Turkish guns did good work, and nowhere where they able to get nearer than a mile to the river.

A few days later, the 11th squadron went on a little expedition towards the bridge, and paid its respects to Turks who held a trench west of it, while British field guns did some excellent practice on a machine-gun " possie." That night the Turks blew up the bridge, a wooden affair 80 feet long and 12 feet wide, and thereafter patrols were able to approach within a few hundred yards of the river. The weather was now becoming uncomfortably hot, and the Aucklanders had a foretaste of the heat they were to endure down in that malaria-stricken valley during the summer.

Some days later the infantry made a local push northward, and the A.M.R. was used on both flanks. They had no fighting, but plenty of shell fire. On this occasion two troops of the 11th squadron, under Major Herrold, added mountaineering to the list of their experiences. Their task was to get in touch with the 53rd Division on En Nejmeh, a rough peak, 2,391 feet above sea-level, and therefore another 1,000 feet above the level of the Jordan Valley. Riding west from the Wadi Obeideh, the party crossed some broken country, and then found itself in a veritable paradise among rolling hills. The vegetation was luxuriant, and among the grass and wild flowers of every colour, deer and flocks of partridges were seen. On reaching the old Roman road, the horses were left behind, and in three parties the men went forward. The party which essayed the direct ascent toiled on, but always the top seemed as far off as ever. Eventually the rifles had to be sent back, and eight men crawled upward, helping each other over the dizzy ledges. Figures could be seen on the crest, and the party signalled, but got no reply. They had to climb on, scaling a high cliff before they could signal from the site of some old ruins. From this lofty point of vantage a view of the whole of the Jordan Valley was obtained and every move of the successful advance of the infantry was observed.

One day the 11th squadron, which had gone out to get into touch with the enemy, had a particularly severe shelling, but as usual, speed beat the gunners. Later in the day a troop of the 3rd squadron was ordered out to try to cut off a cavalry patrol, but the guns opened on them, and they had to scatter. During this stunt the 4th squadron had been kept busy keeping an eye on four possible fords.

An amusing incident of the time must not be overlooked. It was the habit of the officers to bathe in the Sultan's Spring, near Jericho. One day the padre, the doctor, and another officer were enjoying themselves in the water when the adjutant came along. The bathers promptly splashed the adjutant before he undressed. The adjutant decided not to have a bathe, and he went off, taking the padre's clothes with him. The padre could not go home naked, so he was left there alone. At dinner time his messmates sent him a tin of bully beef, a biscuit and an empty beer bottle. His clothes went up later. It is rumoured that that evening the man of peace was willing to fight the whose mess.

CHAPTER XXXI.
Across the Jordan.

There was to be little opportunity for practical joking for some time to come, however. The Commander-in-Chief had decided to make a raid into Gilead, through which ran the Turk's lines of supply to the forces operating against the Arabs of Hedjaz, named the Sherifian Forces. For the operation a special force known as "Shea's Group" was created. It consisted of the Australian and New Zealand Mounted Division, the 60th (London) Division, the Imperial Camel Corps Brigade, the 10th Heavy Battery R.G.A., the Hongkong Mountain Battery, besides two bridging trains and armoured cars. Reconnaissance had shown that the Jordan, at this time of the year, was unfordable at any available point, and that the only practicable places for throwing bridges across were at Makhadet, Hajlah, and Ghoraniyeh. The intention was that a steel pontoon bridge was to be thrown across the Hajlah for the passage of the cavalry and the "Camels," and a standard pontoon bridge, a barrel bridge, and an infantry bridge were to be built at Ghoraniyeh for the passage of the 60th Division.

At midnight on March 21, the bridging efforts commenced. At Ghoraniyeh repeated attempts by the swimmers of the Londons failed, owing to the force of flood water. The enemy opposite were alarmed, and the attempt had to be abandoned for a time. Better fortune attended the Australians of the Desert Mounted Corps Bridging Train and the Londons at Hajlah, which is about three miles from the Dead Sea. Swimmers got across unobserved, and a raft ferry was started. After dawn the gallant Londons were crossing under heavy enfilade machine-gun fire. Meantime the bridge train had been performing stupendous feats, and by 8.10 a.m. their pontoon bridge was finished, other battalions of the Londons crossing immediately. During the day the infantry were confined to the trees and growth bordering the river, all attempts to extend the protection over the bridgehead being stopped by machine-guns, which opened up at every angle. No crossing had yet been possible at Ghoraniyeh.

Meantime the A.M.R. was waiting for its great chance, the chance which came on the morning of the 23rd. No other regiment of the New Zealand Brigade, nor any regiment of the Light Horse, was to share the honours of this wonderful day. The W.M.R. and the C.M.R. had come over the hills to Talaat Ed Dumm, near Nebi Musa, but there they were to remain for the time being. It was Auckland, and Auckland alone, which was to break the ground below the Mountains of Moab for the Londoners, when the hour struck. The hour struck at 5 a.m. on March 23, when the Regiment moved across to the pontoon bridge at Hajlah to a day of remarkable exploits —a day of the most audacious gallantry ever achieved by the horsemen of this campaign.

The men seemed to realise that a day of days had begun when they stood to their horses in the early dawn and tightened their girths. The horses, for the first time in their varied careers, tramped across a pontoon bridge, below which the river swept fast and deep. At 7.30, the Regiment had passed through the outpost line of the infantry, which was little more than 500 yards from the river. The country was flat, and, excepting the presence of small wadis which cut it, was excellent for fast mounted work. Fast work it was to be. Immediately two troops of the 11th squadron were sent eastward, and one to the north-east, while the 3rd and 4th squadrons were ordered to make a dash north to attack from the rear the garrison defending the crossing at Ghoraniyeh, where bridging operations had so far failed. Engineers were standing by at the spot, but apparently little hope of success was entertained, seeing that guns which had been waiting to cross there had been sent down to the bridge at Hajlah. All pack horses, excepting those carrying Hotchkiss guns, were left behind, and the two squadrons, with the 4th acting as advanced guard, set off at the gallop.

Meantime one of the troops of the 11th squadron—under Lieutenant Tait—had intercepted a squadron of Turkish cavalry 60 strong. Without a second's hesitation, Lieutenant Tait with his 20 men, armed only with rifles, galloped at the sabres. The Turks showed some spirit, and attempted to ride the North Aucklanders down, but they broke and fled before the troopers who fired as they galloped forward. The Arab horses of the Turkish cavalry were no match for the swift and powerful mounts of the riflemen, who, within a few minutes, were on the heels and abreast of the Turks, and shooting with deadly accuracy. Numbers of Turks dropped from their saddles, while their comrades spurred on in panic, yelling in fear, and shooting wildly into the air or blindly backwards. No less than 20 of the Turks were shot down during this wild ride, and seven were taken prisoner. The Aucklanders had only one casualty, the gallant troop leader himself, who was shot dead.

Simultaneously, the 3rd and 4th squadrons were galloping north at breakneck speed. Everything depended on speed, and more often than not the main line was on the heels of what, under ordinary circumstances, would have been a screen. Spur as they would the advance guard could not keep any distance from the squadrons behind, and the colonel's shouts of "Faster, Faster," came clearly to their ears. Those fine horsemen seemed to be possessed of a devil, so reckless was the ride. The dash which the commander put into his regiment was amazing, and staggered the battalions of the Londons which were able to view it.

At 9 o'clock the leading squadron encountered a post of 17 Turks, which they instantly charged and captured intact without suffering a single casualty. The Turks seemed to be mesmerised by the suddenness of the onslaught, and they were prisoners before they knew what had happened. They had not been trained for this sort of warfare, which, according to one trooper, followed the rules of some authority named Rafferty. He could not say where the text book could be obtained, but he was emphatic that Rafferty rules were followed.

While this move had been progressing, the troop of the 11th squadron, which had been sent north from the crossing, had driven a machine-gun post from Kasr El Yehud overlooking the river, and as the Regiment continued the gallop to the north-east, one troop of the 4th squadron, under Lieutenant M. E. Johnson, was detached to cut this party off. Using the fashionable tactics of the day, this troop swooped down upon the party and collected the lot, guns and all.

The " main body " of the Regiment now turned its attention towards the final objective, the Ghoraniyeh Bridge, to repair which the Royal Engineers were waiting for a chance. After a rest in a wadi, the 4th squadron was ordered to seize Shunet Nimrin by rushing it at the gallop, and the 3rd squadron was ordered to rush high ground overlooking Ghoraniyeh. The latter squadron succeeded in galloping into good positions. There were two machine-guns on the left, however, and Lieutenant Collins with his troop of the 3rd squadron was ordered to get them. Unseen by the machine-gunners who were firing vigorously at other targets, Collins and his men swept up a wadi on their flank, and dismounting right under them, rushed them before they could swing the guns round. The whole post was captured, and one of the guns was turned on a party of Turks who were seen bolting for their lives. Eleven of them were killed. This smart action enabled the remainder of the squadron to get into good positions commanding the bridge, the remaining Turks fled, and the Royal Engineers were able to start their work on the bridge. Some men of A.M.R. lent a hand to get the first rope across. Meanwhile, the 4th squadron had come under artillery fire from Nimrin. Later, the two squadrons attempted to cut off the garrison retiring from Ghoraniyeh towards Nimrin, but the artillery of the enemy from the hills put over a barrage which compelled a withdrawal. This was done at the gallop in lines of troop columns at irregular intervals, a formation which proved the best for escaping gun fire.

It was a wonderful day. Events happened so rapidly that when the Regiment was relieved from the outpost line at dusk, the men could hardly realise what they had done. A total of 50 Turks were killed, 60 were captured, besides four machine-guns, at a cost of one officer killed, and one officer and one man wounded. Only six horses were hit. It need hardly be said that the extraordinary success of the day gave the A.M.R. a wonderful reputation among the Tommies. Many of them said they had never dreamed such riding possible. Through quick and courageous decisions, and prompt and intrepid action, one regiment, armed only for dismounted fighting, had cleared some miles of country. At any time hesitation or slow movement might have meant disaster. It was one of those occasions, too, when the results were immediately seen, for by nightfall artillery and supplies were passing over the pontoon bridge at Ghoraniyeh, while the Australian and New Zealand Mounted Division started to cross at Hajleh.

As usual, the day was not without its humours. A sergeant of the 3rd squadron was the victim of the best joke. When the Regiment was standing-to in the wadi near Nimrin, a gun, very close at hand, started to drop shells into the opposite side of the watercourse. The sergeant in the wild gallop had lost his sense of direction, and believing that the gun was a British gun, climbed to the top of the sheltering bank and energetically waved a flag at the gun, which was only a few hundred yards away. The gun immediately roared again, and the sergeant took only half a second to roll down the bank again. "The damn thing's not ours at all," he remarked, amid the laughter, and added somewhat pensively, "And I waved my little flag at it."

CHAPTER XXXII.

Raid into Gilead.

At dawn the next morning, the New Zealand Brigade moved from the crossing in a north-east direction over the ground the A.M.R. had cleared the previous day. The A.M.R. was in reserve, and watched the infantry and various mounted units, including the W.M.R. and the C.M.R., occupy the foothills without serious opposition. Into the Turk's position on the hill of Nimrin, which guarded the valley up which the main road led to Es Salt, the 60-pounders put some shells, while eight aeroplanes dropped bombs. Under this cover the infantry rushed the place, and captured 50 Germans, four field guns and two machine-guns. The advance was immediately pressed on. The New Zealanders, after watering at the fast mountain stream in the Wadi Nimrin (the horses having become accustomed to drinking from troughs or nose bags were perplexed by the current, and showed a tendency to follow the water down in search of a still place) moved along the Es Salt road for a short distance, and then turned to the right up the Wadi Jerria, which was knee-deep in grass and ablaze with bright flowers. The advance guard was commanded by Lieut.-Colonel McCarroll, and consisted of one squadron of the C.M.R. (in the van), the A.M.R., and the Hongkong Mountain Battery, which used camels to carry the guns and ammunition. After five miles had been covered the narrow track became very steep. It was hard for the horses, but terrible for the camels. With all necessary safeguards out, the column bivouacked on the cold heights of

Gilead. The contrast in temperature with that recently experienced in the Jordan Valley was marked. They were now between 2,000 and 3,000 feet above sea level, and they shivered in the cold. To crown all, rain began to fall, and sleep was well nigh impossible. At dawn it was utterly impossible to "boil up" and, feeling as miserable as frozen dogs, the horsemen continued the march. The ration camels had been unable to scramble up the track from the wadi, so no food could be issued for the day, but the iron emergency ration was in every man's holster. When the rain ceased a dense mist enveloped the mountains, and through it the regiments pushed on. At a distance of 100 yards they looked more like phantom horsemen than flesh and blood. Soon the track started to descend to the Wadi Sir. Up this wadi the brigade moved, and suddenly through the mist loomed the Circassian village of Ain Es Sir. In the village was a party of 88 Turks, under two officers, engaged in cutting down poplar trees for fuel for the railway engines on the Hedjaz line. Never were there more surprised men. They were gathered in without a shot being fired. The advanced guard passed through the village, and when the column came up the men were amazed to see Turkish soldiers wandering about the streets, but they were merely being mustered by their officers to be handed over to the beings who had ridden out of the mist. The Circassians, the most treacherous ruffians the New Zealanders were to encounter, slunk about in surly silence, but committed no hostile act. Their chance was to come later.

The wireless men with the brigade set up their instrument, and received a message that the

2nd Light Horse, who had been crossing the mountains by a more southerly route, had been delayed by the atrocious weather. The New Zealanders, therefore, bivouacked just beyond the village, the horses receiving the last handful of grain that had been carried on the saddles. Patrols were sent out a couple of miles further on and captured a patrol of six Germans, and later a German scout. No other enemy troops were seen.

There was still no sign of the ration camels the next morning, and when the fog lifted at 10 a.m. the horses were taken out to feed on the growing oat crops. Later in the day 50 horses were sent back to " pack up " food for the men. By this time hundreds of the men of the Sherif of Mecca, all armed to the teeth, were roaming about and anxious to take a hand in the war against the Turks. That day the brigade was joined by the rest of the Anzac Division, and preparations were made for the attack on Amman the next day.

The column moved at 8 a.m. (March 27), the horses having had nothing but green feed. The plan was for the New Zealanders to attack Amman from the south, with their right flank on the railway, while the Camel Brigade attacked from the west, and the 2nd Light Horse from the north. Leaving the road a couple of miles east of Ain Es Sir, the New Zealanders swung to the south-east to enable them to get into position. The A.M.R., with a section of the machine-gun squadron, formed the advanced guard, the 4th squadron being in the van. About two miles and a-half from Amman the Regiment came under shell fire, particularly when crossing the sky line into a wadi which afforded some cover, as it moved east to its appointed position. When about 1,500 yards

from the railway, the Regiment turned north. On
the left was the C.M.R., which connected with the
Camel Brigade. The W.M.R. was detailed as
escort to a demolition party, whose duty it was to
destroy the railway in the vicinity of Kissar
Station. It was now about noon. As the two
regiments moved on Amman, they were accompanied by a ragged and highly excited mob of
Bedouins, whose chief, a fine old type, shadowed
the Auckland colonel, in the hope of being given a
share in the action. Unexpectedly a train came
in from the south, and stopped opposite the left
flank of the Regiment. Our machine-guns opened
on it, and machine-guns on the train replied. A
squadron was getting ready to charge it when it
steamed on to Amman. The old Arab chief blazed
away at it in good style, but he went to earth very
quick when a bullet whizzed past his ear.

A little later the Aucklanders witnessed a
rare sight. Over the hills east of the railway
came charging a party of Arabs, hundreds following on foot. Their quarry was a party of 60
Turks, who had not been quick enough to board
the train. The 4th squadron set off to see what
was happening, and were just in time to prevent
the Arabs from slaughtering the unfortunate
Turks. One German had been done to death,
however, and most of the Turks had been despoiled
of all their clothing. Meanwhile, the Turkish
artillery and machine-guns had held up the advance on all sides. The attackers had no guns,
and there was no sign of the infantry from Es Salt,
which had fallen early that morning. On front
of the 3rd squadron was Hill 3039, which was
alive with machine-guns. The 11th squadron was
sent to the high ground east of the railway to protect the flank, and the 4th squadron came up from

the line to support the 3rd. A shell dropped among them, and killed two men and wounded seven others, besides knocking out a number of horses. At 6 p.m. the enemy delivered a strong counter-attack against the right of the Canterburys, and succeeded in gaining the ridge, but almost immediately were driven from it at the bayonet point. No further progress was possible that night, but the line reached was held. The Regiment had 13 casualties for the day. No rations came up that night, and odd biscuits had to suffice. The horses fared much better, the wadis being full of grass.

Next morning a force of 300 Arabs went to the colonel for work. Laughingly he pointed to the hill that had held up the advance, but the old boy declined the honour. He used the very sound argument that all his men would be killed before they could reach the top. A handsome young Arab, who had been interpreting, then asked, " Will Amman be captured?" " Yes," replied the colonel. " What will you do with the Circassians?" continued the Arab. " Leave them alone if they don't trouble us," was the reply. " Won't you allow the Arabs to kill them all," queried the young cut-throat, who, by the way, had been taught the English tongue at St. George's in Jerusalem, and was reputed to be a Christian. Soon after a troop of the Regiment was sent off to investigate a report that Turks were coming from the south, and the Arabs swarmed after them. It was a picture of contrasts—the East and the West! Disciplined soldiers and a mob! The Arabs who remained with the Regiment persisted in walking about the sky line until one of their number was killed by a shell nose-cap striking his head. The rest ran for their lives. Then one came back to the body, shied off like a horse when he saw the hideous wound, and then regaining courage rushed forward, grabbed the dead man's cloak and made off with it. Other Arabs then came up, and bolted like hares with the knives and other belongings of the deceased.

During the night the enemy had been heavily reinforced, and his fire again held up the advance. Artillery assistance was asked for, and one section of the Hongkong Mountain Battery was promised. Before it arrived, however, the Turks delivered a very determined counter-attack against a battalion of the Camel Brigade, which had joined the New Zealanders after its demolition work on the railway. The Turks reached within bombing distance, but the camel men, who also had some bombs, held their ground, although suffering casualties. At 11.30, two battalions of infantry and a few guns arrived, and a general advance was ordered for 1 p.m. The line was pushed on, but machine-gun fire from the dominating hill became too severe, and artillery was again requested, the section of the mountain battery not yet having appeared. It reported at 2.30, and went into action immediately. By 4 o'clock the A.M.R. and the Camel battalion had moved forward 500 yards, and reached the lower slopes of the hill, but they could go no further owing to the inadequacy of the artillery support. Steep rocky faces lay above them, and these were swept by the nest of machine-guns which remained intact. At nightfall the Regiment withdrew a distance to a stronger defensive line. No better success had been met with on the other sides of the town. A limited supply of rations had come up during the day, but it was lucky that there was grass for the horses. The

A HALT IN A WADI AT FUSAIL ON THE WAY TO JISR ED DAMIEH.

MOUNTED RIFLEMEN MOVING INTO ACTION NEAR JISR ED DAMIEH.

JERICHO JANE.

A Turkish gun which shelled Jericho. After its capture it was overturned.

4th SQUADRON A.M.R. MARCHING THROUGH ES SALT, IN THE HILLS OF GILEAD.

Arab allies of the Regiment returned during the night, the old chief reporting to the colonel that he had destroyed the telegraph line going south. He was thanked for his work, and told that he could now send his men home to sleep. The old chap made a low salaam, and with great dignity answered " Where the English soldier, my friends, sleep near the enemy, the Turk, there sleep I and my men."

CHAPTER XXXIII.

Attack on Amman.

The night passed quietly, and no further advance was attempted the following day, it having been decided to deliver a surprise attack the next night. The position to be attacked was a very strong one. The defences were distributed with the usual skill of the Turks, across a steep flinty ridge running from south-west to north-east, and so placed that each succeeding position dominated the one in front. At a conference, a plan of attack was drawn up. This plan was to attack up the stem of the ridge in a north-easterly direction, the second line passing over the first as soon as the first of the main positions had been taken. Later, at the suggestion of Lieutenant-Colonel McCarroll, who was to command the whole attacking force, the plan was altered, and it was agreed that the attack should be carried due north against the highest points of the ridge, and that the two trenches further down the ridge should be dealt with after the upper ones had been carried. The A.M.R. and the Camel Battalion were to go straight at the point marked D in the sketch* (the south-eastern corner of the ridge), and the two squadrons of the C.M.R., which were available, were to pass through the line as soon as it had achieved its objective and rush the positions marked E. and F. some 200 yards further on at the north-east corner of the ridge. The W.M.R. were on other duty, and were not available for the attack. The scheme was very similar to that prepared for the opening of the Gallipoli offensive in

---

* See end of book.

August, but without the aid of a diversive bombardment and the glare of searchlights to intensify the gloom. The attack was to be pressed swiftly and silently, and the trenches carried with the bayonet alone. Magazines had to be empty because even an accidental shot might have jeopardised the whole action.

The brigade (dismounted) concentrated at 1.30 a.m. (March 30) in a wadi below their line. The moon shone fitfully, and there was a slight mist in the air. At about 1.45, the first line moved forward to the attack, making hardly a sound. An open flat 800 yards wide, and then a little valley, had to be crossed before the steep ascent could be reached. The minutes passed, the silent line drew nearer and nearer to its objective, and still the enemy remained in ignorance of his danger. When nearing the point from which the rush could be made, a Turkish sentry fired one shot and bolted. Still the trenches remained silent. Then, with the roar of the charge, the Aucklanders and the splendid men of the Camels leaped forward. A splutter of flame broke out from the trench, but it was too late. Shrieks and groans echoed through the night as the bayonets went home with a thud. A young officer suddenly fell down a dug-out, which had been covered with a blanket, on top of a Turk, and blood-curdling yells pierced the night, as the officer and the Turk rolled about on the ground. The men above had their bayonets handy, but they had to allow the officer to deal with the Turk with his hands. They say that the language and sounds which arose from the dug-out were unique. Within a few minutes the only Turks remaining in the trench were those who had been captured and those who were dead. The prisoners totalled 23, and with them were taken five machine-guns. Our losses were slight. On the heels of this attack came the second line, which went on and carried positions E. and F., while the A.M.R. and Camels cleared up B. and C. Owing to the rocky nature of the ground it was impossible to dig trenches, so the men started to build stone sangars. Then came cold rain and shells. At dawn the Turks opened an enfilade machine-gun fire from A, a hill to the left, and the 4th squadron attacked it under cover of rifle and machine-gun fire from the 3rd squadron, capturing every man. Under the fire of a number of guns the men continued to build up the stone sangars to afford some little cover. A few men found cover in a grave opened by Arabs in search of loot.

About 9 a.m., the enemy was seen massing on the north-east slopes of the hill for a counter-attack. Lieutenant-Colonel McCarroll appealed for artillery assistance, but none was available. The section of the mountain battery attached to the brigade had only four rounds to fire. Soon after the Turkish bombardment increased and a determined counter-attack by a large force was delivered. It reached the crest within a very short distance of the A.M.R., but was swept back by rifle and machine-gun fire. The ground in front was strewn with dead Turks.

On the north-east section, part of the C.M.R. and the Camels were so hard pressed by overwhelming numbers that they wavered and started to retire, but within a few yards they were rallied by a most gallant young officer, and with a mighty roar they swept the Turk from their line. So splendid was the recovery, that they were with difficulty prevented from continuing on after the routed Turks. Soon after the young officer had rallied the men he fell mortally wounded, but he had lived for his great hour; in it he had achieved one of the hardest tasks an officer can accomplish, and had gone to his God " trailing behind him clouds of glory." The rout of these Turks was hastened by the heavy fire the A.M.R. was able to pour into them. A war artist would have gloried in the picture of that small body surging back to the attack, which looked so like a forlorn hope, and in the sight of the A.M.R.'s line of resolute men, standing shoulder to shoulder in their wet great coats, on that shell-swept crest, pouring rapid fire into the Turks. Once again the breed held good.

It is worthy of special note that this brilliant bit of work was done without the aid of artillery. The enemy continued to shell the hill, no less than three batteries directing their fire upon it, and heavy losses occurred. The evacuation of the wounded was very difficult and dangerous, owing to the exposed nature of the ground behind the firing line. About five o'clock another counter-attack was delivered against the C.M.R., which had been reinforced by two troops of the A.M.R., on the right, but it was successfully repulsed.

CHAPTER XXXIV.

Retirement.

Only partial success had been achieved by the forces attacking Amman from the west, and the situation had been complicated by the arrival of Turkish reinforcements in the vicinity of Es Salt, and that evening a general withdrawal was ordered.

The retirement could not possibly be attempted until after dark for every movement was met with a terrific storm of shells. No one knows how the men held out on the crest throughout that long afternoon. Some slight rest was obtained when the New Zealand machine-guns found the emplacements of the enemy, and forced them to move. The Turkish artillery continued its heavy fire until darkness fell. What a relief was the arrival of darkness that evening!

Plans were speedily made for the retirement, but owing to the difficulty in evacuating the wounded this could not take place immediately. The forward dressing station was 1,000 yards from the firing line, and from there the wounded had to be carried a further two miles before other means of conveyance could be obtained. But these other means of conveyance were only saddle horses and cacholet camels. The camel apparatus, which was only a double litter fitting over the hump, was reserved for the worst cases. The others had to be strapped to horses. The sufferings those men endured on that terrible journey, over slippery and dangerous tracks through the hills on a night which was piercingly cold, can never be described. Many died, of course, who otherwise would have lived.

Unfortunately, there were hardly any stretchers on which to convey the wounded to the dressing stations, and blankets had to be used for the purpose, some of the cases, therefore, requiring six men to carry them. This increased the difficulty of the retirement, and delayed it. All this time the men on the ridge had to keep a keen watch upon the enemy. "Jacko" was still looking for a chance to get the hill. Our right flank was very open, and there was the chance of the Turks pushing round it at any moment. It was an anxious time, and the appearance of the moon at 8.30, while helping to expedite movement, increased the possibilities of a disastrous retirement.

The colonel issued orders to each unit, giving the exact time for moving back, so that the whole force would meet in one line for the final withdrawal. When the last of the wounded had been got away and the dead buried, the force moved back in silence. Care was taken by everyone to avoid even kicking a stone. The first 1,000 yards was covered without event, the Turks not having any suspicion of what was taking place. The moon was now well up, and was showing up the crest that had been left, but the New Zealanders had got out of an impossible position by the same method they had used to get into it—by stealth. The retirement was now considered safe, and a feeling of inexpressible relief came over the men. Strong men, weary beyond all telling, and still showing signs of the daze which comes from long endurance of shell fire, silently gripped hands. The last of the wounded were picked up by the retiring line at the first dressing station, and carried on their painful way to the horses.

No disgrace attaches to this retirement. What had been started as a raid to cover a railway demolition party had developed into a little war without the necessaries of war, and the raiding force had done surprisingly well to have accomplished what it had. For two days it had existed on emergency iron rations, which, while they can sustain life, are not the food to fight on, nor the food to enable men to stand the intense cold which prevailed. Apart from the lack of proper food the men had had little sleep, and they were just about as wretched as they could possibly be, but the traditional cheerfulness of the A.M.R. shone out. As always, they made the best of things. It was typical of the men that when rations did come up they were more pleased about getting grain for the horses than some hard tack for themselves.

The former bivouac, a mile east of the village of Ain Es Sir, was reached by the column about 4 a.m., and the men of the A.M.R. were soon fast asleep.

The tribulations of this raid were not yet done, however. The whole force was to return to the Jordan, and the New Zealand Brigade was detailed to cover the infantry and Camels going back by this route. At 4 p.m., by which time most of the transport camels had started west, the C.M.R. reported a strong force of Turks advancing on the left flank. The A.M.R. was ordered out to support the C.M.R. The A.M.R. halted 600 yards from the outpost line, and spent one of the most dreadful nights of its existence. A cutting wind blew, and there was no shelter from it. Stiff with the cold the men lay close together, and prayed that the Turks would be frozen too. The regiments began to retire slowly before dawn. The enemy had come within 1,500 yards of the C.M.R. line, but had not attacked. Daylight was breaking by the time they were clear of the village, where the W.M.R. took over the rearguard duties. The column slowly moved down the wadi, along which were scattered the bodies of dozens of camels which had been knocked out by the greasy slopes and the cold, and were now being cut up by the Arabs for food. When the Regiment had reached the point where the road leaves the Wadi Sir and goes up the bank towards the Wadi Jerria, shooting was heard in the rear. The Circassians had opened fire on the Wellingtons from the houses and caves and rocks on either side of the defile. The W.M.R. promptly returned the fire, and the Circassians were severely punished. Unfortunately, the W.M.R. had nine or ten men killed. The A.M.R. and C.M.R. got into position to cover the retreat of the W.M.R., and when a machine-gun and a battery of the 181st Infantry Brigade, which was ahead, opened up, the firing ceased. Meanwhile a strong Turkish force was reported to be advancing, and the march was continued as quickly as possible. A force of Turks was observed working its way down a ridge to the south, but the mountain gun stopped it. At last the mounted men passed through the infantry brigade which was in position to hold the rear, and after drawing rations from a dump, pushed on down the slopes towards the Jordan Valley, the Dead Sea, calm and still, spread out below them. At many places along the track were to be seen the disasters which had overtaken the camel train.

Nimrin was reached by 8 p.m., and there they bivouacked. During the operations, the brigade had captured nine Turkish officers, 188 other ranks, and seven Germans, besides five machine-guns. It had also shared in the capture of three mountain guns. Its total casualties were six officers and 32 other ranks killed, six officers and 116 other ranks wounded, and 13 other ranks missing.

CHAPTER XXXV.

Jordan Recrossed.

The next day the brigade moved across the Jordan, the pontoon bridges of which had had a very severe buffeting through floods during the raid, and camped a mile south-east of Jericho on the banks of the Wadi Kelt.

After this very arduous raid not a few men could be found who were in perfect agreement with Terence Mulvany, immortalised by Kipling. That distinguished character, when describing a "war" on the Indian frontier, said: "Thin the Tyrone, wid the Ould Rig'mint in touch, was sint maraudin' an' prowlin' acrost the hills promishcuous an' onsatisfactory. 'Tis my privit opinion that a gin'ral does not know half his time fwhat to do wid three-quarters his command. So he shquats on his hunkers an' bids them run round an' round forninst him while he considhers on it. Whin by the process av nature they get sejuced into a big fight that was none av their seekin', he sez 'Obsarve my shuperior janius. I meant ut to come so.'" Mulvany, of course, voiced the eternal plaint of the ranks, who may not be taken into the confidence of the Commander-in-Chief. It was a pity, a very great pity, that the rank and file, and more than the rank and file for that matter, did not know that their raid to Amman meant much more than aiding the Arabs of Hedjaz. That was the present and obvious purpose, but it and subsequent operations on the left flank of the Turkish line were all part of the plan to convince the Turks that the next great blow would be delivered there. Events proved that the Turk was so convinced, and no one can say how much was the gain to the British when, towards the end of the year, they smashed his line near the coast, and swept through to final victory. One definite fact, however, is that the enemy kept the whole of his Fourth Army east of the Jordan.

The morning after the Regiment bivouacked near Jericho, enemy aeroplanes came over, and the Aucklanders awakened by the crash of anti-aircraft guns. Within a few seconds a bomb exploded nearby, and the doctor was heard to remark, in that impersonal style common to his kind, " If I am any judge, the next one will be damn close." The doctor had proof that he was right as soon as he got out of his bivvie. The next bomb had landed among the headquarters' horses. Eight men were wounded, and 18 horses were killed and four wounded. The doctor was one of the many who had a narrow escape, a piece of metal striking the earth between him and his bivvie mate.

Nothing of much moment occurred during the month of April. The Regiment had its share of patrolling the Jordan, improving the bridgehead defences, and burying Turkish dead. A good number of awards were announced, the chief of which was that Lieutenant-Colonel McCarroll had received a bar to his D.S.O. The double decoration won by the colonel gave the Regiment very great satisfaction. Then came another " honour" which literally filled the cup to the brim. This was the cup received by the Rugby football team of the A.M.R. as the champion team of the Anzac Mounted Division. The final contests had taken place before the first Jericho stunt, but the cup had not been presented. The prize was formally presented at a brigade parade on April 8 by Lieutenant-General Sir Henry Chauvel, G.O.C. Desert Mounted Corps. With him was General Chaytor. The cup was filled with wine, and full honours were done by the generals, the colonel of the Aucklands, and the team. But it was not the full team. Since the final game of football, they had played the game of war, and war had taken its toll. General Chauvel said a number of flattering things about the New Zealand Brigade, and he particularly mentioned the exploit of the A.M.R. when it made its dash across the Jordan.

He mentioned that a very high authority had rung him up on the telephone on the morning of the Jordan gallop, and in excited tones had said: "The Aucklands are across and riding hell for leather," which, of course, goes to show that generals were once lieutenants, and do not always speak in the language of despatches. It might be mentioned that two of the spectators of the ride across the river were General Allenby and the Duke of Connaught. During the second week of the month the Turks attacked the Ghoraniyeh bridgehead, but were severely dealt with, and they retired, leaving hundreds of dead. Another attack was made further north at Auja, but it met with a similar fate. The New Zealanders had no hand in these defensive actions.

As the month wore on the heat increased, and with it came the flies and mosquitoes and sickness. Malaria did not become very bad, but most of the men were being prepared for it when they should again leave the valley for the hills. A little less discomfort was realised by shifting camp to a spot 200 feet higher, but it can hardly be said that there was much pleasure in this sojourn in the ancient valley.

CHAPTER XXXVI.

Second Raid into Gilead.

A second raid into Gilead was started on April 29. On this occasion the New Zealanders were in reserve, and did what fighting they had to do between the river and the foothills on the eastern side. The general plan was to envelope the right of the enemy's main force about Shunet Nimrin, capture Es Salt, and advance to a line beyond. Infantry were to attack Nimrin at 2 a.m. on April 30, while Australian Light Horse Brigades rapidly pushed north to get astride of the Umm Esh Shert-Jisr Ed Damie and Es Salt-Jisr Ed Damie tracks, thence moving on Es Salt from the north and north-west. This force was known as Hodgson's Force. Simultaneously Shea's Force was to advance over the southern tracks, one of which the New Zealanders knew only too well.

At midnight, the New Zealand Brigade left bivouac and remained in reserve to the 180th infantry, who attacked the first positions at Nimrin at 2 a.m. The W.M.R. and the C.M.R. were ordered to support the right flank of the attack early in the day, but the A.M.R. remained in support for an hour or two. At 9.30, the 4th squadron was sent forward to the right of the C.M.R., but a barrage was put in front of them (the enemy had at least four batteries in action), and the squadron had to take what cover could be found. Soon after the 3rd and 11th squadrons had to be sent back to a spot where cover could be found for the horses. By this time it had become apparent that the Turks were in too great strength to allow the infantry and mounted rifles to make any headway, and all that could be done was to lie low until darkness. The New Zealanders then withdrew to the bridge at Ghoraniyeh, and there bivouacked. Some six officers and men were wounded, including Major Herrold, O.C. 11th squadron, but he remained on duty. The hold up had not affected the raid on Es Salt, however. The Australians, operating over what were little more than goat tracks, got the mountain town and a large number of prisoners.

The next day enemy reinforcements arrived and started to push from the north-west against the line which commanded the Jisr Ed Damie-Es Salt track. During the forenoon, the Turks in great strength pushed south, and although suffering heavily under artillery and machine-gun fire at point-blank range, continued the movement, and compelled the two British batteries to abandon their guns, for which there was no passable road. About this time the A.M.R. was ordered to gallop north to support the sorely pressed line. Soon the Regiment was in position over a distance of two miles, with its left flank resting on the ford. Trooping back were the gunners who had lost their guns, and other disturbing evidences of hurried retreat. The position looked bad, but the men were heartened to see fresh batteries come up at the gallop and go into action. The fact that mattered most was that the track leading from Es Salt to Umm Esh Shert, the only line of retirement for the Australians at Es Salt, lay behind the British position. That night the

3rd and 11th squadrons moved forward to the outpost line, and, with the Camels on the left and the Dorset Yeomanry on the right, toiled like Trojans on earth works. No fighting took place during the night. At Nimrin the Turks still held up the infantry. The Beni Sakhr tribe of Arabs had failed, not unexpectedly, to take its promised action against the enemy down the Wadi Es Sir, and therefore this track was being used by the Turks to reinforce at Nimrin, which therefore became " the southern claw of a formidable pair of pincers," with which the enemy threatened to cut off the cavalry at Es Salt.

May 2 passed "quietly" in the valley and foothills, but at Es Salt the Australians were attacked, and their withdrawal was ordered. May 3, a day of intense heat, saw no action by the river except the continuation of the artillery duel. A feeling of great relief swept over the forces in the valley when at dawn the next morning the Australians, who had raided Es Salt, were seen winding down from the mountains. They had captured no less than 942 prisoners and 29 machine-guns, a very satisfactory " bag " indeed. But the operation achieved much more than this result; it convinced the enemy High Command that the push for Damascus would be made on this flank.

That evening the brigade withdrew to the vicinity of the Auja ford, where a bridge was in the course of construction, the W.M.R. and the C.M.R. returning to the old bivouac near Jericho, but the A.M.R. remained there for a day performing patrol duty and working on the eastern bridge-

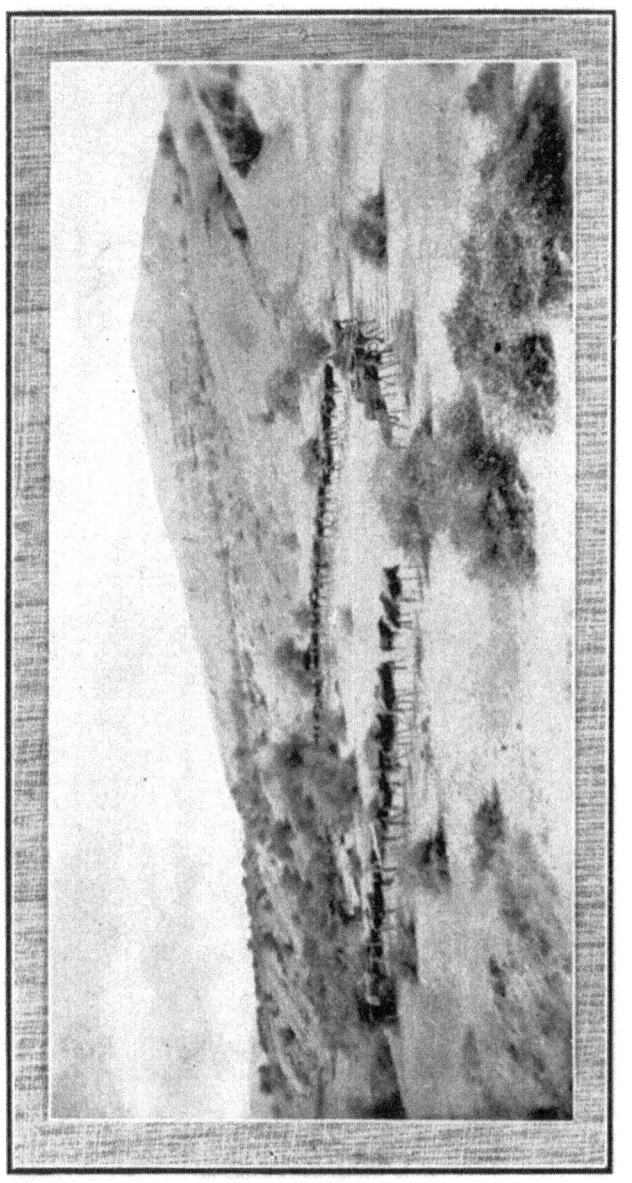

DUMMY HORSES IN THE JORDAN VALLEY, WHICH HELPED TO MISLEAD THE TURKS INTO BELIEVING THE GREAT BLOW WAS TO FALL THERE.

THE JORDAN VALLEY.

1. A.M.R. ready to leave. 2. The Mount of Temptation, showing monastery on face. 3. Last glimpse of the valley.

AN INTERESTING GROUP.

Reading from left to right, the names are: Lieutenant-Colonel McCarroll (A.M.R.), Brigadier-General Meldrum (O.C. N.Z.M.R. Brigade), Lieutenant-Colonel White (O.C. W.M.R.), General Allenby (Commander-in-Chief), General Chaytor (O.C. Anzac Division).

THE REMAINING ORIGINAL OFFICERS OF THE A.M.R. IN DECEMBER, 1918: MAJOR W. HAEATA, LIEUT.-COLONEL McCARROLL, AND LIEUT. W. STEWART.

head defences. Incidentally it might be mentioned that patrols had to retire before a force of 500 Turks, and artillery was asked for. The Camels advised headquarters that Auckland was in for a warm time, and a whole brigade of Light Horse was sent out to relieve the Regiment. "An excellent wheeze," remarked one glad soul. "We'll report thousands of Turks whenever we want relief."

CHAPTER XXXVII.

Trials of the Valley.

Several days of rest were spent at the old "bivvie" ground. They were spent rather than enjoyed, for the steamy heat of summer was now upon the land. The flies were in myriads and the mosquitoes were on an energetic offensive. Odd parties, more or less listless, wandered about with Old Testaments and guide books, and marvelled over the ease with which Joshua made his conquests. Others tried the simple art of floating in the Dead Sea, and ruminated in a lethargic sort of a way at the presence of a naval section with a motor-boat or two on the salt waters. But the thermometer registered anything up to 110 degrees in the shade, and hence it was not surprising that most of the men were inclined to take everything for granted.

Finally, the New Zealanders were moved to a camping ground up in the western hills near Talat Ed Dumm. "Funny sort of place to live," said one trooper. "There's not enough flat ground to play marbles." "Who the devil wants to play marbles," growled his mate, who, it may be inferred, had had enough of the valley.

At the end of May, the brigade shifted to El Khudr, near Bethlehem. There was a difference of 2,000 feet in the altitude, and the change in temperature had a marked effect upon the general health. The country looked a paradise after the desolate valley and the inhospitable hills. The grape vines were green, the barley crops were ripening, and fruit hung upon the trees. It was

Palestine at its best. Leave parties were now going to the rest camp at Port Said, and the campaigners for the time-being forgot the trials of the Jordan.

Towards the middle of June the New Zealanders returned to the Jordan valley for a stretch of patrol duty, the A.M.R. being bivouacked at Wadi Abeid.

Mosquitoes, scorpions, and snakes seemed to increase with the summer, which dragged wearily on. " Jacko " sometimes raised sufficient energy to throw over a few shells, and the British gunners, more through politeness than anything else, threw a few back—at least so it seemed to the men on the horse lines or in the trenches facing north. Fortunately for the well-being of higher officers, a lively paper-war was proceeding over small matters that could affect the winning of the war, but for the rank and file there was little mental stimulus, and that is a sad state of things to happen in the Jordan valley when summer heat saps the system. True the Regiment had to find daily a working party for trench defences—but digging is not a mental stimulus when the shade temperature is 110 degrees and the air seems devoid of oxygen.

At the beginning of July, the A.M.R. took over a sector from the W.M.R., the new bivouac being at Ain Ed Duk beside " the best spring in Palestine." Here shower baths were erected, and they provided the one comfort of the stifling days. About the middle of the month the enemy restored some interest to life by attacking a salient held by Light Horse on the right of the A.M.R. A force of Germans attacked one side of the salient and got possession of sufficient trench to isolate those at the point of it. Turks attempted to attack the other flank of the salient and the line held by the A.M.R., but artillery fire kept them well back. A vigorous counter-attack by Australians closed the gap the Germans had made, and 400 were captured. The Hun prisoners were highly wroth against the Turks for letting them down, and did not hesitate to say so to their captors. During the day the W.M.R. went out after a party of 100 Turks, and captured 60. They were nearly mad with thirst, and no wonder, for the shade temperature that day was 115 degrees. What it was in the sun can be conjectured from the fact that rocks were too hot to touch. The object of the enemy attack was to gain possession of the fine stream behind the British lines. Prisoners stated that they had suffered greatly from a shortage of water, and that they had been promised plenty if they took the position. They certainly found a plentiful supply of water, but in a prison camp.

A few days later the New Zealanders were relieved, and they moved back to Talat Ed Dumm, and thence after a week to Bethlehem and cooler air. During the month the Regiment had evacuated to hospital four officers and 166 other ranks, the majority of them being malaria cases. This was the general experience of all units in the torrid valley, and it emphasised the importance of the efforts to combat the mosquito by "canalising" the creeks and dealing with still water where the insects bred.

Three weeks were pleasantly spent. Regimental and brigade sports were held, and a great deal of sight-seeing took place. On August 16, the brigade left on the return journey to the " melting pot " of Jericho. What was said about the Jordan Valley when the column descended into its heat cannot here be stated. The Regiment camped near Jericho, and found guards and mosquito-squashing parties, and did some training. Yes! It was a very unpopular valley.

The month's hospital list had 109 names. The following were mentioned in despatches by General Sir E. H. H. Allenby for distinguished and gallant services and devotion to duty:—Captain W. Haeata, 3rd squadron; Lieutenant S. L. Wright, attached to Brigade Transport; and Lance-Corporal W. H. Jefcoate, 3rd squadron.

CHAPTER XXXVIII.

Beginning of the End.

Now comes September, the wonderful September which saw the Turk vanquished and Palestine freed. The first indication of the coming move by the Commander-in-Chief was the appearance in the Jordan Valley of dummy camps and lines of dummy horses, in the erection of which the A.M.R. took a hand. These things were for the benefit of enemy aircraft, but the Royal Air Force by this time had almost driven the Taube from the sky. An electric current went through the force as the import of these activities became apparent. "Allenby is about to strike," was whispered down the wind, and there was an atmosphere of subdued excitement along the lines and in the bivouacs. More active patrolling began. To further delude von Sanders, a programme of harassing the enemy in the valley was begun. The mounted patrols had the double purpose of finding out the enemy's strength and positions, and of drawing his gun fire. Through the hot dusty plain the little bodies of horsemen moved, and if they awakened " Jericho Jane " the British gunners thought it was an excellent day. But from the point of view of the horsemen, it was much better when " Jane " directed her attention to shelling the dummy camps. It was really entertaining to see the shells bursting over these empty habitations. Nothing gave the great deception away. As the day fixed for the commencement of the action approached, the Turks could still see great clouds of dust arising from troops coming into the valley, but they did not see the greater clouds caused by the brigades which moved out of the valley at night. Within a few days it was to be proved that the enemy did not know that five infantry divisions were between the high hills on the west of the Jordan Valley and the sea, with three divisions of cavalry in the orange groves behind Jaffa, and 301 guns in position instead of the normal number of 70. One of the cavalry divisions near the coast was the Australian Mounted Division. The Australian and New Zealand Mounted Division (often called the Anzac Division) was to remain on the right flank as part of "Chaytor's Force," which included an Indian infantry brigade, two battalions of Jewish troops and two battalions of infantry of British West Indians. It was not for them to take part in the great ride to Damascus, but their work on the Jordan and then over the hills to Amman was to be none the less important.

Elsewhere has been related how at dawn on September 19 the Turkish line was broken on the coast and how the cavalry poured through like a tidal wave which nothing could stay, how they penetrated to the Jordan behind two Turkish armies, and how they swept on to Damascus. Chaytor's Force was the pivot on which the advance swung. This force had to hold the line of the Jordan River from the Dead Sea, and also to move north with the 53rd Infantry Division as it advanced on its left. To the New Zealand Brigade fell the task of moving up the valley. On the night of September 21, the A.M.R. left Musallabeh, with the 4th squadron as advance guard, and occupied without opposition Kh Fusail and Tel Es Ed Dhiab, some 10 miles north of the Wadi Auja. Patrols were sent forward, but soon they encountered the enemy, who was holding a strong line covering the bridge at Mafid Jozeleh. A small force was found between the left flank of the Regiment and the right flank of the infantry on the hills, and was promptly dealt with, 20 prisoners and two machine-guns being taken. A large quantity of war material was secured during the day. That night the rest of the brigade, with the two battalions of West Indians and the 29th Indian Mountain Battery and the Ayrshire Battery, came up and joined the A.M.R.

The B.W.I's. were sent to guard the right to the river and the right rear, while the Mounted Rifles Brigade continued north to secure the important bridge and crossing of Jisr Ed Damieh, and to cut the road leading from the bridge to Nablus, along which retreating Turks were expected. The march started at midnight, the A.M.R. with one section of machine-guns being the advance guard. Moving cautiously along the Jericho-Beisan road, the Regiment secured without opposition the bridgehead at Mafid Jozeleh. Thence it went forward and got astride the Nablus-Damieh road. It was found that a large force of Turks had just passed towards the bridge, and the 3rd squadron was sent after them. The 11th squadron remained on the road facing west to intercept prisoners, while the 4th squadron occupied El Makhruk to the north-east. The 11th squadron had the pleasure of capturing some enemy transport, which had no idea that the British were in the vicinity until they were in the trap. The 3rd squadron soon caught up with the force moving towards the bridge and captured a number of prisoners. A cavalry outpost line attempted to hold the squadron off, but it was soon driven down to the river flat from the high ground above the bridge. The squadron held the high ground overlooking the bridge until dawn, when the enemy counter-attacked and forced the right of the squadron to retire to a strong position under artillery support. As the enemy were digging in and receiving reinforcements, the commander of the Aucklands recommended an immediate attack, at the same time asking for some assistance. This course was agreed to, and one squadron of the C.M.R. and one company of the B.W.I. were sent to reinforce the regiment. Meantime the artillery was doing some good shooting. The position held by the Turks was in the shape of a crescent with a flat top, the British line running round it at a distance of 500 yards. No weak spot being found in the enemy line it was decided that the whole line should advance, and so close in on the bridge. Lieutenant-Colonel McCarroll distributed his men as follows:—On the left, overlooking the bridge and road, one squadron and a-half with one machine-gun (these troops were not to advance, but to inflict punishment on the enemy when driven in), then came the rest of the A.M.R., less two troops, then the West Indians with one troop of the A.M.R., and then the C.M.R. squadron. The remaining troop of the A.M.R. was held in reserve. At the given time the whole line advanced, the bayonets flashing in the morning sun. Splendid covering fire was put over by the artillery, and the long-range overhead machine-gun fire was also most effectual. The Turk would not face that irresistible line of steel. Some surrendered as soon as they could, while others fled, only to be overtaken by the line on the right. The flat-footed West Indians, who had not been in action before, did splendidly. They chased the Turks down the hill and caught many of them. The C.M.R. closed in rapidly from the right. One of their troops came forward mounted, but it was stopped by a cliff. It at once wheeled to the right and made down a wadi to the river, and was very useful in rounding up the prisoners. The surviving Turks poured over the bridge in disorder, and they made no attempt to destroy the bridge, which was rushed by the reserve troops and secured intact. It was a very smart operation. A total of 350 Turks were captured, besides seven machine-guns. The killed and wounded made a considerable total. The only losses on our side were: A.M.R.: 3 killed, 1 died of wounds and 1 wounded; B.W.I.: 1 wounded. The A.M.R. remained for the rest of the day on the high ground above the bridge, but a C.M.R. squadron went across the bridge and cleared the surrounding country.

CHAPTER XXXIX.

On to Es Salt.

Next morning the brigade concentrated on the east bank of the river, and at mid-day moved east towards Es Salt. In intense heat, the column, led by the C.M.R., crossed the plain, and then started the steep ascent in single file. Touch was gained with the enemy in the foothills, but the advanced guard was not checked, capturing several posts and outflanking a redoubt a mile west of Es Salt. The mountain town was enveloped by 4 p.m. and taken without a fight, over 500 prisoners being secured. Once again the mounted troops had performed a feat which the Turks had not thought was possible. The climb of 3,000 feet through the hills had been exhausting to man and beast, because the pace was fast for such country. The Indian Mountain Battery, which accompanied the New Zealanders, lived up to the reputation of that branch of the service. There was no limit to the admiration won by the mules which carried the guns. In such work in such country the trained mule is master of all four-footed soldiers, and the mounted riflemen take off their hats to him and to the fighting men of India who led him.

That night the A.M.R. bivouacked west of the town. Next morning, after watering in Es Salt, the Regiment moved east along the road to Amman as advance guard to the brigade. The road was filled with the wreckage of a disastrous retreat. Evidently the Air Force had bombed it the previous day. Dead men and animals, abandoned carts and guns cumbered the way. Wounded Turks, who had crawled under the banks of the road, cried piteously for help. It was the hideous side of war. By mid-day the Regiment, close on the heels of the fleeing Turks, had occupied the Circassian village of Suweileh without opposition, and secured a few prisoners. Here a halt had to be made, for the Regiment had been going too fast for the rest of the column. Good water was found, and the horses were watered and fed, and the men " boiled up." During the afternoon, touch was gained with the 2nd Light Horse, which had crossed the hills further south.

That evening, a selected party of 100 men with picked horses was ordered to ride across country to the Hedjaz railway south of Amman and damage the line as much as they could with the few tools available. Each squadron supplied 33 men and an officer, and the whole was under the command of Major Herrold. All saddles were stripped, and all that was carried beyond arms and ammunition was two picks, two shovels, and four spanners. Before darkness fell, the party started on their hazardous enterprise, striking due east. No one had any knowledge of the 10 or 12 miles of trackless country lying between Suweileh and the railway. The party was divided into three sections, one to work on the line and the other two to cover them on either flank, and then it pushed forward into the night, a small advance guard feeling the way. Soon the little column was picking its doubtful way through a jumbled mass of rocky spurs and deep ravines. The ironshod hoofs striking the rocks seemed to make an appalling noise, but luckily there was no one to hear. Finally a track was struck, and as it ran due east it was followed for a mile or two, but with great caution, as it showed signs of recent traffic. Soon sounds of men were heard, and the advance guard, going forward on foot, found a party of Turks digging a trench. The essential thing being to remain unseen, the party turned back and took a track of sorts which ran up a gully on the left. Up this the column moved in single file. The moon had now risen, and while its light aided progress it increased the chance of detection. The luck held, however. From the head of the gully, the party moved on through broken country, passed sleeping Bedouin camps, and finally reached the top of a ridge which overlooked the railway. The men dismounted in a gully, and two officers went forward to reconnoitre. They found that the road running parallel to the line on the far side was filled with Turkish transport, and it seemed too good to hope that a demolition party could escape detection. But the job had to be attempted. They returned to the party, and moved it forward to a depression within 400 yards of the line. Here the men got into position to cover the working party. The latter crept forward, two officers and six men going first with spanners, and then a few men with the picks and shovels.

The spanner men, lying as flat as they could, had only started their task when an engine with an armoured truck full of soldiers came down the line. The workers crawled behind a couple of rocks a few yards from the line and waited. The Turks in the truck were making a great row, and did not notice the prone figures as the train moved slowly past and round a bend beyond. The working party then crawled silently back to the line, and were none the happier when they observed, a matter of 50 yards away, the figure of a man on the ground with a pack horse standing alongside. This individual neither heard nor saw anything, however. Again the work was interrupted, this time by a mounted patrol. One of the horsemen stopped only a chain away, but he did not see the figures on the ground. Eventually all the bolts were removed except one, and then the picks and shovels had to be used to finish the job. Both rails were twisted in such a way as to make them useless, and left in their original positions. The party then crept back to the horses, and the raiders secretly wended their way back, reaching Suweileh soon after dawn. That morning a train was wrecked at the gap made in the line. For his leadership of this daring and highly successful raid, Major Herrold received the D.S.O.

CHAPTER XL.

The Last Fight.

The day following the raid, the New Zealand Brigade moved against Amman, and fought its last definite action. At 6 a.m., the brigade moved east along the main road to attack the town from the north in co-operation with an attack from the west by the 2nd Light Horse. At 7.45 a.m., the W.M.R., who were in advance, came under fire from artillery, and from machine-guns and rifles in advanced posts. The country was of a rolling nature, and did not offer much good cover, even for dismounted men. At 10.30, the A.M.R., less the party which had raided the railway, with one section of the Mountain Battery and one section of the machine-gun squadron, was ordered into action on the left of the W.M.R. A double redoubt held the left of this section, and another held the right. Both positions were protected by wire. One squadron was sent forward dismounted to engage these positions. Observing that the ground between these defences and the main road was undefended, the Auckland colonel sent in one squadron to attack the redoubts from the west over this weak spot. This squadron was very soon under heavy machine-gun fire, but the artillery with the Regiment put over a covering fire and enabled the squadron to move forward by short rushes in small sections. One squadron remained in reserve awaiting a chance to go forward mounted, but the cover was of a very indifferent character. At half-past three o'clock this squadron was galloped up and reached the firing line without casualties, but when the men were dismounting, the enemy opened up an enfilade machine-gun fire from the left, and made it necessary for the led horses to be galloped back. Some casualties, both in men and horses, occurred during the movement. The C.M.R., which had been sent in on the right, was now pushing vigorously against a strong post called the stone tower, and the A.M.R. pressed on in conjunction. Resolutely the 4th squadron moved closer and closer to the double redoubt, and when the final charge was imminent, up went the white flags, and 60 Turks surrendered, while others bolted into the Wadi Amman, which ran north and south behind them. Once again the Turk showed that though he could put up a very determined defence, he had no stomach for the steel. The line pressed on, and soon there was not a Turk who had not taken refuge in the wadi up which part of the C.M.R. was now advancing from the south. About this time the stone redoubt had fallen to a bayonet attack by some of the C.M.R.; another part of that regiment had galloped down the road and into the town, where some prisoners were taken. The rest of the C.M.R. then swept through the town to the high ground east of it, taking these defences in the rear. Already the Amman had been invested on the east by the 1st Light Horse, who had made a wide encircling movement from the left, the railway south of the station had been cut, and dispositions made to meet considerable forces moving north, and there was little more to be done than to gather up the prisoners. Once more the mounted troops had moved too quick and too wide for the Turk. The total captures of the brigade were: 1,734 prisoners, 25 machine-guns, 2 automatic rifles, 1 4.2 howitzer, 2 75 cm. howitzers, 3 75 cm. mountain guns, 3 wireless sets, 298 horses, and a large amount of ammunition and other war material.

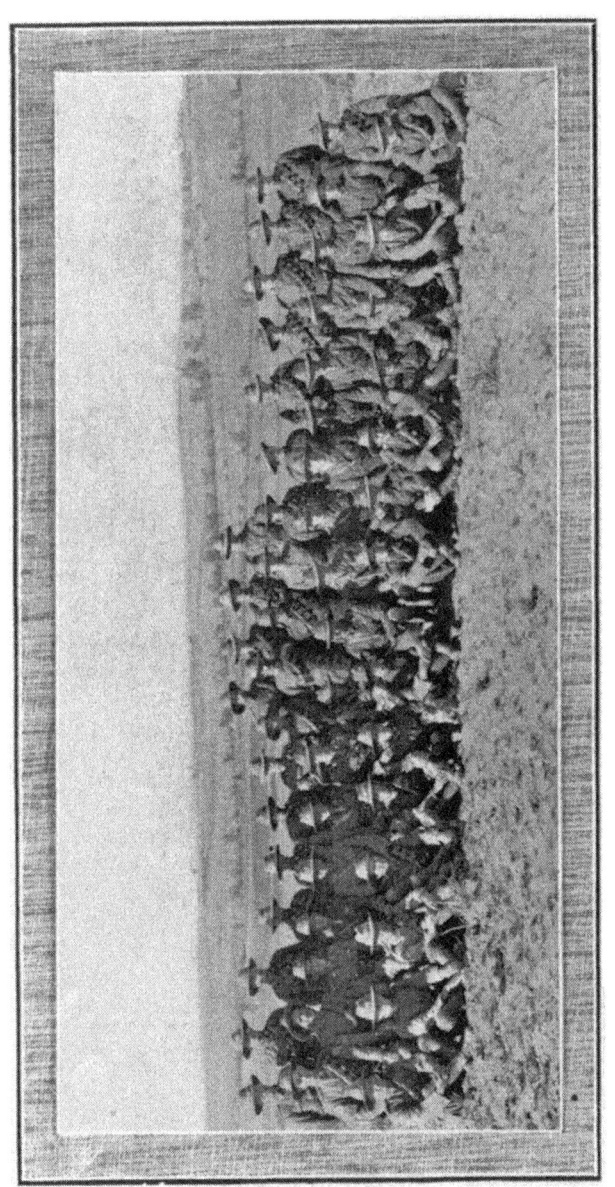

THE MAIN BODY MEN STILL WITH THE REGIMENT IN DECEMBER, 1918.

AN A.M.R. TROOP ON PARADE AFTER HOSTILITIES HAD CEASED.

BACK TO SCHOOL AFTER THE WAR.
1. Wool classing. 2. Motor mechanics.

1. Splendid type of remount. 2. A Main Body veteran which went through the whole campaign, originally owned by the late Sergeant G. S. Bagnall.

The A.M.R. spent the night in the Wadi Amman. No rations had arrived, but the contents of a garden helped to stave off hunger until the arrival of food the following night.

For distinguished work during the past four days the names of the following were brought under the notice of higher authorities:—Major J. H. Herrold, Captain A. C. M. Finlayson, 2nd Lieutenant H. A. Collins, T.-Sergeant E. P. S. Sweetman, Corporal E. Foote, T.-Corporal A. F. Buckland, and Trooper W. E. Tomkins.

The success of Chaytor's Force at Amman cut off between 8,000 and 10,000 Turks, who were being harassed from the east and south by a large Arab force. North of Amman there was hardly a Turk within 40 miles. The remnants of the enemy armies were in headlong retreat, but there was no hope of escape. Cavalry divisions from the coastal sector had crossed the Jordan ready to prey on the flank of the disorganised force, and better still, Lieutenant-Colonel Lawrence's Arab Camel Corps had swooped in from the eastern desert and were co-operating. The delay to the retreat caused by this northern Arab force enabled two cavalry divisions, now south of the Sea of Galilee, to win the race to Damascus.

A few days after the capture of Amman the New Zealanders moved south to support the Light Horsemen, who had found themselves in a Gilbertian situation. The Turkish general had surrendered his whole force to General Chaytor, but the Arab population, now very much anti-Turk, had gathered in great numbers to despoil the Turks. The Turks were so menaced by the Arabs that they did not dare lay down their arms. When the New Zealanders reached the Ziza area, they found that the Australians and Turks had become comrades in arms. In one case the outpost line opposing the Bedouins was held by Turks, with Australians lying in support. It was a rapid change from war to comedy, but from the Turkish point of view the Arabs were too close and too eager for loot to permit the comedy to be thoroughly appreciated. However, the arrival of the brigade ensured the safety of the Turks, who then changed their role from that of brothers in arms to that of prisoners of war.

A very amusing incident occurred at this period. After a busy day in collecting and despatching prisoners, the A.M.R. was resting in bivouac. During the evening, one solitary Turk, who had missed the round up, came in to give himself up. He went to a group of troopers, but they did not want to be bothered with another prisoner, so they refused to have anything to do with him. The unfortunate Turk toddled on to another group, but they also spurned him. Eventually the officers of the Regiment saw him, and they conceived the notion of directing him to brigade headquarters, which, of course, was a very naughty thing to do, but it had been a long war, and they were very keen to give the brigade a chance to make a capture. So the poor Turk, no doubt feeling like Mahomet's coffin, went over to brigade headquarters, and joy of joy, the " spare parts " there employed took the bait. They took it whole. They made the capture, but, it is said, they could not understand the sound of boisterous mirth which came down the wind. The Turk, probably, is still wondering over the extraordinary conduct of this Regiment of " St. George's Cavalry."

CHAPTER XLI.

The Remaining Enemy—Malaria.

The human enemy had been conquered, and one might have expected that the horsemen, who had served their country so well, would have ridden with the proud dignity of conquerors, but, alas! there was still one malevolent enemy which could not be laid low. It was malaria fever. The infection had been brought from the Jordan Valley, and after the excitement of the fighting on the high country had subsided, the men went down by the score. The havoc it wrought in those regiments of strong men was pathetic. On October 2, the day before the column left Amman for the Valley by the well-known track through the Wadi Sir and the Wadi Jeraia, 24 officers and men went down with malaria; from Nimrin, two days later, 76 were evacuated to hospital, at Jericho the next day 58 were fighting with death. The sight of the Regiment on the march—the regiment which had carried itself so gallantly through years of grim war—was tragic. Men, suddenly overcome, stuck to their saddles as long as they could, and then drew out from the column, and were helped into a shady place to await the ambulance men, whose devotion to the sick put the crown on a splendid record. Other men managed to hold out longer, but they swayed in their saddles as the column moved on. By the time Jericho was reached there were hardly enough men left to lead all the riderless horses. By the end of the month, no less than 11 officers and 331 other ranks had gone to hospital. By then only Lieutenant-Colonel McCarroll and Captain W. W. Averill, the adjutant, of all members of the Regiment, had escaped the fever. With a very large number of reinforcements, the New Zealanders continued on to Jerusalem, and after spending a few days there moved on to their old camping place at Richon-le-Zion, via Latron and Ramleh. Following is a list of those who were awarded decorations in connection with the recent operations:—Major J. H. Herrold (11th squadron), D.S.O.; Captain A. C. M. Finlayson (4th squadron), M.C.; Lieutenant H. A. Collins (3rd squadron), M.C.; Corporal E. Foote (4th squadron), Corporal E. P. S. Sweetman (4th squadron), Lance-Corporal A. F. Buckland (11th squadron), and Trooper W. E. Tomkins (11th squadron), M.Ms.

Training was resumed by the New Zealanders, but few there were who took it seriously, for cavalry and armoured cars were pressing on to Aleppo, and everyone knew that the end was near. It came on October 31, when Turkey was granted an armistice, the terms of which meant practically unconditional surrender. The first article of the terms gave infinite satisfaction to the Gallipoli veterans. It stipulated that the Dardanelles and Bosphorus were to be occupied by the Allies. So, after many days, the Gallipoli failure was vindicated.

A couple of days later the New Zealanders attended a function arranged by the Jews of Richon to celebrate the victory and the declaration of the British Government that Palestine would be given to the Jewish nation. The delight of the people, who had suffered the cruel tyranny of the Infidel, was unbounded, and the festivities will never be forgotten by the representatives of " the youngest people in the world."

So began a delirious fortnight. First came the Austrian, and then the German armistice. The scene on the night when the guns ceased on the French front was wonderful. Coloured lights lit the town, and singing and cheering filled the air. The veterans of the campaigns frolicked like youngsters. The A.M.R. officers decided to raid the W.M.R. mess, but no one was at home, for the W.M.R. and the C.M.R. officers had already left to raid the A.M.R. When the Aucklanders returned they were "arrested," and compelled to sing songs and supply all the refreshments. Afterwards the treasurer of the mess declared that the visitors seemed to have had nothing to refresh them for years.

On November 14, the anniversary of the battle of Ayun Kara, the Jewish population formally took over the care of the New Zealand cemetery. The New Zealand Brigade was represented by 50 officers and 150 men, with a firing party. The president of the community gave an impressive address, to which Brigadier-General Meldrum replied. The Rev. Mr. Wilson read a portion of the burial service, and the firing party fired three volleys. Hymns were then sung. Later the bodies of all New Zealanders buried in the neighbourhood were exhumed and interred in this cemetery.

The Regiment remained at Richon until December 18. Some training was done, but the really serious activities related to sport. At first small athletic meetings and rifle "shoots"—yes! the veterans actually were interested in shooting at targets—were the diversions, but these soon gave place to horse racing. The meetings increasing in size and importance until those responsible were giving large prizes, and men were gathering from everywhere to attend and to put their piastres on the " machine." At the Divisional Meeting there was an attendance of about 10,000 men. Among the horses, who had been campaigning for so long, some remarkable racers and steeplechasers were " discovered "—but the " discoveries " were kept dark by the regiments concerned for the confounding of rival units.

From Richon the A.M.R. moved to Rafa, where the men " went to school." An educational scheme was started, and it was typical of the force that the chief " dominie " was found in the ranks, in the person of Trooper J. Robertson, a school inspector in civil life, who had taught not a few of his comrades in bygone days. Trooper Robertson became Major Robertson in a single day —a unique instance of rapid promotion—and under his direction the brigade imbibed knowledge. It was a novel sight to see the classes sitting in groups on the sand in front of black-boards,

CHAPTER XLII.
Return Home.

All eyes were towards home, however, and some of the long service men were able to get away. Arrangements for embarkation were made for about the middle of March, but another duty turned up to delay the home-coming. Nationalist rioting, presaging revolt, broke out in the Delta area of Egypt, and the New Zealanders and some of the Australian Light Horse were rushed to Kantara, hurriedly equipped, and despatched to the infected area, over which martial law was proclaimed. Columns patrolled the whole region, each being responsible for a section of it. In this manner the rising was nipped in the bud. Some amusing incidents occurred through the military administering the law. Through rapid promotion some senior officers were very young in years, and while they were quite competent to order corporal punishment—the most efficacious form of persuasion in the land—they were hardly qualified to decide some of the matters brought before them. For instance, one youthful major of the A.M.R. was applied to by a woman to grant a divorce. Under the circumstances, this matrimonial trouble had to wait until the return of civil law, but it now seems rather a pity that the granting of divorce cannot be included among the achievements of the A.M.R.

A joke popular at the time was to the effect that in the year 1925, the War Office suddenly scratched its head and exclaimed, "Great Scott! The New Zealand Mounted Rifles have been forgotten. They are still in Egypt." All things come to an end, however, and at long last the brigade embarked on the Ulimaroa and Ellinga and sailed for home. The Ulimaroa, which had the A.M.R. on board, reached Auckland on August 8, 1919.

Commenting upon the return of the Regiment, the " New Zealand Herald " said:—" Without wishing to make invidious distinctions, citizens will feel that the officers and men who arrive by the Ulimaroa to-day have a special claim upon their gratitude. They are the first body of fit troops from Egypt to reach the port of Auckland, and they include many veterans who have been on foreign service for years, and who have fought on Gallipoli and chased the Turks from the Nile to Moab. No soldiers deserve a warmer welcome than these mounted men, who count their campaigning in years and their conquests by countries. They may rest assured that New Zealand appreciates all they have done and all they have endured. Bare justice compels the conclusion that the soldiers who served in Egypt and Palestine have had a peculiarly trying experience, unrelieved by many of the relaxations which softened the hardships of the infantry in France. For them there was little pleasant relief behind the lines, no leave in England and no contact with European civilisation and the great movements of national life in Britain. Theirs was the rigorous campaigning of the desert and the torment of the sands. Theirs also was the privilege of participating in some of the most brilliantly planned and executed movements of the whole war, and of sharing in victories which brought renown to British arms, and contributed not a little to the smashing of the hostile combination of Powers. At least they saw war in the form in which every soldier desires to see it, and they acquitted themselves gallantly and skilfully. Auckland honours herself in welcoming them."

In another column it was stated: "Those who were on board the Ulimaroa before she berthed, and saw the partings between the Auckland and southern men, distinguished a phase of comradeship not often observed among homecoming troops. Drafts of troops from England usually are composed of men drawn from many units, who may never have seen one another before, but yesterday's draft was composed of men whose friendships were cemented on Gallipoli or in Palestine. In these campaigns—the most arduous men ever undertook—men were entirely dependent upon one another. Although the differences in rank were honoured in the traditional way, the officers who survived and the men who remained were comrades in the truest sense. Officially they were distinct, but humanly they were friends who had shared their biscuit and 'bully,' whose water-bottles were common property, who thought of each other not as major this or trooper that, but who, in fact, were partners in a dangerous enterprise, the result of which might be annihilation or victory. Yesterday it was a common thing to see colonels and majors saying good-bye to 'Jim' and 'George' and 'Jack,' and there was no restraint or hesitation."

So parted a gallant company of friends. They had done their duty, and had left a record of service which may stand as an example for generations yet unborn.

The Horse—Comrade in Arms.

A trooper's first duty is to his horse, particularly in a campaign in a country when there is little water and sparse natural feed. Only by careful attention to the horses, often at the cost of much-needed rest and sleep, can a mounted regiment, in such a war as that of Sinai and Palestine, undertake the serious responsibilities placed upon it. The A.M.R. was well mounted, but only through unremitting care of the horses could it have accomplished what it did. The swift enveloping movements, which succeeded on a number of occasions, could not have been achieved if these hard-riding, resolute horsemen had not been horse lovers as well as responsible soldiers. The men regarded the horses, which endured so courageously, as comrades in arms, and treated them with self-sacrificing devotion.

Experience taught that a remount must have breeding, otherwise it cannot face the exactions of such a campaign. Further, it must not stand too high, 15 to 15.2 hands being an ideal height. A horse without breeding cannot finish a journey well, and if the soldier has to push his mount constantly he also finishes tired. Without breeding, a horse often has poor withers, in which case the fitting of saddlery becomes difficult, and that is a serious matter when rapid mounting and dismounting is required.

The patient endurance of toil and pain by the horses was constantly a source of wonder to the men, and made almost a human bond between horse and rider. An incident which indicates the wonderful endurance of the New Zealand horses and throws some light upon the close spirit of comradeship existing between the men and their steeds, occurred when the A.M.R. was holding an outpost line in the hills north-east of Beersheba, after the memorable attack on the Saba Redoubt and the subsequent retreat of the Turks along their whole line. For days the Aucklanders had been faced with tremendous difficulties in regard to water. None was to be found in this desolate wilderness. No one in the past had dug a well and planted a tree for shade. For three days the horses had had to be led back to Beersheba, some twelve miles distant, to be watered. The exigencies of the position made it impossible for one or two horses used for packing the Hotchkiss guns to be taken back, and, when the Camel Corps arrived to relieve the Regiment, one of these horses had not had a drink for 72 hours, and he had lain down to die. The Camel men had brought a supply of water with them, but though not over much, they gave the Regiment enough to issue one pint a man before they departed. While this issue was being made, the old pack horse, smelling the water, struggled to his feet and staggered up to the group. "Shout the old chap a pint," said a trooper, and immediately a pint of the precious liquid was poured into the lid of a "dixie" and held out to the animal, which sucked up every drop. He looked so grateful, that another pint was given him and, small though the quantity was, he began to look better immediately. He was then given some barley, and by the time the Regiment was ready to move he had taken a new lease of life, and he was able to make the march back to Beersheba. There he was sent to "hospital," and he lived to return to duty.

Among the finest horses in the Regiment were Colonel Mackesy's original mount and Lieutenant-Colonel McCarroll's "George," both of whom were killed by a bomb from an aeroplane in the Jordan Valley; "Darky," originally owned by the late Sergeant George Bagnall, one of the men who was transferred to the artillery before the desert campaign opened; Sergeant J. Jackson's "Waipa," Major Manner's "Greygown," and Lieutenant-Colonel McCarroll's "Bobrikoff." The last three horses not only endured the hard campaign, but won races against all-comers at meetings held after the signing of the armistice. These races assumed great importance among the mounted brigades and Imperial infantry, and the Divisional race meeting at Rafa was attended by thousands.

The parting of the men from their horses was pathetic. The animals were divided into three classes—those of no further use which were to be shot, those to be sold, and those to be retained by the army of occupation. The men knew that horses sold to Egyptians probably would end their days in miserable slavery, and efforts were made, often successful, to have animals transferred to the class for the kindly bullet. The horse nobly served the Empire in the war, and never better than in the desert campaign.

Roll of Honour.

Deaths.

Following is the list of the fatal casualties suffered by the Auckland Mounted Rifles Regiment. In the absence of a list issued officially by the Government, the information cannot be accepted in every case as absolutely definite and final, but from the information in possession of the Regiment, it is believed to be substantially accurate. In compiling the list, the following system has been followed:—The place where the death occurred follows the number, name, and rank of the soldier; then the date, then the cause where that information is known, and finally the place of burial, where definite information is available on that point. In the many cases where no reference is made to the place of burial, it does not mean that the graves of the men have not been located. It is believed that in a large number of cases the graves have been located, but the final place of interment has not yet been reported. The contractions used are fairly obvious. "K. in A." means "killed in action;" "D. of W." means "died of wounds;" "D. of D." means "died of disease," fever accounting for many deaths under this heading. Where the term "Deceased (C. of E.)" is used, definite information as to the cause of death has been lacking, Courts of Enquiry having found that death took place on or about the dates mentioned. From the nature of the Gallipoli campaign, in some actions of which units were cut down to mere handfuls of men, many of such enquiries were inevitable, although survivors had every reason for believing that missing comrades were killed in action during advances over broken and well-nigh impossible country. The list does not include the names of men who died after their discharge:—

GALLIPOLI.

13/963a **Alker, E.**, Tpr., Anzac, 8.8.15, deceased (C. of E.)
13/965a **Armstrong, W. P.**, Tpr., Anzac, 8.8.15, deceased (C. of E.)
13/970a **Bailey, A. H.**, L/Cpl., Anzac, 8.8.15, K. in A.
13/159 **Baillie, R. P.**, Tpr., Anzac, 8.8.15, deceased (C. of E.)
13/532 **Barnes, J.**, Cpl., Anzac, 8.8.15, K. in A.
13/294 **Bartrop, L. M. La C. F.**, Tpr., Anzac, 8.8.15, deceased (C. of E.)
13/22 **Bayliffe, R. E.**, Tpr., ship "Devanha," 29.8.15, D. of W., at sea.
13/885 **Beattie, N. J.**, Tpr., Anzac, 30.8.15, K. in A., not located.
13/2549 **Beaumont, D. G.**, Cpl., No. 3 General Hospital, 19.1.16, D. of D., Old Cairo Cemetery.
13/166 **Beaumont, O.**, Sgt., Anzac, 8.8.15, K. in A.
13/25 **Beer, V. C. S.**, S.S.M., 15th Gen., Alex., 8.9.15, D. of D., Chatley Military Cemetery.
13/386 **Benner, A. G.**, L/Cpl., ship "Neuralia," 16.8.15, D. of W. at sea, Chatley Military Cemetery.
13/13 **Best, F. Te K.**, Cpl., Anzac, 8.8.15, deceased (C. of E.)

13/664	**Bird, J. H.**, Tpr., Anzac, 8.8.15, K. in A.
13/232	**Birdsall, W. J.**, Tpr., Malta, 22.6.15, D. of W., Pieta Cem.
13/886	**Black, L.**, Tpr., Anzac, 28.8.15, deceased (C. of E.)
13/887	**Blackburn, S.**, Tpr., Anzac, 28.8.15, K. in A., Hill 60.
13/889	**Blaza, E. W.**, Tpr., Eng., 23.8.16, D. of D. fol. Wounds, Shakerston Cemetery.
13/281	**Bluck, A. C.**, Capt., Anzac, 22.5.15, K. in A., Walker's Ridge, No 1 Cemetery.
13/493	**Bowie, A. H.**, Tpr., Mudros, 8.9.15, D. of W., Partianos Cem.
13/980	**Boyd, A. C.**, Tpr., Anzac, 28.8.15, K. in A.
13/296	**Bradley, T.**, Tpr., Anzac, 19.5.15, K. in A., Walker's Ridge, No. 1.
13/304	**Briscoe W.**, Tpr., Anzac, 19.5.15, K. in A., Walker's Ridge, No. 1.
13/657a	**Brookfield, G. L. P.**, Lieut., Anzac, 8.8.15, K. in A.
13/671	**Brown, H. B.**, Tpr., Anzac, 19.5.15, K. in A., Walker's Ridge, No. 1.
13/23	**Bryan, C.**, Tpr., Anzac, 19.5.15, K. in A., Walker's Ridge, No. 1.
13/564	**Bull, C. F.**, Cpl., Anzac, 8.8.15, K. in A.
13/18	**Burrage, H. D.**, Tpr., Anzac, 27.7.15, K. in A., Ari Burnu Cemetery.
13/779	**Burrowes, E. F.**, Tpr., Anzac, 8.8.15, deceased (C. of E.)
13/567	**Cameron, J. S.**, Tpr., Malta, 17.8.15, D. of W., Pieta Cem.
13/549	**Catchpole, T. E.**, Tpr., Anzac, 8.8.15, K. in A.
13/319	**Chamberlain, C. S.**, Tpr., Heliopolis, 20.4.15, D. of D., Old Cairo Cemetery.
13/634	**Chapman, F.**, Major, Anzac, 8.8.15, K. in A.
13/892	**Clark, F.**, Tpr., Anzac, 28.8.15, deceased (C. of E.)
13/33	**Clark, T. L.**, Tpr., Anzac, 8.8.15, K. in A.
13/29	**Clarke, S. M.**, Tpr., Anzac, 6.8.15, K. in A.
13/983a	**Conolly, E. T.**, Tpr., Anzac, 8.8.15, deceased (C. of E.)
13/175	**Cook, A. D.**, Tpr., Anzac, 8.8.15, deceased (C. of E.)
13/678	**Corleison, W. A.**, Tpr., Anzac, 11.6.15, K. in A., Walker's Ridge, No 1.
13/896	**Corner, H. E.**, Tpr., 15th Gen., Alex., 7.9.15, D. of W., Chatley Military Cemetery.
13/318	**Cory, D. H.**, Tpr., Anzac, 8.8.15, K. in A.
13/652	**Cottingham, R. J.**, Tpr., Anzac, 2.7.15, D. of W., No. 2 Outpost Cemetery.
13/308	**Crickett, W.**, L/Cpl., Anzac, 19.5.15, D. of W., Ari Burnu Cemetery.
13/317	**Crosley, G. W.**, Tpr., Anzac, 6.8.15, K. in A.
12/26a	**Cuthbertson, J.**, Tpr., Anzac, 8.8.15, K. in A.
13/897	**Dawes, C. L.**, Tpr., Anzac, 28.8.15, K. in A.
13/989	**Day, A. C.**, Tpr., England, 20.9.16, D. of W., Wandsworth Cemetery.
13/2178	**Deeney, J.**, Tpr., 15th Gen. Hosp., 2.1.16, D. of D., Chatley Military Cemetery.
13/157	**Dimick, F. M.**, Sgt., Anzac, 8.8.15, K. in A.
13/320	**Dobson, C. R.**, Tpr., Anzac, 8.8.15, K. in A.
13/480	**Douglas, G. A.**, Tpr., Anzac, 8.8.15, K. in A.
13/323	**Douglas, J. J.**, Sgt., Anzac, 8.8.15, deceased (C. of E.)
13/680	**Downes, A. O.**, Tpr., Anzac, 27.8.15, K. in A.
13/179	**Durham, D.**, L/Cpl., Anzac, 8.8.15, K. in A.
13/327	**Fairs, C. S.**, Tpr., Malta, 5/10/15, D. of D., Pieta Cemetery.

13/903	**Falkner, V. A.**, Tpr., Anzac, 28.8.15, deceased (C. of E.)
13/185	**Farr, A. J.**, Tpr., Anzac, 8.8.15, K. in A.
13/796	**Farrelly, L.**, Tpr., Anzac, 28.8.15, K. in A. (assumed).
13/334	**Farrelly, O. L.**, Tpr., Anzac, 8.8.15, K. in A.
13/333	**Farrer, C.**, Sgt., Anzac, 19.5.15, K. in A., Walker's Ridge, No. 1.
13/556	**Fletcher, S.**, Tpr., Anzac, 8.8.15, deceased (C. of E.)
13/799	**Fletcher, W.**, Tpr., Anzac, 8.8.15, K. in A.
13/50	**Forrest, L. G.**, Tpr., Anzac, 8.8.15, K. in A.
13/335	**Fotheringham, J.**, Tpr., Anzac, 28.8.15, deceased (C. of E.)
13/172	**Francis, C. W.**, Tpr., Anzac, 8.8.15, deceased (C. of E.)
13/330	**Fryer, A. T.**, Tpr., Anzac, 8.8.15, deceased (C. of E.), not located.
13/61	**Gale, J. H.**, Tpr., Anzac, 19.5.15, K. in A., Walker's Ridge, No. 1.
13/341	**Gibson, N. P.**, Tpr., Anzac, 28.8.15, deceased (C. of E.)
13/188	**Gibson, W. E.**, Tpr., Anzac, 27.7.15, K. in A.
13/805	**Gleeson, R. L.**, Tpr., Anzac, 28.8.15, deceased (C. of E.)
13/60	**Gillard, F.**, L/Cpl., Anzac, 8.8.15, K. in A.
13/907	**Godfrey, H. A.**, Tpr., Anzac, 28.8.15, deceased (C. of E.)
13/347	**Goodwin, D. P.**, Tpr., Anzac, 29.8.15, K. in A. (assumed).
13/274	**Gould, K.**, Tpr., Anzac, 19.5.15, K. in A., Walker's Ridge, No. 1.
13/687	**Gowland, R.**, Tpr., Constantinople, 28.8.15, D. of D.
13/688	**Grant, D.**, Tpr., Anzac, 8.8.15, K. in A.
13/1034	**Greenwood, G. C.**, Tpr., Anzac, 2.12.15, believed D. of W.
13/487	**Hacker, A.**, Tpr., Anzac, 19.5.15, K. in A., Walker's Ridge, No. 1.
13/356	**Haddock, W.**, Tpr., Anzac, 17.6.15, K. in A., Ari Burnu.
13/69	**Hannah, A.**, Tpr., Anzac, 1.7.15, K. in A., Canterbury Cem.
13/909	**Harmer, W. J.**, Tpr., Anzac, 28.8.15, deceased (C. of E.)
13/66	**Harrison, C. B.**, Tpr., Anzac, 8.8.15, deceased (C. of E.)
13/352	**Harrison, R.**, Cpl., Anzac, 28.8.15, deceased (C. of E.)
13/548	**Harrison, H. H.**, Tpr., Anzac, 12.7.15, K. in A., Ari Burnu.
13/812	**Haydon, F. R.**, Tpr., Anzac, 8.8.15, deceased (C. of E.)
13/190	**Hayward, J. H.**, Tpr., Anzac, 8.8.15, K. in A.
13/277	**Henderson, J.**, Lieut., Anzac, 8.8.15, K. in A., (C. of E.)
13/691	**Hewitt, E.**, Tpr., Anzac, 28.8.15, deceased (C. of E.)
13/914	**Hickman, T. H. T.**, Tpr., Anzac, 28.8.15, deceased (C. of E.)
13/354	**Hill, G. A.**, Sgt., Anzac, 8.8.15, K. in A.
13/1004a	**Hill, R. M.**, Tpr., Anzac, 19.5.15, K. in A., Walker's Ridge, No. 1.
13/1007a	**Holmes, W. J.**, Tpr., Anzac, 8.8.15, K. in A. (assumed).
13/881	**Hooper, F. J.**, Tpr., Anzac, 24.8.15, D. of W.
13/694	**Hunter, R.**, Tpr., Anzac, 28/8/15, K. in A.
13/372	**Jackson, G. C.**, Tpr., Anzac, 5.6.15, D. of W., Ari Burnu.
13/278	**James, C.**, Lieut., Anzac, 19.5.15, K. in A., Walker's Ridge, No. 1.
13/2208	**Johnson, C. B. N.**, Tpr., N.Z. Cairo Gen. Hosp., 27.1.16, D. of D., Old Cairo Cemetery.
13/821	**Johnston, G. J.**, Tpr., Hosp. Ship " Andania," 13.8.15, D. of D., at sea.
13/557	**Jones, H. C.**, Tpr., Anzac, 8.8.15, believed dead.
13/700	**Jones, J.**, Tpr., Anzac, 8.8.15, K. in A.
13/371	**Jones, O. S.**, Tpr., Hosp. Ship " Sicilia," 30.6.15, D. of W., at sea.

13/79	Jones, R. R., Tpr., Anzac, 27-28.8.15, K. in A. (assumed).
13/369	Jurd, E. A., 2nd Lieut., Anzac, 8-9.8.15, K. in A. (C. of E.).
13/85	Kearney, W. C., Sgt., Hosp. Ship " Gascon," 9.8.15, D. of W., at sea.
13/702	Kemp, J. A., Tpr., Gibraltar, 17.9.15, D. of W., Church of England Cemetery, Gibraltar.
13/376	Kent, A. W., Tpr., Anzac, 8.8.15, K. in A.
13/876	Kettle, D. F., 2nd Lieut., Anzac, 28.8.15, K. in A.
13/981	King, J., Tpr., Anzac, 28.8.15, K. in A.
13/201	Lamb, E. T., Tpr., Anzac, 27-28.8.15, K. in A.
13/385	Linwood, J., Tpr., Anzac, 23.5.15, D. of W., Ari Burnu.
13/707	Lloyd, G., Tpr., Anzac, 8.8.15, K. in A.
13/155	Logan, P., Lieut., Ship " Galeka," 22.5.15, D. of W. at sea.
13/926	Low, J. C., Tpr., Anzac, 30.8.15, D. of W., Embarkation Pier.
13/708	Lucas, F. W., Tpr., Anzac, 8.8.15, K. in A.
13/591	Lyon, B., Tpr., Anzac, 31.5.15, D. of W., Ari Burnu.
13/502	McCarthy, E., Tpr., Anzac, 8.8.15, deceased (C. of E.).
13/205	McKay, A. D., Tpr., Anzac, 8.8.15, K. in A.
13/250	McKay, A. P., Sgt., Anzac, 8.8.15, K. in A.
13/715	McKenzie, G. G., Tpr., Anzac, 8.8.15, K. in A.
13/409	Mackessack, J., Tpr., Anzac, 6.8.15, K. in A.
13/1042a	McKinnon, J., Tpr., Anzac, 8.8.15, deceased (C. of E.)
13/209	McLeod, A. D., Tpr., Anzac, 8.8.15, deceased (C. of E.)
13/520	McLeod, N. K., Tpr., Anzac, 12.6.15, K. in A., Walker's Ridge, No. 1.
13/108	McMillan, N., Tpr., Anzac, 6.8.15, K. in A., No. 2 Outpost C.
13/574	McNaughton, J., Tpr., Anzac, 8.8.15, K. in A.
13/1046a	McNaul, R., Tpr., 1st Aust. G. Hosp., Heliopolis, 1.9.15, D. of W., Old Cairo Cemetery.
13/210	McNeish, G. F., Sgt., Anzac, 8.8.15, K. in A.
13/254	Mackesy, H. F. E., 2nd Lieut., Anzac, 7.8.15, K. in A.
13/423	Marr, J., S.S.M., Anzac, 18.5.15, K. in A., Walker's Ridge, No. 1.
13/389	Marsh, F. G., Tpr., Anzac, 8.8.15, K. in A.
13/558	Marshall, J., Tpr., Ship " Galeka," 25.5.15, D. of W., at sea.
13/95	Metcalfe, J. H., Tpr., Anzac, 8.8.15, deceased (C. of E.)
13/279	Milliken, M. J., Lieut., Anzac, 8.8.15, D. of W.
13/238b	Milling, C. C., Tpr., Anzac, 28.8.15, deceased (C. of E.)
13/555	Moloney, J. E., Sgt., Anzac, 8.8.15, K. in A.
13/410	Moody, W., Tpr., Anzac, 19.5.15, K. in A., Walker's Ridge, No. 1.
13/217	Morgan, M., Tpr., Hosp. Ship " Gascon," 1.6.15, D. of W., at sea.
13/187b	Mossman, J. D., Tpr., Anzac, 19.5.15, K. in A., Walker's Ridge, No. 1.
13/221	Muldrock, W. H., Tpr., Anzac, 29.8.15, D. of W.
13/412	Munn, C. J. V., Tpr., Hosp. Ship " Sicilia," 10.6.15, D. of W., at sea.
13/559	Munro, L. G., Sgt., Anzac, 8.8.15, K. in A.
13/106	Munro, R. W., Tpr., Anzac, 19.5.15, K. in A., Walker's Ridge, No 1.
13/712	Musk, G. C., Tpr., Anzac, 8.8.15, K. in A.
13/111	Nicholas, S. M., Tpr., Anzac, 8.8.15, K. in A.
13/93	Nolan, D. L., Tpr., Anzac, 8.9.15, K. in A.
13/110	Northcroft, H. C., L/Cpl., Anzac, 19.5.15, K. in A., Walker's Ridge, No. 1.
13/537	Olen, V. A., Tpr., Anzac, 8.8.15, K. in A.
13/579	Olsen, N., Tpr., Anzac, 8.8.15, K. in A.

13/936	**O'Sullivan, J. D.**, Tpr., Hosp. Ship "Maheno," 2.9.15, D. of W., at sea.
13/720	**Otter, G. W. W.**, Sgt., Anzac, 28.8.15, K. in A., Hill 60.
13/122	**Page, G. A.**, Tpr., Anzac, 19.5.15, K. in A., Canterbury Cem.
13/117	**Palmer, P. G.**, Tpr., Anzac, 8.8.15, deceased (C. of E.)
13/561	**Paton, J. S.**, Tpr., Anzac, 8.8.15, K. in A.
11/1050a	**Paulsen, H. W.**, Tpr., Anzac, 8.8.15, deceased (C. of E.)
13/726	**Penman, E. J.**, Tpr., Anzac, 19.5.15, K. in A., Walker's Ridge, No. 1.
13/728	**Phillips, T. W.**, Tpr., No. 3 Hosp., Walton, 18.10.15, pneum. foll. W., Walton-on-Thames Cemetery.
13/729	**Picard, C.**, Tpr., 8.8.15, K. in A.
13/941	**Poole, M.**, Tpr., Anzac, 28.8.15, deceased (C. of E.)
13/730	**Price, J. P.**, Tpr., Anzac, 8.8.15, K. in A.
13/130	**Redfern, F. S.**, Tpr., Anzac, 8.8.15, K. in A.
13/2243	**Richardson, W. R.**, Cpl., Anzac, 5.12.15, K. in A., Embarkation Pier Cemetery.
13/509	**Richmond, R. A.**, Tpr., Anzac, 8.8.15, deceased (C. of E.)
13/439	**Riddell, J.**, L/Cpl., Hosp. Ship "Gloucester Castle," 5.8.15, D. of W., at sea.
13/438	**Rollett, R. R. C.**, Sgt., Hosp. Ship "Devanha," 29.8.15, D. of W., at sea.
13/437	**Rose, J. H.**, Cpl., Anzac, 27-28.8.15, K. in A.
13/194	**Ross, J. A.**, Cpl., Anzac, 28.11.15, K. in A., 7th Field Ambulance Cemetery.
13/443	**Sampson, W. B.**, Tpr., Anzac, 20.7.15, K. in A., Ari Burnu.
13/1056a	**Scott, J. E.**, Tpr., Hosp. Ship "Devanha," 4.9.15, D. of W., Pieta Cemetery, Malta.
13/954	**Simpkins, T.**, Tpr., Hosp. Ship "Gloucester Castle," 1.9.15, D. of W., at sea.
13/442	**Simpson, A. C.**, Tpr., Hosp. Ship "Soudan," 22.5.15, D. of W., at sea.
13/447	**Spurr, C. J.**, Tpr., Anzac, 8.8.15, deceased (C. of E.).
13/139	**Stockley, F. H.**, Cpl., Anzac, 22.7.15, K. in A., Ari Burnu.
13/860	**Strong, E. H.**, Tpr., Mudros, 25.9.15, D. of D., Portianos Cem.
13/545	**Sullivan, F. A.**, Tpr., Anzac, 19.5.15, K. in A., Walker's Ridge, No. 1
13/571	**Swinton, J. H.**, L/Cpl., Anzac, 8.8.15, K. in A.
13/1069a	**Tebbutt, A.**, Tpr., Anzac, 27-28.8.15, K. in A.
13/464	**Terry, F. W.**, Cpl., Anzac, 8.8.15, K. in A.
13/465	**Thomas, A. F.**, Tpr., Anzac, 6.8.15, dead, cause not decided, Embarkation Pier Cemetery.
13/144	**Thompson, G. T.**, Sgt., Anzac, 7.8.15, K. in A.
13/510	**Thompson, J.**, Tpr., Anzac, 19.5.15, K. in A., Canterbury C.
13/147	**Trimble, W.**, Tpr., Anzac, 8.8.15, deceased (C. of E.)
13/466	**Turton, L. C.**, Tpr., Malta, 25.8.15, D. of W., Pieta Cem., Malta.
13/470	**Verner, A.**, Tpr., Anzac, 26.6.15, K. in A., Ari Burnu.
13/47	**Watts, H. H.**, Sgt., Anzac, 19.5.15, K. in A., Walker's Ridge, No. 1.
13/428	**Weir, F. J.**, Lieut., Anzac, 2.6.15, K. in A., Walker's Ridge, No. 1.
13/244	**Wellington, T. H.**, Sgt., Anzac, 8.8.15, K. in A.
13/1172	**Wheatley, P.**, Tpr., Anzac, 28.8.15, deceased (C. of E.)
11/617	**Wheatley, M. L.**, Tpr., 7.8.15, K. in A., unlocated.
13/750	**Whitcombe, G. A.**, Tpr., Anzac, 8.8.15, K in A.
13/476	**White, A. H.**, Tpr., Anzac, 19.5.15, K. in A., Walker's Ridge, No. 1.

13/243	**Wild, J.**, Tpr., Anzac, 8.8.15, deceased (C. of E.)
13/988	**Wilkinson, A. E.**, Capt., Hosp. Ship "Formosa," 28.8.15, D. of W., at sea.
13/258	**Williams, H. L.**, Tpr., Anzac, 19.5.15, K. in A., Walker's Ridge, No. 1
13/478	**Willis, P. A.**, Tpr., Hosp. Ship "Delta," 10.8.15, D. of W., at sea.
13/481	**Willoughby, H.**, Tpr., Anzac, 18.6.15, D. of W.
13/475	**Wilson, L.**, Tpr., Anzac, 8.8.15, deceased (C. of E.)
13/154	**Wilson, R. D.**, Sgt., Hosp. Ship "Sicilia," 9.8.15, D. of W., at sea.
13/758	**Winder, H. E.**, Lieut., Anzac, 8.8.15, K. in A.
13/472	**Woodward, G. F.**, L/Cpl., Anzac, 19.5.15, K. in A., Walker's Ridge, No. 1.
13/754	**Wright, A. F.**, Tpr., Anzac, 28.8.15, K. in A.
13/977	**Wright, W. J.**, Tpr., Anzac, 24.8.15, K. in A.
13/219	**Wynter, R. C.**, Tpr., Anzac, 8.8.15, K. in A.

SINAI AND PALESTINE.

13/283	**Ashton, S. C.**, Capt., Palestine, 31.10.17, K. in A., Beersheba Cemetery.
13/884	**Astridge, N. W.**, Tpr., Canal Zone, 12.8.16, K. in A., unlocated.
16/058	**Atkinson, B. E.**, Tpr., 75th Cas. Clearing Station, Palestine, 8.11.17, D. of W., Beersheba Cemetery.
13/1004	**Barrett, W.** (M.M.), Tpr., Palestine, 31.3.18, D. of W., unlocated.
13/2295	**Bates, A. T.**, Tpr., Canal Zone, 9.8.16, K. in A., Kantara Mil. Cemetery.
13/2296	**Bates, W. H.**, Tpr., 74th C.C.S., Palestine, 2.8.17, D. of D., El Arish Cemetery.
16/065	**Birnie, A.**, Tpr., Palestine, 14.11.17, D. of W., Ramleh Cemetery.
35730	**Black, C.**, Tpr., 66th C.C.S., Palestine, 18.11.17, D. of W., Dier-el-Belah Mil. Cemetery.
13/2418	**Blong, C.**, Tpr., Palestine, 31.10.17, K. in A., Beersheba Cemetery.
58369	**Boles, K.**, Tpr., 47th Stat. Hosp., 16.10.18, D. of W. and malaria, Gaza Mil. Cemetery.
56216	**Bowden, J. S.**, Tpr., 34th C.C.H., 31.10.18, D. of D., Jerusalem Mil. Cemetery.
13/2414	**Bowen, C. C.**, Tpr., Turkey, 6.1.17, D. while prisoner of war, no burial report.
31062	**Brake, E. V.**, Tpr., Amman, 2.10.18, deceased, unlocated.
13/3118	**Bright, J. D.**, Tpr., 76th C.C.S., 26.10.18, D. of D., Ramleh Cemetery.
13/2163	**Browne, J.**, Tpr., Palestine, 19.4.17, K. in A., unlocated.
57836	**Brown-Ross, W.**, Tpr., 78th Gen. Hosp., 24.10.18, D. of D., Dier-el-Belah Cemetery.
57546	**Bruce, C. D.**, Tpr., 24th Stat. Hosp., Kantara, 14.10.18, D. of D., Kantara Mil. Cemetery.
13/2536	**Bruce, R. A.**, L/Cpl., Palestine, 14.11.17, K. in A., Ramleh Cemetery.

13/2305	**Burrell, J.**, L/Cpl., Anzac Receiving Station, 7.10.18, D. of D., Jerusalem Mil. Cemetery.
31065	**Burrow, R. H.**, Tpr., Palestine, 31.10.17, D. of W., Beersheba Cemetery.
13/1013	**Campbell, J. B.**, L/Sgt., 44th St. Hosp., 21.10.18, D. of D., Kantara Mil. Cemetery.
13/3011	**Campbell, W. A.**, Tpr., 66th C.C.S., 1.4.18, D. of W., Mt. Scopus New Cemetery.
13/315	**Carter, A. C.**, T/Sgt., Palestine, 14.11.17, K. in A., Ramleh Cemetery.
13/2022	**Carter, A. J.**, Tpr., 26th C.C.S., 21.10.18, D. of D., Ramleh Cemetery.
18339	**Clarke, J.**, Tpr., 71st Gen. Hosp., Cairo, 2.11.18, D. of D., Old Cairo Cemetery.
13/991	**Coates, W. H.**, Lieut., in the field, 22.7.17, K. in A. (C. of E.), unlocated.
11/1533	**Coutts, E.**, Palestine, 14.11.17, K. in A., Ramleh Cemetery.
31069	**Craig, J. H.**, Cpl., Govt. Fever Hosp., Abbassia, 10.4.19, D. of D., Old Cairo Cemetery.
13/786	**Cranston, M. J.**, Cpl., Palestine, 25.11.17, K in A., Ramleh Cemetery.
13/2031	**Cross, A. J.**, Tpr., Rafa, 9.1.17, K. in A., El Arish Cemetery.
24877	**Cunningham, J.**, Tpr., Rafa, 9.1.17, D. of W. (C. of E.), El Arish Cemetery.
13/2981	**Dale-Taylor, T.**, 2nd Lieut., Cairo, 15.8.16, D. of W., Old Cairo Cemetery.
13/578	**Delaney, A.**, Sgt., 27th Gen. Hosp., Cairo, 17.8.16, D. of W., Old Cairo Cemetery.
43170	**Dennis, F.**, Tpr., Palestine, 31.10.17, K. in A., Beersheba Cemetery.
13/2280	**Duffey, A.**, Cpl., 34th C.C.H., Jerusalem, 12.10.18, D. of D., Jerusalem Mil. Cemetery.
13/2429	**Duncan, G.**, Tpr., Palestine, 14.11.17, K. in A., Ramleh Cemetery.
13/795	**Emmerson, S. L.** (D.C.M.), Sgt., 34th C.C.S., Palestine, 19.10.18, D. of D., Jerusalem Mil. Cemetery.
13/2431	**Ericksen, H. C.**, Tpr., 74th C.C.S., Palestine, 22.11.17, D. of W., Dier-el-Belah Cemetery.
13/605	**Fitton, C. R.**, L/Sgt., 2/4, London Field Ambulance, 2.4.18, D. of W., Jerusalem Mil. Cemetery.
62201	**Fletcher, T. H.**, Tpr., Palestine, 25.9.18, K. in A., Damascus West Mil., No. 2.
13/2102	**Foote, W. H.**, Tpr., 26th C.C.S., 11.4.18, D. of W., Ramleh Cemetery.
13/2269	**Francis, G.**, Tpr., Palestine, 22.9.18, K. in A., unlocated.
9/419	**Fraser, E.**, Tpr., Palestine, 14.11.17, K. in A., Ramleh Cemetery.
36136	**Freckingham, W.**, Tpr., 2nd A.S. Hosp., 25.11.18, D. of D., Ismailia Cemetery.
13/2191	**Gamble, D. H.**, W.O., II., Canal Zone, 9.8.16, K. in A., Kantara Cemetery.
17579	**Gardner, C.**, Tpr., Palestine, 22.9.18, K. in A., unlocated.
13/2320	**Gibson, G. W.**, Tpr., Canal Zone, 9.8.16, K. in A., Kantara Cemetery.
36056	**Gibson, W. B.**, Tpr., Palestine, 30.3.18, K. in A., unlocated.
7/958	**Gibson, W. W.**, Cpl., 27th Gen. Hosp., Abbassia, 2.12.17, D. of W., Old Cairo Cemetery.

35881	**Gillott, W.,** Tpr., 24th Stat., Kantara, 22.11.17, D. of W., Kantara Cemetery.	
13/2972	**Godkin, A. G. W.,** Tpr., No. 1 Aus. Stat., 12.3.16, D. of D., Ismailia Cemetery.	
13/908	**Grant, E.,** Tpr., Palestine, 1.4.18, K. in A., unlocated.	
13/1035	**Gulbransen, C. W.,** Tpr., 31st Gen. Hosp., Alexandria, 22.1.17, D. of D., Port Said Cemetery.	
16883	**Hamilton, J. H.,** Tpr., 27th Gen. Hosp., Abbassia, 19.10.18, D. of D., Old Cairo Cemetery.	
13/911	**Harney, J. A.,** Tpr., Turkey, 19.11.16, D. of D. while prisoner of war, no burial report.	
13/2201	**Harris, E. J.,** Tpr., Palestine, 14.11.17, K. in A., Ramleh Cemetery.	
24861	**Harris, W. T.,** Tpr., Rafa, 9.1.17, K. in A., El Arish Cemetery.	
13/3161	**Haswell, H. G.,** Tpr., Palestine, 14.11.17, K. in A., Ramleh Cemetery.	
17593	**Hawkins, W. H.,** Tpr., Palestine, 31.10.17, K. in A., Beersheba Cemetery.	
7/965	**Henderson, H. F.,** Tpr., 27th Gen. Hosp., Abbassia, 20.10.18, D. of D., Old Cairo Cemetery.	
11/1559	**Hepworth, W. C.,** Tpr., 2nd Auckland Stat. Hosp., Moascar, 21.9.18, D. of D., Ismailia Cemetery.	
58454	**Hill, H. L. G.,** Tpr., 34th C.C.S., 17.10.18, D. of D., Mt. Scopus New Cemetery.	
13/2336	**Hollis, C.,** Tpr., Palestine, 14.11.17, K. in A., Ramleh Cemetery.	
16405	**Huband, R. C.,** Tpr., Palestine, 20.2.18, K. in A., unlocated.	
13/3037	**Hueston, J. R.,** Tpr., Rafa, 9.1.17, K. in A., El Arish Cemetery.	
13/368	**Johns, W. H.,** Lieut., Palestine, 31.10.17, K. in A., Beersheba Cemetery.	
13/152	**Johnson, O. P.,** Capt., Canal Zone, 9.8.16, K. in A., unlocated.	
13/3039	**Jones, S. T.,** Tpr., Transport "Ulysses," 18.2.18, D. of D. at sea.	
11/1569	**Kay, J. A.,** Sgt., Palestine, 14.11.17, K. in A., Ramleh Cemetery.	
13/2210	**Kendall, T.,** Tpr., Palestine, 25.11.17, K in A., Ramleh Cemetery.	
13/3094	**Kilmister, W. R.,** Tpr., Canal Zone, 4.8.16, K. in A., unlocated.	
16307	**King, G. L.,** 2nd Lieut., Palestine, 15.11.17, D. of W., Ramleh Cemetery.	
12679	**Lowe, L. H.,** Tpr., 1st L.H. Field Ambulance, 15.11.17, D. of W., Ramleh Cemetery.	
13/1062	**Lunnon, W. J.,** Tpr., Palestine, 16.11.17, D. of W., Ramleh Cemetery.	
13/1025a	**Lyes, H. C.,** Tpr., Palestine, 19.4.17, K. in A., unlocated.	
12558	**McCarthy, F. J.,** Tpr., Canal Zone, 9.8.16, K. in A., Kantara Cemetery.	
71042	**McCaw, D. V.,** Tpr., 34th C.C.H., 18.10.18, D. of D., Jerusalem Mil. Cemetery.	
35867	**McIndoe, N. C.,** Tpr., 2nd L.H. Field Ambulance, 28.3.18, D. of W., Damascus West Mil. Cemetery, No. 2.	

11/1572 **McLarin, F. W.**, Tpr., 44th St. Hosp., Kantara, 21.10.18, D. of D., Kantara Cemetery.
13/930 **McLeod, C. D.**, Tpr., Angora, Turkey, 4.1.17, D. of D. while prisoner of war in Turkey.
11/1044 **McNamara, H. C.**, Sgt., Rafa, 9.1.17, D. of W., El Arish Cemetery.
13/2608 **McRae, M. I.**, Tpr., Palestine, 30.3.18, K. in A., Damascus West Mil. Cemetery, No. 2.
13/1066 **Mahoney, E. L. G.**, Tpr., Canal Zone, 9.8.16, K. in A., Kantara Cemetery.
36118 **Mannix, P.**, Tpr., Palestine, 5.11.17, K. in A., unlocated.
13/2843 **Mansel, H. P.**, Tpr., 34th C.C.H., 23.10.18, D. of D., Jerusalem Mil. Cemetery.
13/404 **Martin, A. M.**, 2nd Lieut., Nasrieh Hosp., 10.9.16, D. of W., Old Cairo Cemetery.
13/2573 **Miller, R. T.**, Tpr., Palestine, 31.10.17, D. of W., Beersheba Cemetery.
58396 **Moon, K. A.**, Tpr., 26th C.C.S., 13.10.18, D. of D., Ramleh Cemetery.
74111 **Morgan, L. M.**, Tpr., 47th St. Hosp., Gaza, 24.10.18, D. of D., Gaza Mil. Cemetery.
13/2232 **Murray, V. O.**, Tpr., 27th Gen. Hosp., 28.5.18, D. of W., Old Cairo Cemetery.
13/506 **Nowland, W.**, Sgt., N.Z. Mounted Field Ambulance, 22.9.18, D. of W., unlocated.
11/353 **Oberhuber, O.**, Tpr. and Cadet, attached R.A.F., Ismailia, 15.11.18, accidentally killed flying, Ismailia Cemetery.
57594 **O'Carroll, F.**, Tpr., 34th C.C.S., 11.10.18, D. of D., Jerusalem Mil. Cemetery.
13/2235 **Oxenham, F. G.**, Tpr., Palestine, 14.11.17, K. in A., Ramleh Cemetery.
13/1082 **Parry, W. N. G.**, Tpr., Canal Zone, 9.8.16, K. in A., Kantara Cemetery.
16433 **Pattie, R. S.**, Tpr., Palestine, 14.11.17, K. in A., Ramleh Cemetery.
13/1171 **Payne, C. D.**, Tpr., Palestine, 14.11.17, K. in A., Ramleh Cemetery.
16044 **Perry, E. H.**, Tpr., Rafa, 9.1.17, K. in A., Kantara Cemetery.
50038 **Pike, E. N.**, Tpr., Palestine, 30.4.18, K. in A., unlocated.
13/1084 **Pulman, W. V.**, Tpr., Palestine, 17.11.17, D. of W., Ramleh Cemetery.
13/2616 **Quinney, C.**, Tpr., Canal Zone, 11.8.16, D. of W., Kantara Cemetery.
13/942 **Quintal, D. L.**, Tpr., Turkey, 20.12.16, D. of D. while prisoner of war, no burial report.
17534 **Richardson, J. W.**, Tpr., Palestine, 22.9.18, K. in A., unlocated.
13/2245 **Roberts, W. C.**, Tpr., Palestine, 14.11.17, K. in A., Ramleh Cemetery.
13/432 **Rope, C. M.**, Cpl., Rafa, 9.1.17, D. of W., El Arish Cemetery.
13/436 **Ryan, R.**, Tpr., Canal Zone, 9.8.16, K. in A., Kantara Cemetery.
13/949 **Saunders, J. H.**, Tpr., Angora, 26.2.17, died while prisoner of war in Turkey.
35382 **Scott, A. E. L.**, Tpr., Palestine, 27.3.18, K. in A., Damascus West Mil. Cemetery.

13/1093	**Shanahan, R.**, Cpl., 24th St. Hosp., 20.10.18, D. of D., Kantara Cemetery.	
24935	**Slater, A. J. S.**, Tpr., 27th Gen. Hosp., Abbassia, 24.10.18, D. of D., Old Cairo Cemetery.	
13/2485	**Stanbury, H.**, Tpr., 1st L.H. Field Ambulance, Palestine, 14.11.17, D. of W., Ramleh Cemetery.	
13/2487	**Steel, G.**, Cpl., England, 20.2.18, D. of W., Gravesend Cemetery.	
16/514	**Stewart, J. D.**, Lieut., Palestine, 14.11.17, K. in A., Ramleh Cemetery.	
13/1065a	**Stratford, R. C.**, Tpr., Palestine, 30.3.18, D. of W., unlocated.	
13/2084	**Sutherland, H. C.**, Tpr., Canal Zone, 9.8.16, K. in A., Kantara Cemetery.	
13/2494	**Sutherland, W. J.**, Cpl., Palestine, 30.3.18, K. in A., unlocated.	
1/185	**Tait, K. J.** (M.C.), Capt., Palestine, 23.3.18, K. in A., unlocated.	
13/2086	**Thompson, W. W.**, Tpr., Palestine, 25.11.17, K. in A., Ramleh Cemetery.	
13/2497	**Turnbull, T.**, Tpr., Rafa, 9.1.17, D. of W., no burial report.	
9/662	**Twisleton, F. M.** (M.C.), Major, Palestine, 15.11.17, D. of W., Ramleh Cemetery.	
3/2629	**Vaile, W. R.**, Tpr., Rafa, 10.7.17, drowned, El Arish Cemetery.	
13/562	**Vipond, M.**, Sgt., Canal Zone, 9.8.16, K. in A., Kantara Cemetery.	
35866	**Walker, G.**, Tpr., N.Z. Mounted Field Ambulance, Palestine, 15.11.17, D. of W., Ramleh Cemetery.	
13/174	**Wallace, L.**, Sgt., Canal Zone, 7.8.16, D. of W., Kantara Cemetery.	
13/1106	**Waters, M. L.**, Sgt., Canal Zone, 4.8.16, K. in A., unlocated.	
13/867	**Welsh, F. D.**, Tpr., N.Z. Mounted Field Ambulance, 30.3.18, D. of W., Damascus West Mil. Cemetery. No. 2.	
17548	**West, J.**, Tpr., Anzac Receiving Station, 24.9.18, D. of W., Jerusalem Mil. Cemetery.	
12887	**White, P. G.**, Tpr., Palestine, 31.10.17, K. in A., Beersheba Cemetery.	
13/1114	**Wood, A. O.**, Tpr., Canal Zone, 9.8.16, K. in A., Kantara Cemetery.	
13/581	**Wood, C.**, L/Sgt., 31st Gen. Hosp., Port Said, 19.8.16, D. of D., Port Said Cemetery.	
50436	**Wright, C. W.**, Tpr., Cit. Mil. Hosp., 29.10.18, D. of D., Old Cairo Cemetery.	

DIED, OTHER CAUSES.

7/9845	**Clarke, H. W.**, Tpr., 19.12.18, lost at sea en route to New Zealand.	
13/927	**Magnusson, J. W.**, Tpr., 4.5.17, drowned through vessel being torpedoed en route to England.	

Wounded.

Following is the list of wounded, the rank given being that held by the soldier at the time:—

GALLIPOLI.

13/280	Abbot, G. M., Lieut., 6.7.15.		13/303	Bonnington, H., Tpr., 6.8.15.
13/285	Abbot, M. B., Tpr., 28.8.15 and 24.11.15.		13/168	Booth, A. C., Tpr., 8.8.15.
13/882	Acklom, H. R. N., Tpr., 28.8.15 and 24.11.15.		13/20	Brady, W., Tpr., 14.6.15.
13/658	Aldrich, R. J. F., Tpr., 27.5.15 and -.8.15.		13/069	Bradley, W., Tpr., 6.8.15.
13/264	Allsopp, F., Sgt., 8.8.15.		13/300	Breingan, P. E., Tpr., 28.8.15.
13/601	Anderson, E. J., Tpr., 27.8.15.		13/17	Brinsley, G. F., 2nd Lieut., 27-28.8.15.
13/284	Anderson, R. A., Tpr., 11.8.15.		13/14	Brooke, M. A., Tpr., 15.6.15.
13/770	Anderson, W., Tpr., 8.8.15.		13/248	Callaghan, W. H., Tpr., 2.8.15.
13/2275	Appelbe, W. J., Tpr., 2.12.15.		13/543	Cargill, G. D., Tpr., 19.5.15 and 7.8.15.
13/986	Appleton, F. A., Tpr., 28.8.15.		13/310	Carter, W. R., Sgt., 21.5.15 and 8.8.15.
13/5	Armstrong, L. J., Tpr., 29.5.15.		13/673	Catchpole, T. E., Tpr., 6.8.15.
13/282	Ashley, R. A. T., Tpr., 6.8.15.		13/535	Champney, N. D., Tpr., 8.8.15.
13/271	Bagnall, G. S., Sgt., 6.8.15, wounded later in France, and was paralysed, and died subsequently in N.Z.		13/305	Chater, E. W., Sgt., 6.8.15.
			13/31	Cheetham, E. W., Lieut., 6.8.15.
			13/1119	Clark, W. G., Tpr., 2.12.15.
13/542	Balle, J. T., Tpr., 13.8.15.		13/893	Coates, G. P., Cpl., 27-28.8.15.
13/662	Basley, C. O., Tpr., 30.5.15.		13/675	Coldstream, L. M., Tpr., 6.8.15.
13/25	Beer, V. C. S., S.S.M., 22.5.15.		13/37	Collins, H. J., Tpr., 27.8.15.
13/386	Benner, A. G., L/Cpl., 12.8.15.		13/27	Collins, S., Tpr., 13.8.15.
13/775	Bigg-Wither, L. F., Tpr., 6.8.15.		13/536	Connors, W. J., Tpr., 8.8.15.
13/777	Bishop, L. G., Tpr., 8-9.8.15.		13/36	Connoly, W., Tpr., 19.5.15
13/19	Bishop, K., Sgt., 27.6.15.		13/307	Coubrough, N., Sgt., 20.5.15.
13/878	Blackie, A. S., Tpr., 28.8.15.		13/2028	Couldrey, A., Tpr., 30.11.15.
13/2161	Blake, D., Tpr., 20.11.15.		13/786	Cranston, M. J., Tpr., 18.7.15.
13/665	Blennerhassett, B., L/Cpl., 6.8.15.		13/40	Cullen, E. J., Sgt., 12.7.15.
13/666	Blennerhassett, N., Cpl., 9.8.15.		13/316	Culleton, J., Tpr., 6.8.15.
13/291	Bluett, R., Tpr., 12.7.15.		13/986a	Cunningham, D. J., Tpr., 6.8.15.
13/288	Bond, T. H., Cpl., 8.8.15.		13/34	Cutfield, G., Tpr., 24.8.15.

13/267	Dalziel, G. S., Tpr., 8.8.15.	13/873	Furniss, J., Tpr., 8.8.15.
13/41	Dawson, J., Tpr., 8.8.15.	13/338	Garland, G., Cpl., 6.8.15.
13/524	Dawson, J. W., Tpr., 27-28.8.15.	13/350	Garratt, H. G., Tpr., 6.8.15.
13/898	Day, A. C., Tpr., 26.8.15.	13/349	Gibbison, F. B. M., Sgt., 31.5.15 and 12.8.15.
13/791	De Latour, A. G., Sgt., 8.8.15.	13/340	Gilbert, M., Tpr., 6.8.15.
13/1019	Deveney, J. M., Tpr., 5.12.15.	13/351	Gill, J., Tpr., 8.8.15.
13/563	Dickey. E. M., Tpr., 8.8.15.	13/345	Gillanders, C. M., Tpr., 8.8.15.
13/178	Donaldson, T. D. S., Tpr., 8-9.8.15.	13/64	Glass, A., Tpr., 14.6.15.
13/655	Dore, P., Chap. Capt., 22.8.15. (Died in N.Z.)	13/685	Glass, E. R., Tpr., 28.8.15.
13/323	Douglas, J. J., Sgt., 24.5.15.	13/347	Goodwin, D. P., Tpr., 24.6.15.
13/180	Drake, E. R., Tpr., 8.8.15.	13/1034	Greenwood, G. C., Tpr., 2.12.15.
13/45	Drinnan, W. A., Cpl., 15.6.15.	13/57	Grey, A. E., Tpr., 27-28.8.15.
13/321	Duffull, A. G., L/Cpl., 24.5.15.	13/62	Grey, A. S., Sgt., 12.8.15.
13/224	Dunning, A. R., Tpr., 27.6.15.	13/355	Hair, J. L., Tpr., 8-9.8.15.
13/179	Durham, D., L/Cpl., 21.5.15.	13/363	Hall, E. S., Tpr., 28.8.15.
13/48	Eisenhut, H., Tpr., 14.6.15	13/1000a	Hatton, J. T., Tpr., 10.7.15.
13/253	Ellis, G. E., Tpr., 8.8.15.	13/649	Haughton, W. E., Cpl., 31.5.15.
13/681	Evans, H. T. P., L/Cpl., 27.5.15 and 8-9.8.15.	13/811	Haycock, R. H., Tpr., 8.8.15.
13/327	Fairs, C. S., Tpr., 7.9.15.	13/116	Haylock, W. S., Tpr., 6.8.15.
13/150	Finlayson, A. C. M., Lieut., 8.8.15.	13/496	Heath, J. H., Tpr., 24.8.15.
13/183	Finlayson, C. H., Tpr., 24.5.15.	13/266	Heays, R. J., L/Cpl., 6.8.15.
13/184	Finlayson, M., Tpr., 28.8.15.	13/358a	Herbert, H. S., Tpr., 28.8.15.
13/56	Finn, P. A., Tpr., 6.8.15.	13/365	Hercus, A. F., Tpr., 27-28.8.15.
13/328	Fisher, W. F., Tpr., 8.8.15	13/70	Hinman, A. C., Sgt., 14.5.15.
13/556	Fletcher, S., Tpr., 27.6.15.	13/411	Holden, W. R., Sgt., 24.5.15.
13/495	Ford, L. H., L/Cpl., 18.6.15.	13/497	Hollis, R. H., Tpr., 8.8.15.
13/220	Foster, H. M., Tpr., 24.8.15.	13/1007a	Holmes, W. J., Tpr., 7.7.15 and 8.8.15.
13/326	Foster, W. J., S.Q.M.S., 31.5.15.	13/881	Hooper, F. J., Tpr., 23.8.15.
13/684	Foulkes, J., Tpr., 14.8.15.	13/2204	Howie, A. W., Tpr., 1.12.15.
13/336	Fox, J. S. Tpr., 20.5.15 and 6.8.15.	13/695	Hunter, N. E., Tpr., 7.8.15.
13/993a	Fraser, J., Tpr., 8.8.15.	13/918	Hunter, S., Tpr., 28.8.15.
13/214	Frost, E. E., Tpr., 14.6.15.	13/195	Inder, E. W., Tpr., 5.6.15.
13/800	Fryers, A., Tpr., 8-9.8.15.	13/78	Inder, F. L. R., Tpr., 8.8.15.
13/331	Fuller, R. H., Tpr., 16.6.15 and 8.8.15.	13/374	Innes-Jones, E. S., Tpr., 6.8.15.
13/204	Fulton, P., Cpl., 17.6.15.		

13/765	Innis-Jones, M., Tpr., 30.5.15.		13/2218	Longdill, P. W., Tpr., 14.12.15.
13/99	Jackson, J. J., L/Sgt., 8.8.15.		13/827	Lord, E. J., Tpr., 8.8.15.
13/370	James, D., Tpr., 19.5.15.		13/926	Low, J. C., Tpr., 30.8.15.
13/196	Jenkins, C. J., 2nd Lieut., 8.8.15.		13/380	Luxford, F. M., Tpr., 31.5.15.
13/368	Johns, W. H., Tpr., 6.8.15.		13/381	Luxton, L. W., Tpr., 31.5.15.
13/2208	Johnson, C. B., Tpr., 8.12.15.		13/1025a	Lyes, H. C., Tpr., 27-28.8.15.
13/699	Johnson, M. E., Tpr., 24.5.15.		13/109	McArthur, A. C., Tpr., 24.5.15.
13/152	Johnson, O. P., Capt., 8.8.15.		13/148	McCarrol, J. N., Major, 20.5.15.
13/698	Johnson, P. L., Tpr., 14.6.15.		13/212	McClure, R. E. L., Lieut., 6.8.15.
13/197	Johnson, R. N., Cpl., 11.8.15.		13/104	McDonald, A. G., Tpr., 27.8.15.
13/922	Jolly, W. J., L/Cpl., 27-28.8.15.		13/105	McDonald, A. F., Tpr., 19.5.15.
13/529	Jones, C., Cpl., 16.6.15.		13/1039a	McGee, J. A., Cpl., 27-28.8.15.
13/83	Jones, C. F., Tpr., 2.6.15 and 8.8.15.		13/102	McGill, J. C., Tpr., 21.5.15.
13/557	Jones, H. C., Tpr., 28.5.15 and 8.8.15.		13/517	McKenzie, A., Tpr., 8.8.15
13/79	Jones, R. R., Tpr., 11.6.15		13/409	MacKessack, J., Tpr., 19.5.15.
13/611	Keeley, F., Sgt., 4.7.15 and 8.8.15.		13/716	McKinney, R. H., Tpr., 12.7.15.
13/825	Keith, G. V., Tpr., 6.8.15.		13/324	McLellan, J. C., Tpr., 20.5.15 and 8.8.15.
13/702	Kemp, J. A., Tpr., 15.7.15		13/209	McLeod, A. D., Tpr., 30.5.15.
11/680	King, G. A., Lieut.-Col., 27-28.8.15.		13/834	McMahon, S., Tpr., 8.8.15.
13/86	Knight, F., Sgt., 8.8.15.		13/931	McNamara, F. D., Tpr., 28.8.15.
13/522	Langdon, G., Tpr., 24.5.15		13/582	McNaughton, C., Tpr., 6.8.15.
13/379	Lauer, G., Tpr., 8.8.15.		11/1045	McNaul, J. H., Tpr., 8.8.15.
13/706	Lees, R. L., Tpr., 27.5.15.		13/392	McPherson, J. W., Tpr., 10.6.15.
13/89	Leighton, G. C., Sgt., 6.8.15.		13/261	Macey, W. P., L/Cpl., 15.7.15.
13/1021a	Lennard, G. B., Tpr., 27-28.8.15.		13/568	Mackereth, R., Tpr., 26.7.15.
13/1022a	Le Noel, N. H., Tpr., 28.8.15.		13/254	Mackesy, H. F. E., Sgt., 19.5.15.
13/198	Leslie, W. C., Tpr., 24.5.15.		13/145	Mackesy, C. R. E., Major, 29.8.15.
13/87	Lewis, A. W., Cpl., 28.8.15.		13/256	Maddren, R. H., Tpr., 18.6.15.
13/654	Lister, H. R., Tpr., 8.8.15.		13/2001	Mahan, A. G., Major, 7.10.15.
13/523	Little, H., S/Sgt., 8.8.15.		13/498	Maidens, G. H., Tpr., 8.8.15.
13/925	Llewell, A. G., Tpr., 27-28.8.15.			
13/707	Lloyd, G., Tpr., 27.6.15.			
13/488	Lloyd, W. E., Tpr., 8.8.15.			
13/539	Lochead, J. W., Tpr., 8.8.15.			

13/499	Martin, S. A., Tpr., 8-9.8.15.	13/215	O'Reilly, N. W. B., Tpr., 10.8.15.
13/869	Martin, W. M., Tpr., 28.8.15.	13/609	Orr, A. C., Tpr., 6.8.15.
13/273	Mason, A., Tpr., 8.8.15.	13/121	Page, R. H., Tpr., 27-28.8.15.
13/91	Matthews, A. J., Tpr., 15.6.15.	13/528	Palmer, W., Tpr., 19.5.15.
13/397	Melhose, L., Tpr., 8.8.15.	13/119	Palmer, W. T., Lieut., 29.8.15.
13/399	Meyer, E., Tpr., 19.5.15.	13/426	Park, W. H., Cpl., 31.5.15.
13/1031a	Melling, J., Sgt., 15.7.15.	13/937	Partridge, A. E., Tpr., 28.8.15.
13/401	Middleton, H. C., Tpr., 12.8.15.	13/938	Patterson, J. S., Tpr., 28.8.15.
13/97	Mildon, H. A., Tpr., 7.8.15.	13/123	Patterson, J., L/Cpl., 6.8.15.
13/709	Miles, W. E., Tpr., 23.8.15	13/722	Pattison, W. R., Tpr., 19.5.15 and 8.8.15.
13/100	Millen, J. H. D., Cpl., 8.8.15.	13/88	Paxman, G. R., Cpl., 6.8.15.
13/2230	Millar, J., Cpl., 25.11.15.	13/839	Pearce, A., Tpr., 28.8.15.
13/406	Miller, R. J. H., Tpr., 16.5.15.	13/939	Pearson, H., Tpr., 27-28.8.15.
13/54	Milne, J. G., Sgt./Major, 8.8.15.	13/727	Perkins, W. J., Tpr., 24.5.15.
13/710	Mitai, B., Tpr., 8.8.15.	13/728	Phillips, T. W., Cpl., 8.8.15.
13/933	Mooney, J. K., Tpr., 28.8.15.	13/420	Picot, E. H., Tpr., 28.8.15.
13/874	Moore, D. G., Lieut., 29.8.15.	13/449	Potter, W. H., Tpr., 8-9.8.15.
13/103	Moore, W. T., Cpl. 8.8.15.	13/731	Price, W. J., Cpl., 8.8.15.
13/396	Morison, M., Tpr., 27.8.15.	13/397	Prosser, T., Tpr., 18.6.15.
13/527	Morrison, J. H., Tpr., 8.8.15.	13/425	Pryor, F. T., Tpr., 9.6.15.
13/218	Muldrock, V., Cpl., 8.8.15.	13/127	Read, W. H., Tpr., 8.8.15.
13/221	Muldrock, W. H., Tpr., 28.8.15.	13/227	Redfern, A. J., Q.M.S., 6.8.15.
13/717	Nea(ber, C. W., L/Cpl., 8-9.8.15.	13/129	Reid, S. C., Tpr., 8.8.15.
13/504	Neilson, P., Tpr., 28.8.15.	13/945	Richards, H. E. A., Tpr., 28.8.15.
13/413	Nesbit, F. J., L/Cpl., 8.8.15.	13/879	Richmond, H. S., Tpr., 21.8.15.
13/414	Nesbitt, C. W., Tpr., 21.5.15.	13/434	Riddell, W. E., Cpl., 6.8.15.
13/247	Nichols, E., Tpr., 11.7.15.	13/439	Riddell, J., Cpl., 4.8.15.
13/112	Nicol, C. G., Sgt., 19.5.15 and 12.7.15.	13/946	Risk, T. T., Cpl., 28.8.15.
13/572	Noble, A. C., Cpl., 6.8.15.	13/182	Roberts, J. M., Lieut., 19.5.15.
13/505	Norman, A., Tpr., 28.5.15.	13/226	Roberts, P. C., Tpr., 8.8.15.
13/719	Norman, C., L/Cpl., 8.8.15.	13/337	Roberts, T. V., Tpr., 8.8.15.
13/506	Nowland, W., Tpr., 8.8.15	13/435	Robinson, C. H., L/Cpl., 8.8.15.
13/215	Nugent, W. B. C., Tpr., 10.8.15.	13/432	Rope, C. M., Cpl., 8.8.15.
13/1079	Oakden, P. V., Sgt., 28.8.15.	13/194	Ross, J. A., Cpl., 6.8.15.
13/114	O'Hara, C. W., Cpl., 1.7.15.		
13/113	O'Neill, T. L., Tpr., 6.8.15.		

13/229	Saunders, A. G., Tpr., 8-9.8.15.		13/465	Thomas, A. F., Tpr., 6.8.15.
13/454	Saxby, W. J., Cpl., 31.5.15.		13/554	Thomas, C. W., Tpr., 28.8.15.
13/235	St. Clair, J. P., Tpr., 9.8.15 and 27.8.15.		13/960	Thomas, W. E., Tpr., 28.8.15.
13/132	Scanlen, B. A., Tpr., 6.8.15.		13/589	Thompson, W. J. J., Tpr., 19.5.15.
13/636	Schofield, S. C., Major, 8.8.15.		13/590	Thomson, T. R., Tpr., 19.5.15.
13/737	Schollum, E., Tpr., 21.5.15		13/902a	Tomasi, J., Tpr., 7.8.15.
13/1056a	Scott, J. E., Tpr., 28.8.15.		13/511	Travis, A., Tpr., 6.8.15.
13/455	Seaward, C. F., Tpr., 28.8.15.		13/173	Treweek, C., Tpr., 17.6.15
			13/467	Troup, J., Sgt., 6.8.15.
13/451	Self, R., L/Cpl., 24.5.15.		13/964	Vanstone, A., Tpr., 25.8.15
13/955	Sigvertsen, C. A., Tpr., 28.8.15.		13/246	Wade, L., Tpr., 29.5.15.
			13/865	Walker, C. H., Tpr., 28.8.15 and 8.12.15.
13/577	Sharplin, W., Tpr., 20.5.15			
13/1011a	Singh, Jagt, Tpr., 8.8.15.		13/174	Wallace, L., L/Cpl., 8.8.15
13/738	Smith, J., Tpr., 6.6.15.		13/521	Walters, F., Tpr., 8.8.15.
13/134	Snell, G. V., Tpr., 6.8.15.		13/149	Warder, H., Cpl., 6.8.15.
13/135	Speight, H. V. B., Tpr., 6.8.15.		13/968	Warren, A., Tpr., 25.8.15.
			13/479	Watson, J. W., 2nd Lieut., 2.6.15.
13/461	Sperry, F., Tpr., 25.8.15.			
13/230	Spick, A. G., S/Sgt., 28.5.15.		13/2093	Webster, L. S., Tpr., 2.12.15.
			13/975	White, A., Tpr., 25.8.15.
13/237	Stevens, K. M. Lt./Sgt., 8.8.15.		13/976	White, K. C., Sgt., 28.8.15.
13/234	Stewart, F., L/Cpl., 19.5.15 and 8.7.15.		13/477	Williams, E. J., Tpr., 6.7.15.
13/234	Stewart, F., L/Cpl., 8.7.15.		13/759	Williams, H. D., Lieut., 8.8.15.
13/956	Stichbury, C. G., Tpr., 25.8.15.		13/485	Williamson, J., Sgt., 13.8.15.
13/131	Stichbury, T., Tpr., 14.6.15 and 28.8.15.		13/868	Wilson, A. H., L/Cpl., 8.8.15.
13/42	Stringer, T. W., Tpr., 6.8.15.		13/153	Wilson, J. G., Tpr., 25.8.15.
13/84	Sutton, O. A., L/Cpl., 19.6.15 and 8.8.15		13/587	Wilson, K. S., Sgt., 8.8.15.
13/459	Swayne, A. J., Tpr., 7.8.15.		13/581	Wood, C., Tpr., 20.5.15.
13/446	Sweetman, E. P. S., Sgt., 31.5.15.		13/633	Wood, F. A., Major, 8.8.15.
13/239	Taylor, J., Tpr., 12.5.15.		13/156	Woolley, T., Sgt., 12.8.15.
13/462	Taylor, W., Sgt., 29.5.15.		13/753	Wrenn, J. V., Tpr., 27.6.15.
13/199	Tebbutt, C. R., Cpl., 6.8.15.		13/158	Wyman, R. Major, 8.8.15.

SINAI AND PALESTINE.

35726	Adams, C. J., Tpr., 31.10.17.	16277	Cleary, H. M., L/Cpl., 9.12.17.
13/2510	Aldred, M., Capt., 9.8.16 and 9.1.17.	43162	Clements, V. E., Tpr., 14.11.17.
57570	Anderson, J., Tpr., 12.7.18.	16353	Colbeck, R. W., Lieut., 9.1.17 and 27.3.18.
17371	Anderson, G. A., L/Cpl., 28.3.18.	13/2313	Cole, L. J., Tpr., 9.8.16.
13/2013	Armstrong, A. M. L., L/Cpl., 14.11.17.	13/307	Conbrough, N., Sgt., 30.3.18.
18322	Armstrong, J. H., Tpr., 23.3.18.	13/1016	Court, H. P. F. W., Sq.M.S., 14.11.17.
43199	Baird, R. H. F., T/Cpl., about 27.3.18.	13/2172	Cox, A. O., Tpr., 25.11.17.
16059	Ball, A. C., Tpr., 30.3.18.	13/2553	Cramp, J. R., Tpr., 25.11.17.
16523	Barnes, E., Tpr., ,9.1.17 and 19.4.17.	13/1017	Creighton, J. W., Tpr., 7.8.16.
17474	Barugh, F., Tpr., 14.11.17.	16745	Crosado, A. C., Tpr., 25.11.17.
35868	Bedford, R., Tpr., 27.3.18.	13/2032	Cross, E. W., Cpl., 31.10.17.
17477	Bellingham, W., Tpr., 14.11.17.	11424	Curtis, A., Tpr., 3.4.18.
13/292	Bennett, W. A., 2nd Lieut., 31.10.17.	31070	Darrington, A. W., Tpr., 31.10.17.
13/19	Bishop, K., Sgt., 19.4.17.	18206	Davidson, N. S., Tpr., 3.4.18.
17555	Bisleye, E. A. H., Lieut., 14.11.17.	35391	Deans, J., Tpr., 3.4.18.
13/2533	Black, G., Tpr., 19.4.17.	11/1789	Delaney, A. H., L/Cpl., 7.8.16 and 30.3.18. 7.8.16.
13/878	Blackie, A. S., 2nd Lieut., 9.1.17.	13/791	De Lautour, A. G., Sgt., 14.11.17.
16505	Bradstreet, J. H., Tpr., 9.1.17.	13/1019	Deveney, J. M., Tpr., 19.4.17 and 30.3.18.
13/1010	Brooks, Arthur J., Cpl., 30.3.18.	13/1019	Deveney, J. M., Tpr., 30.3.18.
13/16	Brown, T. G., Tpr., 9.1.17.	13/222	Dill, F. G., Sgt., 9.1.17.
50403	Bull, H. C., Tpr., 25.9.18.	31072	Donaldson, G., Cpl., 30.3.18.
12582	Byers, E. S., Tpr., 11.8.16.	13/178	Donaldson, T. D. S., Sgt., 9.1.17 and 27.3.18.
13/35	Campbell, C. G., Tpr., 25.11.17 and 30.3.18.	13/178	Donaldson, T. D. S., Sgt., 27.3.18.
13/3009	Canavan, J. W., Sgt., 31.10.17.	13/2759	Douglas, A. H., Tpr., 11.8.16.
13/2309	Carter, A., Tpr., 31.10.17.	13/2103	Dowd, D. H., Tpr., 14.11.17.
13/2023	Carter, J. McN., Tpr., 9.1.17.	13545	Doyle, H., Tpr., 14.11.17.
10733	Cavers, F., Tpr., 27.3.18.	5/226	Drinnan, H., Tpr., 14.11.17.
17572	Chapman, R. C., Lieut., 31.10.17.	13/2033	Dunn, C. L. J., Tpr., 25.11.17.
13312	Chatfield, S. N., Tpr., 5.11.17.	11/1535	Durham, R. S., Sgt., 14.11.17.
13/2270	Clark, F. R., Tpr., 19.4.17.		
13313	Clark, J. P., Cpl., 31.10.17.		
7/945	Clarke, H. W., Tpr., 6.11.17.		

16286	Dwyer, E. J., Pte., 14.11.17.		13/2200	Harper, T., Cpl., 9.1.17 and 14.11.17.
13/602	Eisenhut, J. J., Sgt., 9.1.17 and 14.11.17.		13/362	Hastie, F., Sgt., 14.11.17.
13/49	Elsmore, B. T., Sgt., 20.2.18.		13/910	Haultain, E. C., Tpr., 27.3.18.
13/2034	Fargher, H. W. J., L/Cpl., 9.1.17 and 31.10.17.		13/161	Herrold, J. H., Major, 30.4.18.
13/2006	Farnsworth, J. L., Sgt., 9.1.17 and 31.10.17.		13/2335	Hird, L. C., Tpr., 14.11.17.
13/150	Finlayson, A. C. M., Capt., 9.1.17 and 30.3.18.		13/2043	Hirst, E. P. I., Tpr., 9.1.17.
16292	Finlayson, A. A., Tpr., 9.1.17.		13/67	Hodder, C., Sgt., 6.8.16 and 19.4.17.
35993	Finlayson, H. J., Tpr., 25.11.17.		13/2045	Houghton, H. R., Tpr., 14.11.17.
11/1550	Finlayson, J. B., Sgt., 14.11.17.		43338	Hunt, W., Tpr., 30.3.18.
13/2432	Finlayson, L. B., Tpr., 9.1.17.		13/695	Hunter, N. E., L/Sgt., 14.11.17.
57815	Finn, T. W., Tpr., 25.9.18.		13/553	Hynes, J., Cpl., 9.1.17.
13/228	Fisher, W. F., Sgt., 9.1.17.		17417	Jackson, C. G. R., Lieut., 14.11.17.
35960	Fitzpatrick, L. R., Tpr., 14.11.17.		10097	Jamieson, A. E., Tpr., 4.8.16 and 9.1.17.
43309	Fleming, S., Tpr., 30.4.18.		13/1054	Jefcoate, W. H., Cpl., 30.3.18.
13/2187	Foote, F. J., L/Cpl., 14.11.17.		13/2452	Jeffs, J. E., Cpl., 27.3.18.
13/2036	Forsyth, W. A., Tpr., 9.8.16.		13/196	Jenkins, C. J., Cpl., 8.8.15
13/2565	Foster, A. I., Tpr., 14.11.17.		13/1013a	Jenkins, J., Tpr., 7.8.16.
13/1029	Foster, H., Tpr., 9.1.17.		35863	Johansen, W. T., Tpr., 14.11.17.
13/2566	Frost, H. C., Tpr., 9.8.16.		13/2822	Johnson, J. W., Cpl., 20.2.18.
13/331	Fuller, R. H., Cpl., 14.11.17.		57827	Johnston, H., Tpr., 25.9.18
17579	Gardner, C., Tpr., 25.11.17		13/922	Jolly, W. J., L/Cpl., 6.8.16 and 19.4.17.
13/351	Gill, J., Tpr., 27.3.18.		13/2584	Jupp, W. F., Sgt., 5.11.17.
16294	Gillanders, W. G., Tpr., 30.3.18.		11/1569	Kay, J. A., Sgt., 9.8.16.
13/2040	Going, L. R., Sgt., 6.8.16.		43190	Keene, S. H., Tpr., 25.11.17.
13/908	Grant, E., Tpr., 25.11.17.		13/2032	King, H. S., Tpr., 12.8.16.
13/2572	Grant, G. Z., Tpr., 9.8.16.		43340	King, T. J. J., Tpr., 2.12.17.
7/960	Gray, H., Tpr., 9.5.17.		50024	Kingston, S., Tpr., 30.3.18.
11/1564	Greenwood, B. A., L/Cpl., 9.1.17.		13/66	Knight, F., Sgt., 19.4.17.
42987	Grey, J., Tpr., 20.2.18.		13/2457	Lange, D., Sgt., 14.11.17.
13/363	Hall, E. H., Cpl., 14.11.17.		13/2587	Lawrie, W. B. D., Tpr., 19.4.17 and 14.11.17.
12600	Hamilton, John, Tpr., 19.4.17 and 31.10.17.		18376	Laycock, A., Tpr., 27.3.18.
13/2199	Hanham, J. N., S/Major, W.O. I., 9.1.17.		13/2214	Leaming, H. G., Tpr., 9.1.17.
13/2559	Hardy, F. H., Sgt., 9.8.16.		13/560	Lee, C. G., Farr./Sgt., 14.11.17.
			35744	Leherty, L. M., Tpr., 31.10.17.
			13/2272	Lister, D., Tpr., 19.4.17.
			13/3045	Lomas, A. R., Cpl., 9.1.17 and 19.4.17.

13/148	McCarroll, J. N., Lieut.-Col., 14.11.17.		13/593	Palmer, D. H., Cpl., 9.1.17.
16571	McGill, A., Tpr., 14.11.17.		13/528	Palmer, W., W.O. I., 14.11.17.
16250	McKay, T. E. A., Tpr., 3.4.18.		13/2007	Parrish, A., 2nd Lieut., 31.5.16.
13/2058	McKenzie, L. D., Cpl., 19.11.16.		13/486	Pascoe, W., Sgt., 9.1.17.
7/983	McKercher, D., Sq.M.S., 9.1.17.		18088	Paterson, L. M., Lieut., 30.3.18.
11/1572	McLarin, F. W., Tpr., 9.8.16.		16054	Paton, J. S., Tpr., 14.11.17.
13/931	McNamara, F. D., Tpr., 9.1.17.		13/2359	Pearson, J. A., Cpl., 9.8.16.
13/833	McNamara, S. A., Sgt., 31.10.17.		13/2276	Penny, B., Sgt., 14.11.17.
13/2226	Maisey, J. M., Tpr., 9.8.16.		36013	Perry, E. G., Tpr., 14.11.17.
13/2589	Marchant, R. G., Tpr., 25.11.17.		13/2362	Petley, G. H., Cpl., 31.10.17 and 30.3.18.
43314	Matchett, G., Tpr., 27.3.18.		13/841	Phillips, G. M., Tpr., 8.11.17.
13/501	Maxwell, F. J., Sgt., 9.1.17.		11/1590	Pollard, A. W. T., Sgt., 9.8.16.
13/2573	Miller, R. T., Tpr., 19.4.17.		13/990	Reed, M. R., Lieut., 9.1.17.
24914	Mitchell, J. W. H., Cpl., 3.4.18.		13/129	Reid, S. C., Lieut., 14.11.17.
13/2636	Moore, H. A., Tpr., 30.4.18.		13/946	Risk, T. T., L/Cpl., 3.4.18.
13/96	Morgan, J. W., W.O. II., 21.6.18.		13/226	Roberts, P. C., Tpr., 3.4.18.
13/2066	Mudford, J. E., Cpl., 9.1.17.		13/1087	Robins, A., Tpr., 14.11.17.
13/757	Munro, D., Capt., 23.3.18.		13/531	Rodgers, J. L., Tpr., 3.4.18.
13/2232	Murray, V. O., Tpr., 31.10.17.		30292	Roger, W. P., Tpr., 30.3.18.
13/2459	Muir, J. C., Sgt., 9.1.17.		16586	Rolfe, F. J., Tpr., 19.4.17.
13/2067	Nankivell, W. J., Sgt., 14.11.17.		16504	Rorke, H. M., Lieut., 19.4.17 and 25.11.17.
13/2068	Nesbitt, D. D., Cpl., 14.11.17 and 30.3.18.		13/2617	Rossiter, N. E. J., Cpl., 14.11.17.
13/506	Nowland, W., Sgt., 31.10.17.		34989	Rouse, E. G., Tpr., 14.11.17.
13/1080	O'Connor, C. J., Tpr., 14.11.17 and 19.9.18.		13/125	Ruddock, W. D., Lieut., 9.1.17.
13/2469	O'Dowd, C. T., Cpl., 30.4.18.		16955	Rule, E. J., Tpr., 19.12.16.
13/419	O'Leary, M. J., Sh./Sm., 25.11.17.		13/3075	Rusden, L., Tpr., 9.8.16 and 25.11.17.
9/2260	Olsen, B., Tpr., 19.4.17.		18089	Ryan, L. C., Lieut., 25.11.17.
13/2279	Ormiston, T. D., Cpl., 14.11.17.		13/2619	Ryan, M., Tpr., 9.1.17.
13/609	Orr, A. C., W.O. II., S.S.M., 14.11.17 and 30.3.18.		13/1090	Sands, D., Tpr., 4.8.16.
			17587	Schlaepfer, R., Tpr., 14.11.17.
13/721	Owens, J., Cpl., 9.9.16.		13/3097	Scott, A., Tpr., 7.8.16.
			13/2368	Scott, J. L., Sgt., 26.3.17.
			13/2367	Searle, T., Cpl., 11.8.16.

13/2621	Secombe, C. F., Sgt., 9.8.16.	13377	Tunstall, C. W., Tpr., 14.11.17.
50055	Serjeant, C. R., Tpr., 30.4.18.	9/2138	Twaddle, T., Tpr., 14.11.17.
13/1093	Shanahan, R., Cpl., 8.7.17.	16450	Walker, H. C., Tpr., 4.6.17.
16442	Simcock, R. A., Tpr., 9.1.17.	31106	Walker, T. E., Tpr., 29.3.18.
24935	Slater, A. J. S., Tpr., 31.10.17 and 28.3.18.	13/2945	Wallace, M., L/Cpl., 25.11.17 and 1.3.18.
43783	Smellie, W. McL., Tpr., 5.11.17.	13298	Walsh, M. J., Tpr., 14.11.17.
13367	Smith, C. B., Tpr., 14.11.17.	13/2090	Waters, P. H. G., L/Cpl., 30.3.18.
30457	Southcombe, E. M., Tpr., 30.3.18.	13/1107	Waters, R. L., Sgt., 19.4.17 and 14.11.17.
13/231	Spick, R. M. P., Sgt., 25.11.17.	13/479	Watson, J. W., 2nd Lieut., 14.11.17.
13/2486	Stark, J., Tpr., 9.8.16.	13/2628	Watt, G. S., Sgt., 25.11.17.
13291	Sterling, F., Cpl., 14.11.17 and 20.2.18.	13/2269	Wells, G., Cpl., 4.8.16.
13/440	Stewart, A., Tpr., 31.10.17.	16139	Whelan, S. L., Tpr., 19.4.17.
13/2489	Stichbury, H., L/Cpl., 9.1.17 and 14.11.17.	13/1111	White, C. H., L/Cpl., 30.3.18.
13/3085	Storey, E. J., Tpr., 29.3.18.	13/483	White, C. N., 2nd Lieut., 14.11.17 and 30.3.18.
17450	Street, A. A., Tpr., 14.11.17.	13/656	Whitehorn, H. S., Major, 9.1.17.
13/2085	Swan, W. F., Tpr., 4.8.16.	13/2095	Wilkinson, J., L/Cpl., 14.11.17.
13371	Swayne, F. H., Tpr., 25.11.17.	36024	Williams, J., Tpr., 31.10.17.
13/489	Sylverton, C. V., Tpr., 25.11.17.	35795	Wilson, J. Tpr., 30.3.18.
11/2548	Dale-Taylor, I., L/Cpl., 14.11.17.	13/587	Wilson, K. S., Sgt., 9.1.17.
1,185	Tait, K. J., Lieut., 14.11.17.	13/2101	Wood, E. G., Tpr., 3.10.18.
13/746	Thompson, H. V., Tpr., 30.3.18.	16463	Woods, W., Tpr., 30.4.18.
13/2086	Thompson, W. W., Tpr., 14.11.17.	13/2267	Woolnough, H., Tpr., 31.10.17.
16135	Trounson, R. H., Tpr., 14.11.17 and 30.3.18.	13/512	Wyatt, J. C. E., 2nd Lieut., 9.8.16.
		13/1078a	Yeo, T. F., Tpr., 14.11.17.
		36027	Young, A. G., Tpr., 14.11.17.

Honours and Awards.

13/610	**Mackesy, C. E. R.,** Colonel, C.M.G., C.B.E., D.S.O., mentioned in despatches three times.	
13/158	**Wyman, R.,** Major, D.S.O., mentioned in despatches.	
13/148	**McCarroll, J. N.,** Lieut.-Col., C.M.G., D.S.O., Bar to D.S.O., mentioned in despatches.	
13/161	**Herrold, J. H.,** Major, D.S.O.	
13/150	**Finlayson, A. C. M.,** Major, M.C. and Bar, mentioned in despatches three times.	
13/699	**Johnson, M. E.,** Capt., M.C. and Bar.	
13/395	**McGregor, E. J.,** Lieut., M.C., mentioned in despatches.	
13/129	**Reid, S. C.,** Lieut., M.C.	
	McCathie, D. S., Lieut., M.C.	
	Collins, H. A., Lieut., M.C.	
13/528	**Palmer, W.,** W.O. I., M.C., mentioned in despatches.	
13/5	**Armstrong, L. J.,** Lieut., D.C.M., mentioned in despatches.	
13/178	**Donaldson, T. D. S.,** Sgt., D.C.M.	
13/791	**De Lautour, A. G.,** Sgt., D.C.M.	
13/48	**Eisenhut, H.,** W.O. I., D.C.M.	
13/2559	**Hardy, F. H.,** T/Cpl., D.C.M.	
13/438	**White, C. N.,** Sgt., D.C.M.	
13/479	**Watson, J. W.,** 2nd Lieut., M.M.	
13/340	**Gilbert, M.,** 2nd Lieut., M.M.	
13/994	**Clarke, S. B.,** W.O. II., M.M., mentioned in despatches.	
13/2040	**Going, L. R.,** Sgt., M.M.	
13/2571	**Grant, C. O.,** T/Sgt., M.M.	
13/2473	**Pilcher, D.,** Sgt., M.M.	
13/3082	**Smillie, J.,** Sgt., M.M.	
13/446	**Sweetman, E. P. S.,** Sgt., M.M.	
13/2628	**Watt, G. S.,** Sgt., M.M.	
13/164	**Buckland, A. F.,** L/Cpl., T/Cpl., M.M.	
13/2587	**Laurie, W. R. D.,** Tpr., M.M.	
24941	**Tomkins, W. E.,** Tpr., M.M.	
13/963	**Underwood, H.,** L/Cpl., M.M.	
13/149	**Warder, H.,** Cpl., M.M.	
13/2095	**Wilkinson, J.,** L/Cpl., M.M.	
13/245	**Young, O. F. T.,** T/Cpl., M.M.	
13/634	**Chapman, F.,** Major, mentioned in despatches.	
13/633	**Wood, F. A.,** Major, M.C., mentioned in despatches.	
13/264	**Allsopp, F.,** Capt., mentioned in despatches.	
13/75	**Haeata, W.,** Capt., mentioned in despatches twice.	

13/301	Bigg-Wither, C. V., Lieut., mentioned in despatches.
13/119	Palmer, W. T., 2nd Lieut., mentioned in despatches.
13/607	Patten, J. C., W.O. II., mentioned in despatches.
13/990	Reed, M. R., Capt., mentioned in despatches.
	Wright, S. L., Lieut., mentioned in despatches.
13/237	Stevens, K. M., L/Sgt., mentioned in despatches.
13/1054	Jelcoate, W. H., Cpl., mentioned in despatches.
13/273	Mason, A., Tpr., mentioned in despatches.
13/438	Rollett, R. R. C., Tpr., mentioned in despatches.
13/2096	Wilkinson, R., Tpr., mentioned in despatches.

CIVIL DECORATIONS.

13/73 Hovey, G., T/Major, O.B.E.
13/160 Smedley, C. F., Capt., M.B.E.

FOREIGN DECORATIONS.

Whitehorn, H. S., Major, Croix de Chevalier.
13/23a Carpell, J. M., Sgt., Belgian Croix de Guerre.
13/448 Simpkins, J., Sgt., Medaille Militaire, mentioned in despatches.
13/2309 Carter, A., Tpr., Russian Decoration, Medal St. George, third class.
13/535 Champney, N. D., Tpr., Serbian Decorations, Silver Medal, mentioned in despatches.

Message to the Troops

from the Commander-in-Chief after the Final Victory.

I desire to convey to all ranks and all arms of the Force under my command, my admiration and thanks for their great deeds of the past week, and my appreciation of their gallantry and determination, which have resulted in the total destruction of the VIIth and VIIIth Turkish Armies opposed to us.

Such a complete victory has seldom been known in all the history of war.

26th September, 1918.

Allenby
General
C.i.C.

19020

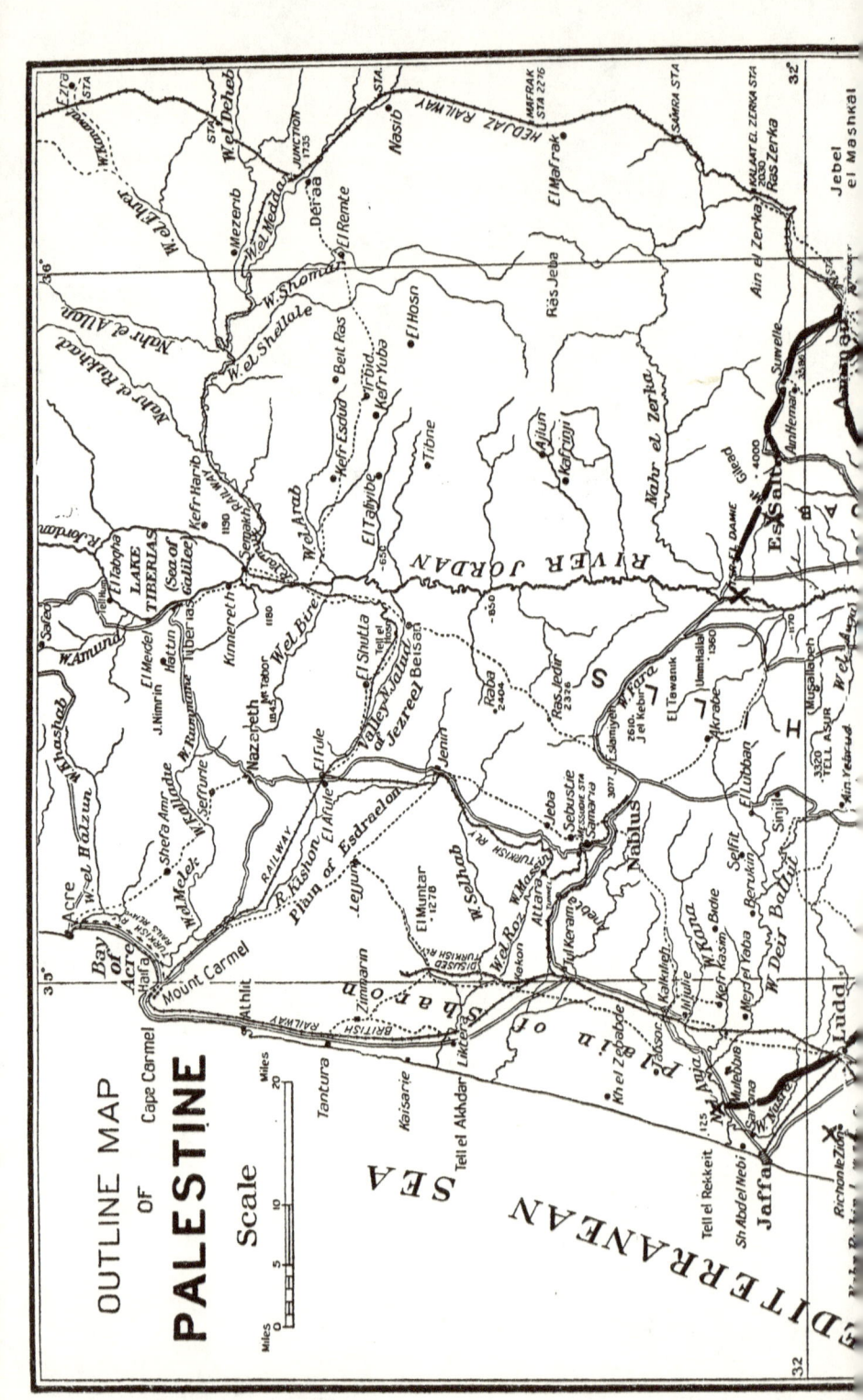

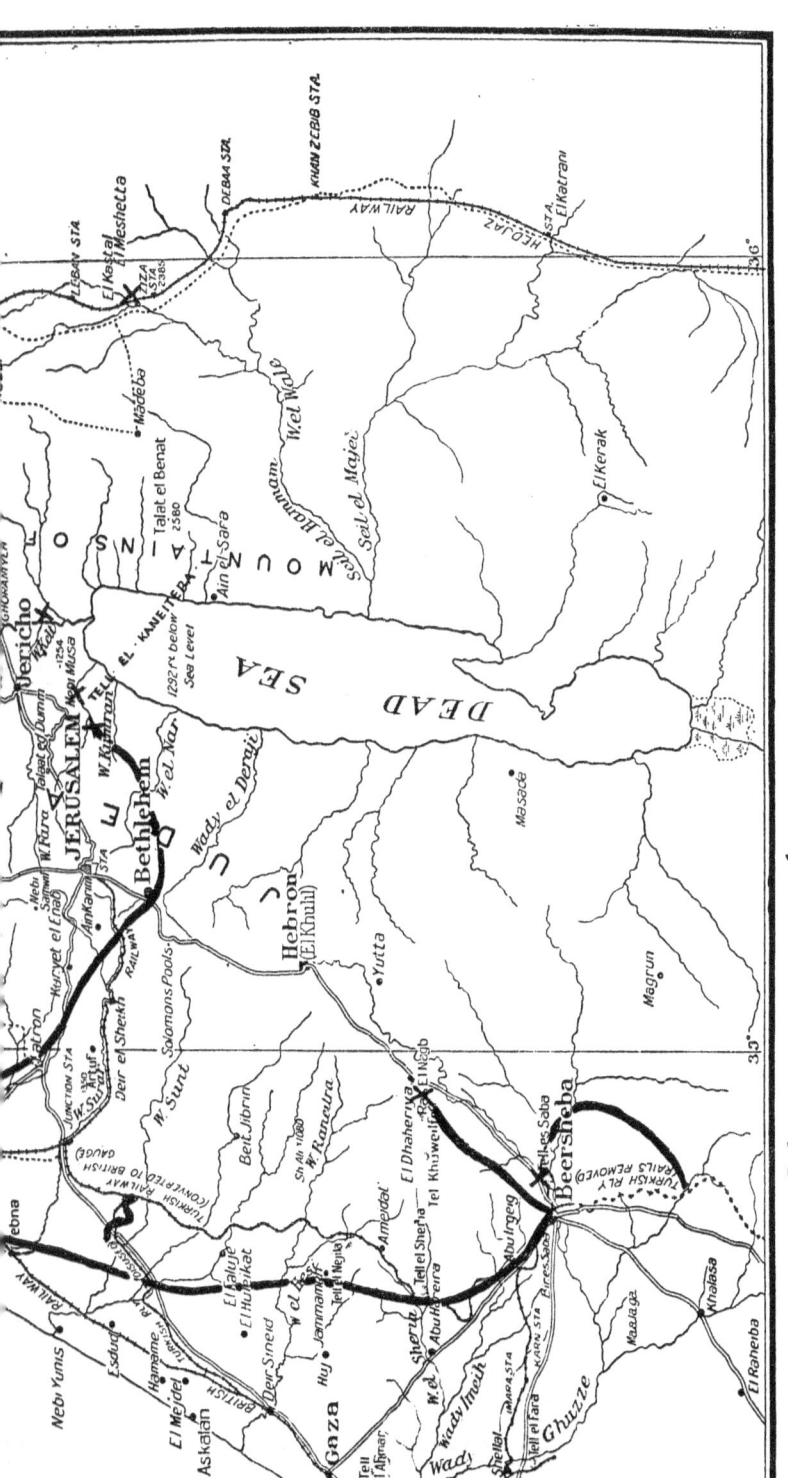

The places where the Auckland Mounted Rifles Regiment was engaged are marked by crosses. The heavy line from Ras El Nagb to Beersheba, and from Beersheba to Richon le Zion is the route of the long trek; that from the Auja to Bethlehem shows the route of the regiment when it was sent to the right flank of the British line, and those from the Jordan to Amman indicate the regiment's movements described.

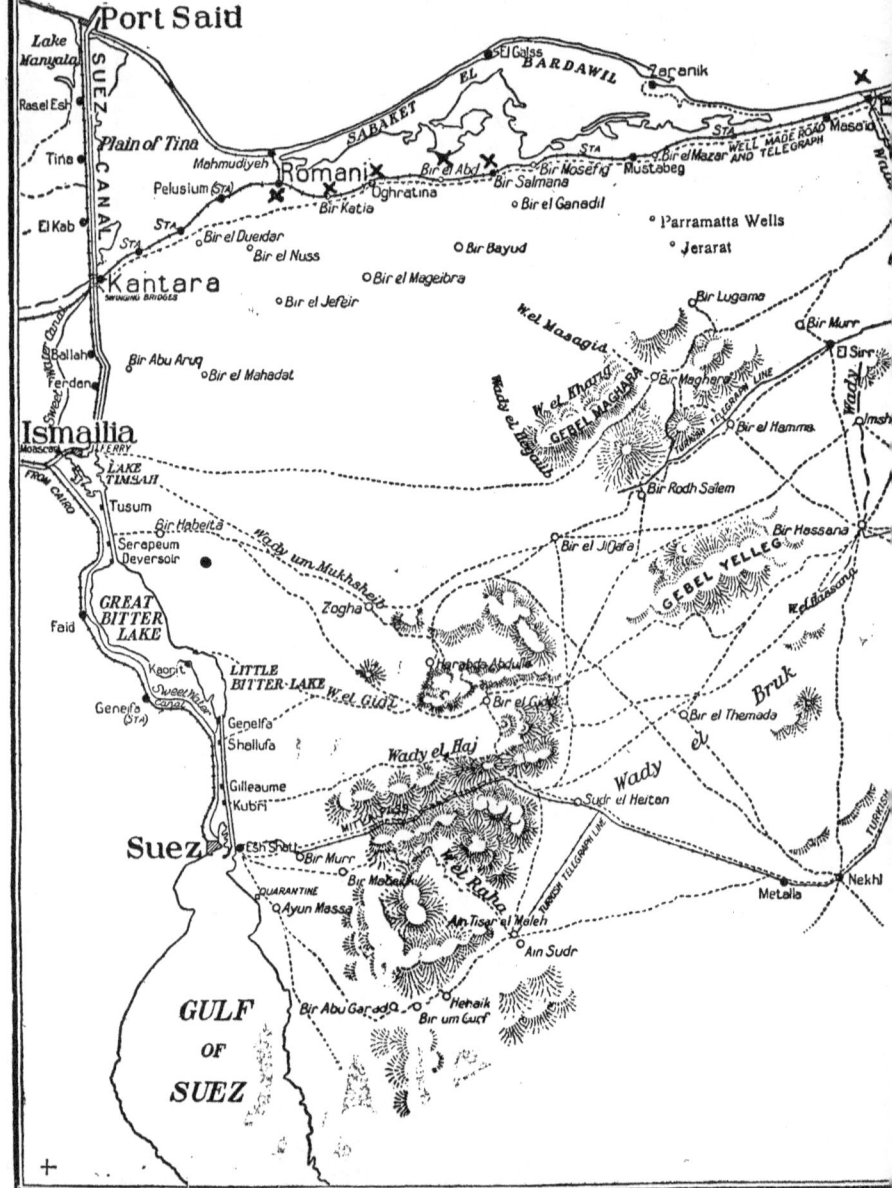

References: Ain, Ayun, Well. Bir, Spring. Gebel, Mountain. Ras, Bl

The places where the Auckland Mounted Rifles Regiment was engaged are marked by crosses. The l

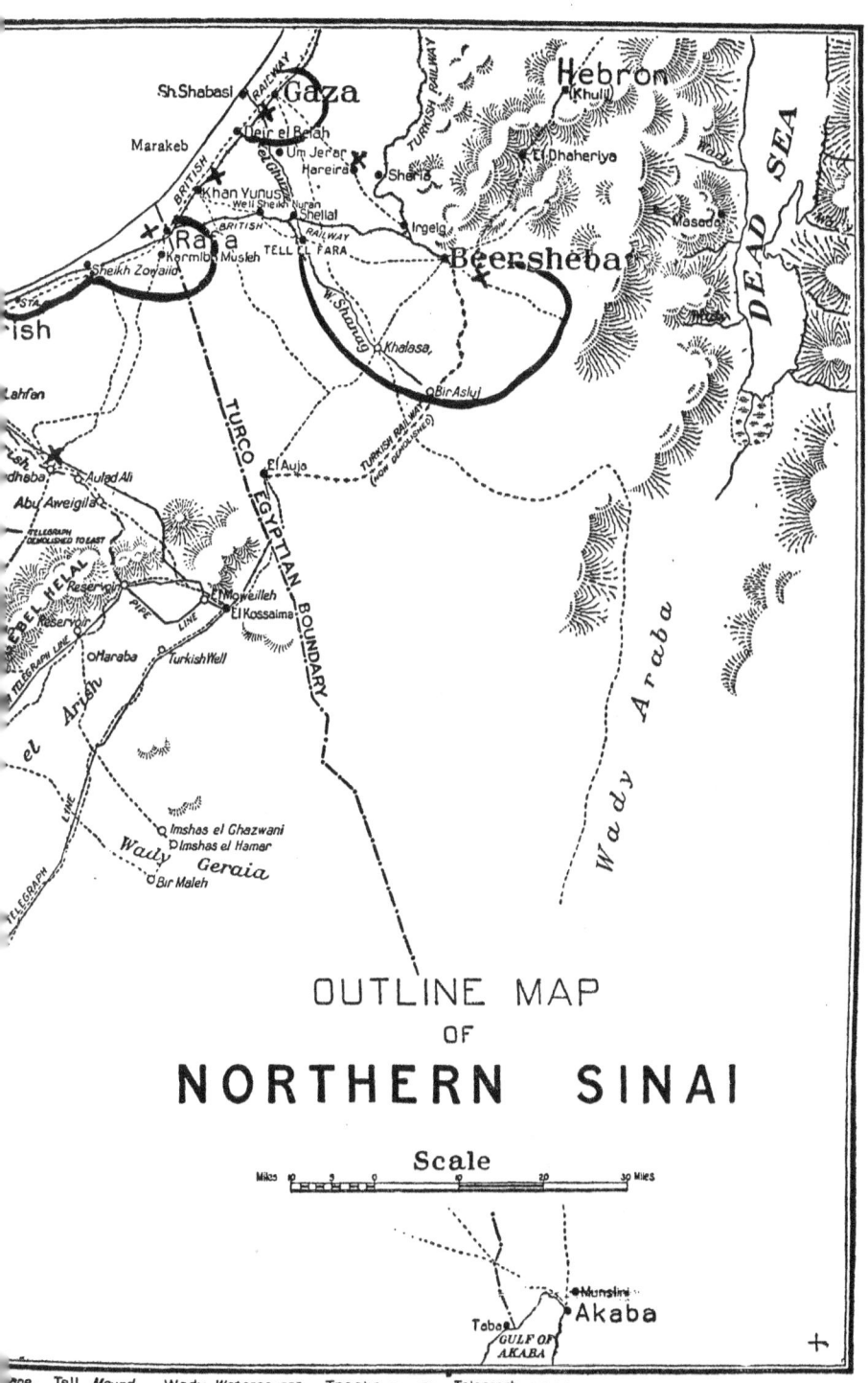

pe, Tell, Mound. Wady, Watercourse. Tracks, ... Telegraph ←←←←

curved lines indicate roughly the enveloping movements in which the regiment took part.

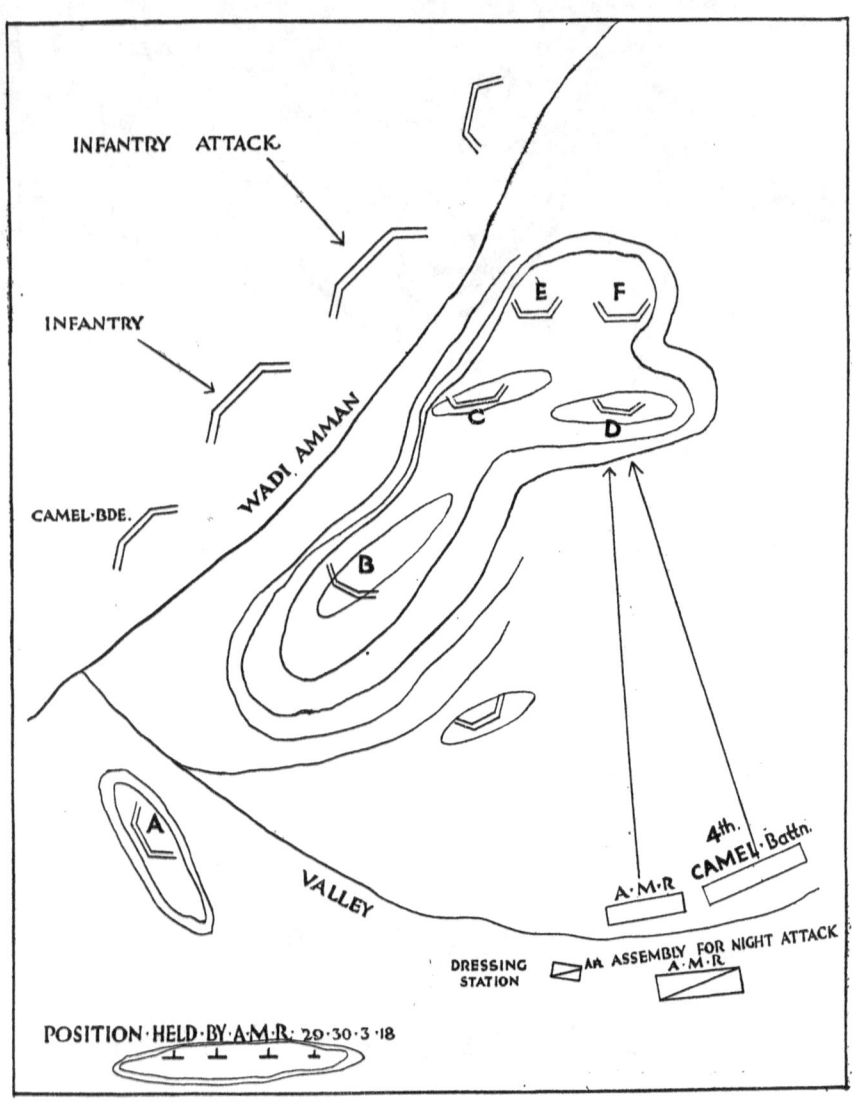

SKETCH (not drawn to scale) **OF HILL 3039, AMMAN NIGHT ATTACK, 30.3.18.**
A.M.R. (Major Cheeseman) and 4th Battalion Camels (Lieut.-Colonel Mills) attacked trench D. When this was completed A.M.R. swung to the left, taking trenches B and C, while C.M.R. (Major Acton-Adams) went through and took E. and F.

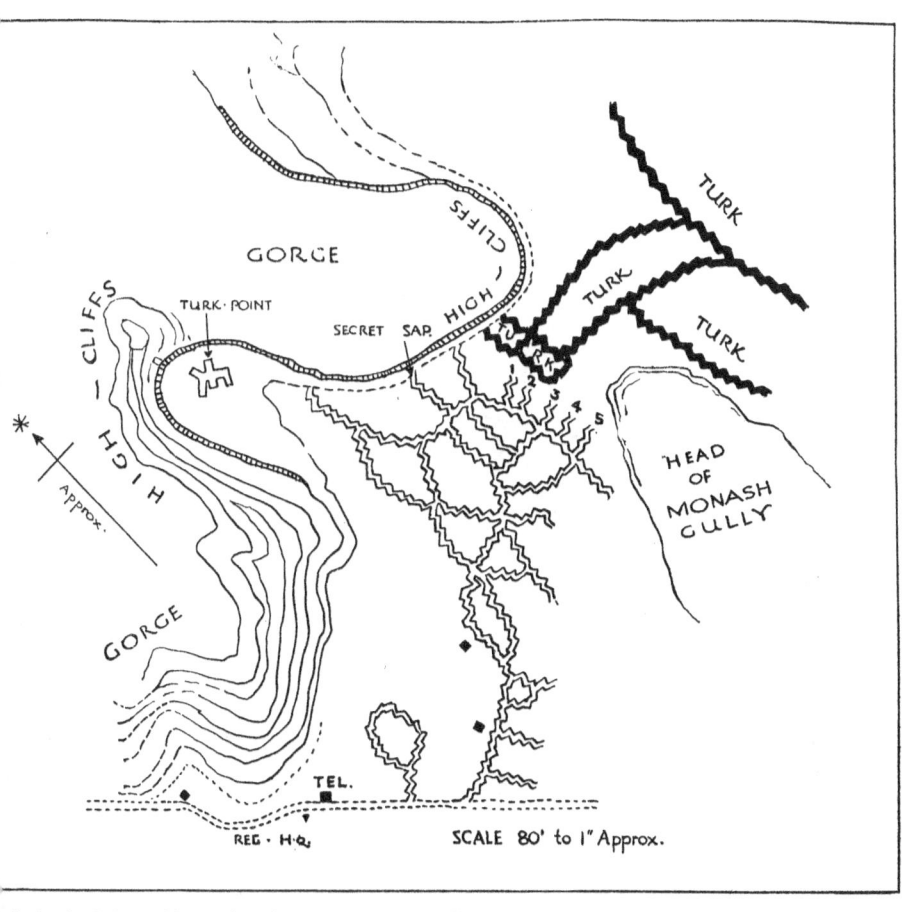

Rough sketch of the position on Russell's Top, showing the Nek. The Turkish attack of May 19 was delivered before the saps shown had been constructed, and before the line from which they ran was completed.

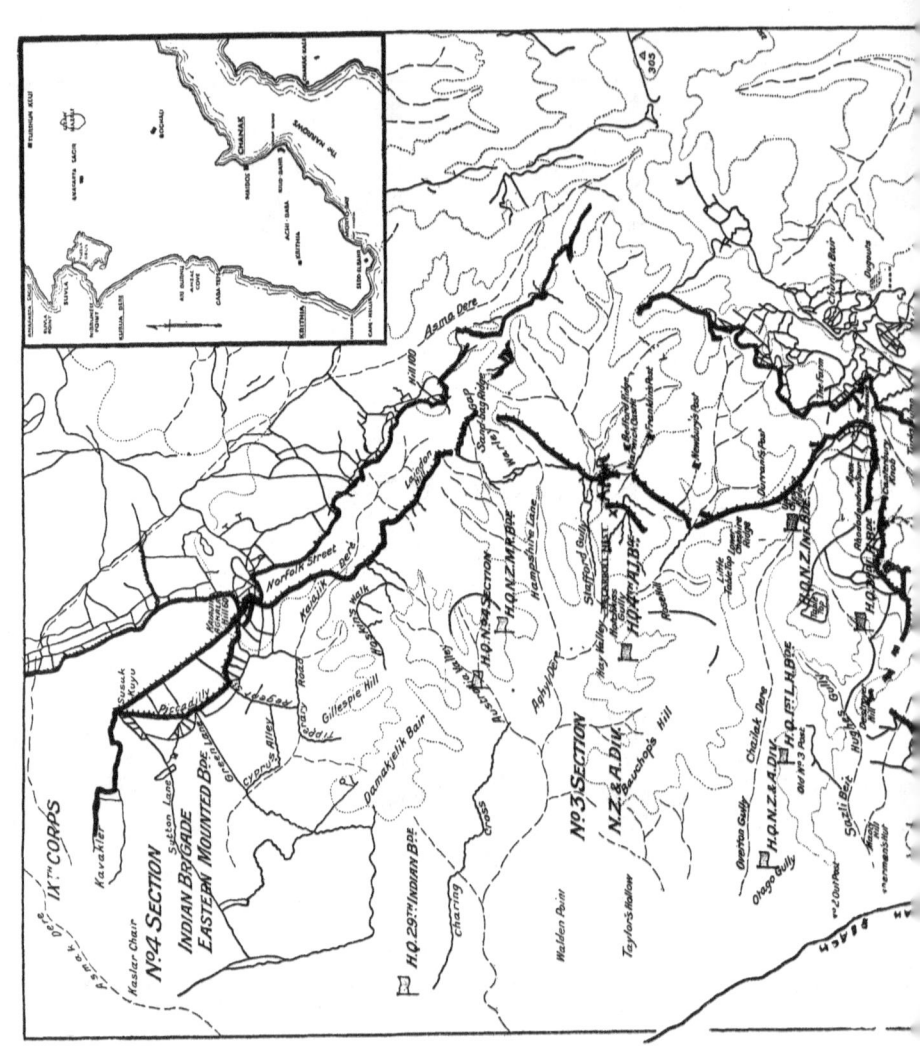

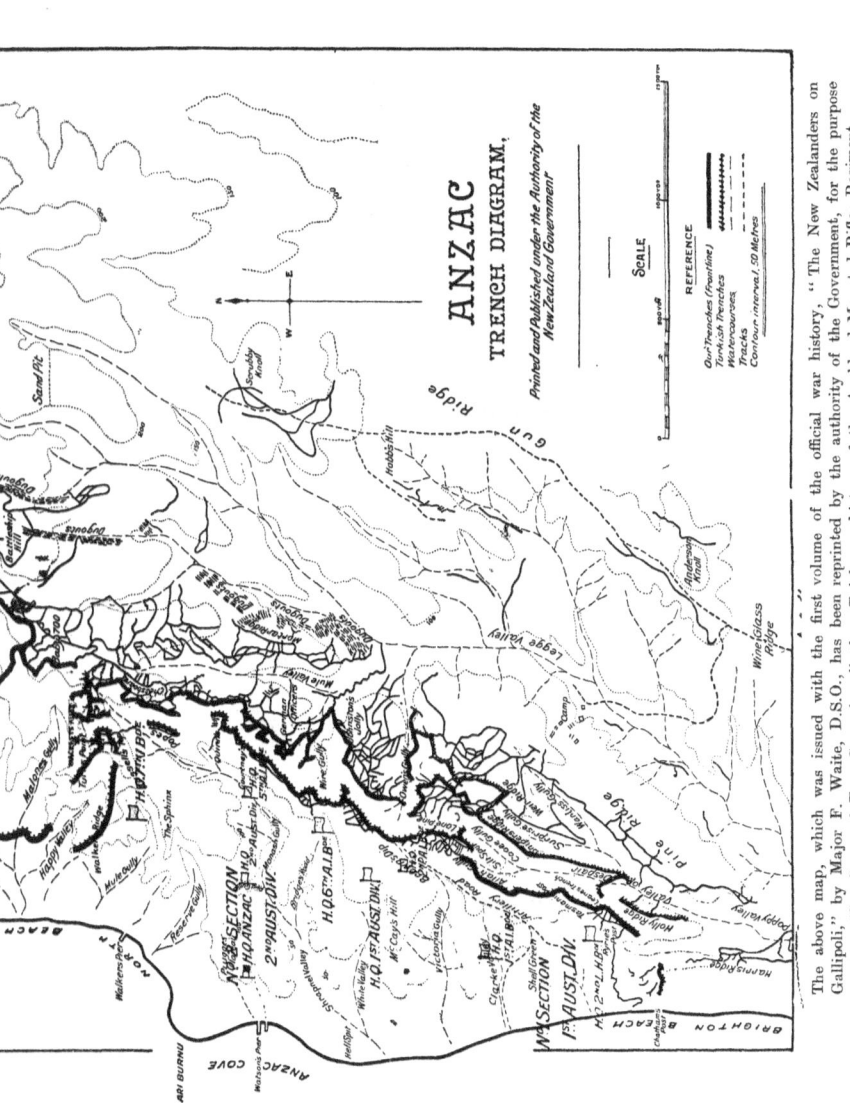

The above map, which was issued with the first volume of the official war history, "The New Zealanders on Gallipoli," by Major F. Waite, D.S.O., has been reprinted by the authority of the Government, for the purpose of "The Story of Two Campaigns," the official war history of the Auckland Mounted Rifles Regiment.

3rd (Auckland).

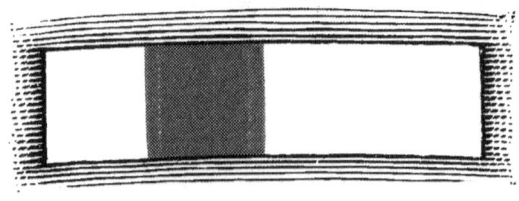

4th (Waikato). 11th (North Auckland).

A.M.R. Squadron Badges and Regimental Colours worn on hat band. The white-red-white strip was taken from the diagonal crosses in the Union Jack.

www.ingramcontent.com/pod-product-compliance
Lightning Source LLC
Chambersburg PA
CBHW021831220426
43663CB00005B/199